The Rules
Reclaiming Your Freedom, Your Manhood, and Your Sanity

Brant von Goble

Loosey Goosey Press
Bowling Green, Kentucky

Loosey Goosey Press
1111 Shive Lane #200
Bowling Green, KY 42103

ISBN: 978-0-9820991-7-9
LCCN: 2019950649

Contents

Introduction

Men, let us begin with what you already know: A great deal of the machinery of our society sees you as the enemy. Our government is, at best, indifferent to you, concerned only with your ability to serve as cannon fodder and as a source of revenue. At worst, such as is the case in the family courts, it regards you as purely evil. You are hated by the academic community, which would rather see our schools close outright than much longer tolerate *foul, foul men.*[1] Our media consider you fools, useful but to the extent you can be ridiculed as halfwits and parasites or demonized as rapists and murderers. Even marketers regard you as a lost cause, believing you to be so singularly incapable of making any purchasing decisions on your own that even products *for men* must be advertised to women.[2]

All of these are fine. All of these are what they are. Reality is neutral, as is time. Your sole concern is what you make of them.

As I suspect you may well have heard at least once in your life, *the world does not owe you a damn thing!*[3] This is true. There is no reason to be bothered by it, and there is no reason to complain. What is less often mentioned is the other side of the coin: *You do not owe the world a damn thing either.*

You have been sold one of the oddest, most contradictory models of masculinity to have ever existed—that a man can prove his independence and strength through no other means than by subordinating himself to others, who are obliged to treat him with contempt and contempt alone. According to the model perpetuated by all sides—left, right, and center—a man should be a slave to his employer, a footman to his wife, and a serf to his bank (assuming he has a mortgage). These he should all do gladly. Yet despite being a servant to all and sundry, a man should stand up for himself, somehow without offending any of his many masters, and if by some small miracle he does find himself freed from the fetters of work, women, and property taxes, a man should immediately find new overlords and beg them to shackle him yet again. Failure to do this is irrefutable proof that a man is abnormal, immature, immoral, selfish, or *irresponsible*, because a *good man* is responsible for assuming as many responsibilities as possible, regardless of what is in his best interests.

This is wrong. This is nonsense. This stupidity will become the bane of your existence if you allow it to do so.

I am not arguing that you do not owe anything to *anyone*, only that you owe nothing without receiving something in return. The legal term for this is *consideration*.[4] No contract in the common law is valid without it, which is to say that an agreement is not binding unless each party receives something in exchange for something else. *Give something; get something.* This is a fundamentally fair principle, one that has been recognized for many years. You do not owe *the world*, *Western civilization*, *the market*, or *humanity* your loyalty or love, nor do you owe them maximum economic contributions, productivity, blind social conformity, offspring, or anything else. No one owes *anything* to any of these constructs. They are abstractions, and abstractions cannot owe anything nor can they be owed anything.

Somewhat less negatively, I encourage you to remember anyone who has helped you in your times of need. Family (almost always excluding wives or sexual partners), friends, and even understanding bosses can make the difference between life and death. I am not advocating that you abandon these people. If anything, I urge you to build stronger relationships with them, so long as you do not allow yourself to become a sucker—one who forgets the significance of consideration.

Isolation is what your oppressors want for you. Isolated men are easier to control. A revolution may start with one man, but it cannot be of much effect unless it is supported by a community of revolutionaries.

I have prepared this self-study curriculum because I have seen too many men driven over the edge—to drink, to drugs, and to violence (usually against themselves, only rarely against others). Every Western man I have gotten to know well has said or clearly intimated that he has seriously considered suicide at least once in these past few years. *Every! Single! One!*

Think about that.

I have known a few who have gone through with the act outright and a great many others who have killed themselves by small measures (something millions do every day)—poisoning their livers, drugging themselves into oblivion, or taking so many risks that they eventually ended up dead by the side of the road or in some other lonesome, forgotten place. These men were not fools or idiots, and they were not cowards.

Were this only an insubstantial number of people, I might be willing to believe that these actions were the results of bad biochemistry, traumatic childhoods, or flawed genetics. But the sheer numbers suggest something else: A declaration of no confidence, an act of protest against society itself. Even if my non-random sample is far from representative of the whole, even if only *half* of all men are driven by our culture and way of life to contemplating ending their existences, half is still far too many.

The better part of the chattering classes regards this as unworthy of note. Our media will make much of even slight increases in the suicide rate of women, but the welfare of men is quite obviously a topic they have deemed to be of far less concern, despite men being more likely to die by their own hands.[5] If you have noticed this profound silence, you may well have become annoyed. You may have had no response at all—meaning you have become too resigned to the existing order to think much about it.

Ultimately, it is anyone's right to be indifferent, which is all the more reason for you to care about yourself.

Suicide is an extraordinary demonstration of hopelessness. For whatever voting with your feet is worth, voting with your life is worth far more. A great many men are expressing their disgust in less overt ways—by withdrawing from their work, their communities, and anything else connected to society at large. This is a rational response—one that has been examined by other writers—and I have no reason to repeat what has already been written about at length, and well.[6]

This course is something different. It is not an analysis. It is not a rant, and although it may sometimes be written from a position of frustration, it is not a work of hate. The Rules were born of compassion—of the concern I feel for my fellow man.

Perhaps this sounds inauthentic. Perhaps you think me dishonest. That is fine. I welcome your skepticism. Read, consider, and make up your mind for yourself. This is not a collection of ponderous prose or a never-ending lament for the decline of civilization. It is not a philosophical discourse. It is a detailed analysis of the problems we, as men, face and a plan of action that *you* can use in your everyday life to improve your existence while sabotaging those who sabotage you.

The Rules were written to help you step back from the chasm of despair.

I have considered the sources of the struggles facing Western men, and I elaborate on these as needed, but I have not allowed myself to become bogged down in the details. *How and why did we get here?* are worthwhile questions, but they are only relevant to the extent that they help us better answer the big question: *What should you do (or not do) to make your life better?*

There is no one group or person to blame. Feminists, as bad as they are, cannot take all of the credit for this suffering. Let us not make them into something mythical: the witches behind the curtain. Government, media, educational institutions, and the collapse of the agrarian and industrial economies have all played a role in driving men to misery and death. Recognizing this requires no belief in a conspiracy: Sometimes the wrong chemicals are mixed together and toxic gases results. People have died from this. As often as not, the accidental chemists had no idea of what they were doing. Such is the confluence of factors facing Western men. They are being poisoned, and who poured the ammonia into the bucket of bleach is beyond the scope of the Rules.

This course is predicated on honesty: It is about being honest with *yourself* regarding all things—who you really are and what you are capable of doing; who (if anyone) cares about you; why people are interacting with you and what they are trying to get from you; how much time you have remaining on this earth (which is not long, for no one has very long); and, most importantly, what *you* need and what *you* want. The Rules cannot be followed by the man who does not know these things. The Rules cannot be followed by the man who has not taken the time to consider his true nature—to understand himself—to the best of his abilities.

There are answers throughout this series, and there are questions as well. The answers are useful. The questions, more so. By answering these *honestly*, you will make yourself stronger, and I urge you to review the study materials throughout this text. This material is purely for your own benefit—food for thought, if you will—and there are no grades. The only right answers to most of these questions are the answers that you craft for yourself—the ones you *know* to be true and to be right for you and your life and goals.

Every lie you tell yourself binds you to a harmful delusion. Every time you break one of these chains of deceit, you are that much closer to liberating your mind.

The man without self-deception is nearly impossible to fool. You can be that man. I do not care if you lie to anyone else. If you ever meet me and choose to lie to me, fine. Lie so hard that it hurts. Claim you are a Scottish nobleman or a Nigerian prince. Such makes no difference to me.

Either way, I am not going to give you any money, and if you live in accordance with the Rules, you will have all the money you need.

This self-contained instructional program is divided into several sections. It begins with an examination of *the Rules*. These are what you need to know first. Every subsequent section explains concepts critical to understanding the Rules, why the Rules need be used, or how to use them. Study the Rules first. If you cannot abide by the Rules, the rest of the course will be a waste of your time, and I have no desire to waste anyone's time. Time is valuable. Time is the only thing you have that you cannot replace.

Understand this: The Rules are disruptive. If you apply them systematically, they will change both your life and the way others think about you. You may face some criticism, but this should prove to be relatively mild. The most common attacks you will face will be subtle: namely, attempts to degrade your masculinity, which are efforts at shaming you into compliance and submission, so that you may better serve as a cog in a vast and indifferent machine, one that will wear you down to nothing more than scrap. Ignore these attacks, and they will go away. Ignore these attacks, and you will be that much closer to achieving *true freedom*, which is the ability to pursue your interests without outside interference or distraction and having the resources to do so.

A final thought, and the single most important lesson of the Rules: We are all *real men*. How could you be anything else? A real man is his own master. No one can take your manhood from you. Only you can surrender it. Even then, it is yours to reclaim whenever you wish, and no one can stop you.

So, are you ready to stand up for yourself?

Are you ready to break free from the bondage of falsehoods?

If not you, who will? If not now, when?

1) The Rules

Let us start with the Rules, of which there are only four.

They are:

1. Give as little as possible.
2. Take as much as possible.
3. Always have an exit.
4. Enjoy your life to the fullest.

These may seem self-explanatory, and to a certain extent, they are. But I urge you to read carefully before trying to follow them. As is the case with many things in life, the devil is in the details.

First, I stress that I am not advocating robbing liquor stores and shooting up government offices. These actions might well be fun, but they are self-defeating. Unless you have truly gotten to the point that you no longer care if you live or die—exactly how your enemies want you to feel—years in prison may not be the best of times for you. Do *not* do anything self-destructive. *Enjoy your life to the fullest* is not meant to suggest that you develop a cocaine habit. Such stands to give you short-term pleasure, but it would make you feel worse in the long term. The Rules were not written to encourage you to take the leap into darkness. Rather, they were devised to help you step back from that ledge and to make the most of your remaining time on this spinning ball of dirt and rock.

Living by the Rules is not reckless. It is rational self-interest. Remember, the odds are that few people care much about your welfare, so you must assume this responsibility.

Men, Morals, and Game Theory

The theory underlying the Rules is based on a pragmatic understanding of human psychology (with a limited emphasis on evolutionary psychology), a very small amount of philosophy, a bit of Western culture and law, some data on current and probable future economic conditions, a fair amount of personal and expert information on the practical operation of educational institutions, and the lightest touch of game theory. I mention religion but very briefly, and only to the extent I demonstrate that it is oftentimes misquoted or misinterpreted. I am not a proselytizer. Your faith is your business.

From the perspective of game theory, you will find three major approaches to winning at life. The Rules were developed with the idea that you should take the third.

Now, I offer simplified explanations of each.

The first is the *maximax* strategy, which assumes that you should make *max*imum effort to achieve *max*imum outcomes, regardless of risk. This is the sort of overly optimistic strategy encouraged by those who argue that opportunities are boundless and that a life of infinite prosperity is yours for the taking. I hope you recognize this sheer absurdity of this approach. If not, I have a unicorn trotting across a bridge over prime swamp land in Florida, and I think you may well be interested in all three. I'll happily draw up a quitclaim deed for the land and the bridge and a bill of sale for the unicorn. Unfortunately, I only accept briefcases filled with cash or gold bullion as payment. But given the modest price of 90,000 dollars for the lot, you are getting a steal, I promise.

The second is the *maximin* strategy, which makes *max*imum effort to *min*imize loss. This is extreme cautiousness, which if followed perfectly, would lead you to try nothing and to *take* nothing, as there might be some chance of loss.

The third strategy—the one used in this course—is *minimax*, which is designed to *mini*mize losses by avoiding *maxi*mum negative outcomes. Stated another way, minimax is about *minimizing regret*, or for our purposes, minimizing *substantial regret*, with *substantial regret* itself being a tricky notion we will examine throughout these lessons.[1]

I built this program on a *minimally moral perspective,* which is an extension of the minimax approach. This is distinct from a *maximally moral perspective,* which places moral values and abstractions above the well-being of the individual practitioner— think Gandhi, Mother Theresa, or whomever else you deem to be of the strongest moral fiber. It is also distinct from a truly *amoral perspective*—one in which a person has no moral compass or sense of concern for anyone other than himself. A minimally moral approach is one in which you avoid undue moral regret. You behave morally *enough* so that you do not find yourself to be *too much* of a bastard, with the understanding that you are better off erring slightly on the side of bastardry than on the side of decency, if only because it is better to be the *screwer* than the *screwee.*

A point I frequently made to my students in my teaching days and that I reiterate now: *Good enough is good enough.* Here we are generally going for passing grades, not straight A's in all of our endeavors.

Next, let's evaluate the dangers of the life strategies many of our fathers used.

Dad's Doomed and Dying Dreams

Let me be clear about this: The game has changed. If you are 40 years of age or younger, you will almost certainly never make money as easily as did your father. His world is gone, as are the good jobs, generous benefits, and decades-long retirements. Barring a lottery win, a lucky accident, extraordinary skills or abilities on your part, or some other peculiar turn of fate or circumstance, you *will* have less than did your father, unless you work *much* harder.[2] You will be expected to do more, to receive less, and to be eternally anxious. Your relationships with your company, your children, and your wife/partner/significant other (to the extent you have relationships of consequence with any of the aforementioned) will be far more tenuous than were those of the Baby Boomers. Our fathers lived in a peculiar moment in human history—one in which the maximax strategy appeared to work, at least temporarily—and such odd circumstances are unlikely to arise again before anyone and everyone breathing today shuffles off this mortal coil.

Understanding these facts is the first step to liberation.

Think about your father. If he was anything like mine, he spent his days trying to make others happy. For men of that generation, life was more often than not defined by what they could accumulate—houses, cars, wives, promotions—and what they ended up getting was not necessarily what they wanted: It was what they were *told* that they wanted and what they were told that they should have.

There is no reason to attack these men. Good luck is just that —luck—and even good luck can be a mixed blessing. The richest and most powerful of these men might well have sold us down the river, but most men were not rich or powerful, although many of

4

them had more than you ever will. The vast majority, like you, had relatively little say in the big decisions.

Nothing in this course is intended to promote a generational divide—something that is aggressively cultivated by various actors (including those in government, media, and the academic community) to set fathers and sons against each other. And that *is* the purpose of sowing intergenerational discord—to put groups of men at odds with other groups of men. Notice that in almost all of the reports that compare the generations, women (young and old alike) come out unscathed and smelling of patchouli oil and innocence, while men (sometimes young and sometimes old) are invariably presented as idiots, bums, or psychopaths. Few of the changes that have occurred in the legal, political, or economic landscapes, or their effects on the behavior of men, are examined in these hypocritical retrospectives and hypercritical evaluations.

Contrary to what you might well think, the great economic and cultural shifts over the past 50 years are not reasons for despair. You *will* destroy yourself if you try to achieve what our father's generation achieved and achieve it in the same way. You will work yourself to death for a house, a car, and a family that will almost certainly be taken from you. Your wife *may* not be the one to take all that you have (although such is quite probable). But even if she does not, you will not have much security. Unlike your father, you will need to incur huge and largely unsustainable amounts of debt to achieve the American nightmare.[3] Miss a few payments due to unemployment or disability, annoy someone—your wife, your boss, or *anyone on the entire internet*—and you may well find yourself out on the street, wondering if you can scrape together enough money to buy a bullet and rent a gun. And no one will have any sympathy for you. Somehow, you will have done wrong. If you had been a more responsible, harder working, more loyal, or overall better husband, father, and worker, you could have kept up with the winners. You could have held fast to all the things other people think you should consider worthy of a lifetime of sacrifice.

Here is the worst part: *You* will have driven yourself to suicide, and the people you tried to impress will not care one way or the other. This is the curse of a multi-decade run of good luck: It conditioned us to believe the impossible. It set us up to fall, and fall hard, into the abyss.

Consider all the demands placed on you by society. If you turn them around carefully in your mind and start to think about how they fit together, you will realize that they are oftentimes contradictory. Here are a few of them. See if you can recognize how half preclude the other half.

1. You should be an infinitely loyal employee—a bitch for hire.

2. You should be completely independent—your own man (and not take shit from anyone).

3. You should always be at work, trying to make as much money for your family as possible.

4. You should never miss anything important in the lives of your wife or your significant other or your children (despite always being at work).

5. You should care nothing for the opinions of others.

6. You should be intent on making a good first impression.

7. You should be willing to sacrifice anything for your wife, for your significant other, or for your children.

8. You should be entirely fine with your wife or significant other disappearing with your children, thereby preventing you from seeing or interacting with them ever again.

9. You should regard women as your superiors in every way.

10. You should (discretely) help women do all of the things they cannot do for themselves (and then apologize for making them feel helpless).

11. You should show no weakness, no vulnerability.

12. You should be sensitive.

No matter what you do or do not do, you will be doing something wrong. You will somehow be in error—damned if you, and damned if you do not. *Something* will be your fault. If you try to play by these rules, you have already lost. The only question is by how much.

So play by different rules. Play by *the Rules*.

Look out for yourself. Take care of yourself. Set your own goals based on what benefits *you*, and realize that almost anything you do for anyone else will go unappreciated. Most people cannot respect those who offer help and expect nothing in return. Remember the importance of *consideration. Give something; get something.* Get it now, and do not wait for delayed payment. Do not accept promises of intangibles, such as love, affection, or appreciation. And never sell the value of your efforts short. You owe no loyalty to those who have no loyalty to you. Ignore this advice and risk earning truckloads of contempt. No one respects a sucker.

Honestly, do you?

The Rules are not about cheating. What they *are* about is getting the best deal for yourself from society, from government, from your employer, and from everyone else around you. Do you negotiate? Did you try to get the best possible deal when you last bought a house, a car, a motorcycle, or a plane ticket?

You should have. If not, why did you let yourself get reamed?

The Rules are an all-encompassing strategy to thrive. Apply them to every aspect of your existence, and you will start to see that almost every moment of your life is transactional. For every deal, you should demand consideration, and that which you receive should be *at least* proportional to your efforts. It is not your job to see that the other party gets a fair deal—that is their problem—and if they do not want what you are selling, they can walk away. This last statement also applies to you. You do not really *need* much. Most things are *wants*. Air is free, food is cheap, and you can find a rattrap of an apartment somewhere. If you are feeling adventuresome, forget the apartment: Buy a tent. You *have* options.

The world does not owe you a damn thing, but you can bet that almost everyone—government, girlfriends, landlords, and lawyers—will take all that you *let* them take. They will gladly push you head first into a wood chipper and toss what remains of your mangled carcass into a shallow grave and think nothing of it.

The first two Rules are about flipping the script. The other side wants to *give as little (to you) as possible*. What do you think your government, your company, and your girlfriend/wife/casual lay are doing every time they interact with you? They also want to *take as much (from you) as possible*. Chances are that you are not getting much in the way of charity from those around you.

If by some miracle you have benefited from the genuine kindness of others, remember those who have helped you: They are rare souls. I do not encourage you to mistreat them. There are a few points of light in the darkness of life, but not many: Do not extinguish them. Be careful though. Your eyes are probably just playing tricks on you.

The Third Rule (*Always have an exit*) is one that the better part of our economic leadership, businesses, and government would prefer that you ignore. *Being trapped*, be it in a marriage, a job, a home, a middle-class identity, a school, or even a country, is what all of these people and organizations want you to be. Marriage traps men. The American work ethic—one which emphasizes subsuming your identity into your job title—traps men.[4] Mortgages trap men. Status and externally validated identity trap men. Educational institutions trap men, at least until said men graduate or abandon their courses of study. Patriotic duty traps men.

A great many people want to trap men. A great many people want to trap *you*. Do not let them. Do not attach yourself to anyone or anything that you do not truly want or need, and be flexible. Even if you are interested in accumulating some things that are conventionally valued, remember that the less you care, the better a position you are in to drive a hard bargain. If your identity is truly tied up in something—if you *must* have it—you are all but guaranteed to be conned. Also remember that most of these —marriage, work, middle-class status, and formal education—put nearly all of the obligation on you. *You*—not your wife, not your company, not your college, and not your country—are the one most vulnerable to things going south when investing in these. One of the few parties that has as much skin in the game as do you is the bank that financed your (really, *your wife's*) home: If you walk off in the middle of the night, the bank may stand to lose real money. Money matters.

The Fourth Rule (*Enjoy your life to the fullest*) is about having well-defined priorities, and it is surprisingly hard to follow, because you can only fully enjoy your life *if you know what you want*. You can easily learn to detect chicanery *reactively*: Somebody makes you an offer and you weigh it. *Is this fair, and how can I make this deal sweeter for myself?* you may reasonably ask, and this requires intelligence and effort, but it does not demand much introspection. You can study the market: for cars, for jobs, for women, or for anything, really, and figure how much a good or service should cost and if a deal is sound in the general sense of it.

But this is pointless if you do not know your *wants* and *needs*. I could go out today and get a great deal on an ottoman from one of the local junk stores, but *what the hell would I do with an ottoman?* (What does anyone do with an ottoman, rest his feet on it while eating Turkish delight?) A deal is bad *for you* if it provides you with something that you do not want or need. *Enjoying your life to fullest* is about knowing what *you* want and what you think you should have. It is the most personal of the Rules, because a *full and enjoyable life* for you might well mean nothing to me, and vice versa.

Chances are that you have made a critical mistake your entire life—that of underestimating the worth of your efforts. Your father probably did this as well (but in a slightly different way). He was almost certainly too busy keeping up with Joneses to ask himself what he really wanted or what was the fair value of each one of his irreplaceable days. You are *not* too busy. You *do* have the time. You have it right now. Start thinking. The next chapter will help.

10

2) The Lists

We spend our lives in bondage to our wants and needs. As for *needs*, there is only so much we can do to be rid of them. Short of uploading our consciousnesses to the cloud, we cannot liberate ourselves from our physical forms while continuing to exist: For the time being, we're stuck with the limitations and weaknesses of our stinking bags of skin and bones. With *wants*, however, nature does not so limit us.

These are the *Evil Five* (Ev5):

1. Alcohol consumption

2. Drug consumption

3. Socializing

4. The pursuit of sex, sex, and the consequences of sex (collectively: *coitus, et cetera*)

5. Status seeking and maintenance (collectively: *status struggle*)

I have given the Ev5 their own section, in which they are examined at length. For the time being, we can simply categorize them as *wants*, not needs, and although they are not inherently bad, one must guard himself against indulging in them to excess or in a harmful manner. They are significant because their pursuit takes up a non-trivial percentage of many men's waking hours. Without judging anyone's values, I ask you four questions regarding the Ev5:

1. Who (or what) has an interest in encouraging you to pursue the Ev5?

2. How does your pursuit of the Ev5 benefit these people or entities?

3. To what extent does the pursuit of the Ev5 make your life better in the long term?

4. Who benefits more from your pursuit of the Ev5, you or someone else?

If you answer these questions with care, there is a reasonably good chance you will come to the conclusion that the pursuit of the Ev5, beyond a very reasonable point, benefits parties other than the pursuer far more than it benefits the pursuer himself (you). You should carefully evaluate how much you really desire these things versus how much you has been told and conditioned to desire these things. You must also determine how bound you are willing to allow yourself to become to hedonism and materialism.

So who benefits from keeping you as unfree as possible, and what are they trying to achieve? Let us torture another metaphor for a while and see if we can extract any truth from it. I'll grab my pliers and my branding iron. You can supply the jumper cables and the car battery. With some dedication, we should be able to determine how much we naturally, organically want this, that, or the other (the Ev5 included) versus how much we have been brainwashed into wanting one thing or the next.

The Digesting Duck

In the early 18th century, Jacques de Vaucanson built an *automaton* that looked like a duck. The faux duck did not quack like a duck, it did not fly like a duck, and it did not swim like a duck. *It ate, and it shit,* or at least it appeared to do these things. In truth, it had no digestive system, so it did nothing more than artfully move about a bit. This may not seem very impressive to us today, in our era of self-guided drones and industrial robots, but for the time, the *digesting duck* was a big deal.[1]

In a perfectly mature consumer society, you are a slightly improved version of the digesting duck—your eating and excreting are authentic at least—but you *pay* for the privilege. The duck did not.

The duck got a deal. You get fucked.

The digesting duck was a crude machine of consumption. It managed to look as though it was ingesting one thing and turning it into something else. Eat/excrete, eat/excrete—these were the duck's duties, and they are the principal tasks assigned to you as well. Mull over how much what you are encouraged to do is intended to maximize your consumption. Overuse of alcohol and drugs (including prescription medicines); running from one place to the next for social interaction that engages you little (or to attend some singularly useless business function); trying to prove your masculinity through all things related to sex; and consuming or accumulating things that you neither really want nor really need, purely for the sake of improving or maintaining social status —these are some of the ways you play the role of digesting duck 2.0.

Have you ever stopped to ponder the sheer strangeness of the manner in which we establish rank in our society? We do not often evaluate others based on what they can create or what skills they demonstrate, but on how wasteful they can be. Most of us are already familiar with the concept of *conspicuous consumption,* but there is a tendency to frame that notion within the context of very ostentatious displays of wealth. We may define the term too narrowly. In fact, almost *everything* that we are taught to do in our society—everything we are instructed to value—is a form of conspicuous consumption.[2]

The *illusion of ownership* is essential to your duck-ification. But in order for you to become something more than a mechanical quack-er, you must recognize how you are intrinsically similar to our fake feathered friend.

The digesting duck does not own any of what passes through it. It swallows food, but the food is emptied out before long, and it does the duck no good anyway. As is the case for the digesting duck, you own nothing. Let me repeat that. It is important.

You own nothing.

No one owns anything, really. Name anything you possess that cannot be taken away.

My house!

Divorce, eminent domain, failure to pay property taxes, failure to pay your mortgage (assuming you have one), or *civil asset forfeiture*—any of these can lead to the loss of your real estate in short order.[3]

My car!

Divorce (again), repossession, failure to pay your auto loan (assuming you have a loan)—any of these can lead to the loss of your car.

My personal possessions!

Divorce (yet once more), repossession, theft, et cetera.

And intangibles fair no better.

My reputation/social standing!

Slander, legal issues, and even essentially random falls from political favor that are no fault of your own can easily lead to the loss of either of these.

My health!

Disease, injury, et cetera—you get the idea.

The point of all of this is that you do not own anything.

At first glance, one might think that I am attacking the first two Rules—*Take as much as possible* and *Give as little as possible* —as I would seem to be arguing that following them is futile. Such is not the case. In truth, what I am arguing for is a better understanding of what you get when you buy something and what you have when you possess it—and what you get and have is the temporary use of a thing. All uses are temporary, if only because nothing and no one lasts forever, including you. Even the digesting duck, long since destroyed in a fire, did not stand the test of time.

Even ducks get fucked in the end. *Quack!*

Your goal should be to gain the use of things that you find, well, *useful.* You should learn to see all possessions as utilities, not as marks of what you are. If you accumulate utility in a pragmatic and rational way, your quality of life will increase. If you accumulate *symbols*, particularly the type of symbol that is used to convince you or those around you that you are a specific type of person, you will be miserable and vulnerable. A utility can be replaced, but a possession that has become a part of you—that defines you—cannot. A bit of you dies with the loss of the signifier. *You are not your khakis*, but more than that, you are not any of your possessions.

None of the aforementioned is an expression or promotion of strict antimaterialism, at least not in the John Lennon "Imagine" sense of it.

Having nothing sucks. It is difficult to appreciate how much money matters until you've had to survive without any. Nevertheless, *symbols,* without a substantial and overriding utility, are generally a bad deal for the person trying to accumulate them.

Once you absorb these truths and you come to fully understand the tremendous emphasis that is put on becoming a blind and mindless consumer, you can start to think about *the lists*.

The Chain Gang

Much of what you are taught to value amounts to a chain of one form or another. Chains of addiction, chains of debt, chains of status—these are what you are supposed to *desire* and to struggle to accumulate. You should not only be a prisoner but a prisoner who accepts his fate without complaint, who sees his lack of liberty as both desirable and inevitable.[4] *Why* are you encouraged to accept this, and *who* has an interest in encouraging you to pursue these things that keep you forever laboring for the benefit of someone else?

The answer to the first question is obvious: *money and power!* And following the money trail answers the second question. The rich grow richer, the tax coffers are filled, and the entitled remain well-fed largely as a result of the surplus labor of working men. By *surplus labor,* I mean any labor that is in excess of what a man needs to perform to take care of himself.

Even if *no* men were on welfare or disability, even if all of them did enough work to take care of themselves *but not any more than that*, governments would have a difficult time keeping millions of people of questionable worth on their payrolls. Many businesses would survive, but many others, particularly in domains that rely on the purchases made *by* men *for the benefit of women and children*, would see tough times. Without men working more than they need to support themselves and for things that benefit them relatively little, our economy would change drastically.[5]

Eventually, this might be a net positive for much of society and for the planet. Houses might be smaller and more environmentally friendly. Fewer precious metals would be extracted from the earth for useless toys and baubles, leading to less in the way of pollution from mining, and governments would have fewer resources to engage in pointless and destructive wars and to subsidize incompetence and bad behavior.

We, as a civilization, might well learn to be content with more modest material existences, making us happier, less frustrated, and less obsessed with *stuff*, and we, as men, would generally be in a better state as well, as the fruits of our surplus labor frequently benefit quite a few women and a select group of highly privileged men, while actually hurting the majority of us, collectively and individually. The unchaining of working men might well be *good* for almost all of the world (including, in the long-term, a fair number of women), but good or not, large changes are disruptive, and they stand to threaten those already in positions of power.

Making a List, Checking It Twice (or Thrice or Even More)

The first set of lists concerns people and their actions, and the first of the first is of those who encourage you to blindly follow the herd. This is the *sheeple list*—not that all of the people named therein are necessarily sheeple themselves, but that they want *you* to be a sheeple.

17

Some people may have encouraged you to take the conventional route due to reasons very specific to you, rather than merely as a matter of course—a math teacher who encouraged you to go to college because she thought you were a brilliant calculus student, for instance.

Do not include these individuals. Their reasons recognized you as a unique human being, whereas we are looking for those who encouraged *conventionality for the sake of conventionality*.

On the lines below, try to write down the top 10 parties responsible for trying to sheeple-ize you. Also write down the relationships they have to you (be they friends, parents, teachers, bosses, even media personalities, or public figures).

1. _____

2. _____

3. _____

4. _____

5. _____

6. _____

7. _____

8. _____

9. _____

10. _____

Now, look at the list. Do you see any theme or pattern? Did a certain type or category of person encourage you to blindly follow the herd more than did others?

You are going to prepare another list, this one based on the first. On this second list, you should write what each of the people previously named encouraged you to do simply because *that is what is done*.

Buy a house, marry a girl, go to college—what was the convention these people encouraged you to follow?

1. _____
2. _____
3. _____
4. _____
5. _____
6. _____
7. _____
8. _____
9. _____
10. _____

Again, do you see any patterns? Did a great many people encourage you to take the same conventional path?

I ask that you make a third list on this topic. This time, ruminate on why society encourages you to follow the conventions you wrote down moments ago.

Is the purpose of this convention to make you a debt slave? Is it to make you psychologically vulnerable and dependent on the approval of others? Is it to make you less able to stand up for yourself? Is it to isolate you? Is it because following convention is supposed to make you happy? Maybe you do not know the reason why something is encouraged, in which case you should not dismiss the possibility that *no one* knows why you should follow a given tradition or convention. Sometimes, things are done simply because they have been done, and done a certain way, for a long time.

If you are uncertain of the purpose of a convention, leave the line blank. Some of these things can be confusing.

1. _____

2. _____

3. _____

4. _____

5. _____

6. _____

7. _____

8. _____

9. _____

10. _____

So what shall you do with all of these lists? Well, start by just looking at them. Have you ever thought about the sheeple life and those who encourage it? The people, institutions, and goals you have listed may not be inherently bad; however, you need to start considering their suitability to you more carefully. Now that you know *who* has encouraged you to follow convention, *what* conventions you have been encouraged to follow, and *why* society expects you to follow such conventions—or at least have some reasonable explanations for the last—you can start to disentangle yourself from conventions and the promoters of convention. This makes compiling our next set of lists easier. You should be able to at least partially separate yourself from your programming.

The fourth list is of people you believe to be genuine friends—people who really care about you. You may find some overlap between the people on this list and those on the sheeple list. After all, not everyone who encourages you to follow convention for convention's sake has sinister intentions. Some people may well think that following convention is the shortest route to happiness for you, for me, and for everyone, possibly because they are sheeple themselves.

This list should not exceed five people, which is about all the truly close friends that a person can have.[6] Your list may be even shorter. If so, that is fine as well. The average American is only close to two people—that includes friends *and* family.[7] Five is a rather optimistic number, and it is more important that you be honest with yourself than that you aim for a high score.

Okay, you know the drill.

1. _____
2. _____
3. _____
4. _____
5. _____

We will put aside any more references to people for a minute. The next list—number five—is different. It is based on what *you* want. Include the things that *you want because you want them,* not because you were told to want them. A review of the previously prepared pages should help you to exclude the latter. Possessions, such as motorcycles or musical instruments, might be worthy of mention, but the list does not need to be restricted to that which one may have or hold.

Experiences count as well. *To travel to another country* might also be *something that you want*, even though it is not really a *thing*. Whatever you really want, write it here. Chew over each item for a moment or two before you put pen to page. You may be tempted to add something without much thought—*$10,000,000 and a private island* seems to be a fairly obvious answer, for example—but that which is included for no other reason than that *it sounds like a good thing to want* will not do you much good.

For some people, the list of all that they desire could be a book unto itself, but a list too long to be practical is not much better than no list at all. Try to keep your number of items to ten. After all, your days are numbered, so you must prioritize.

1. _____
2. _____
3. _____
4. _____
5. _____
6. _____
7. _____
8. _____
9. _____
10. _____

Now refer to the previous items and write down *why you want what you want* for list six. What will you get from having each thing or experience? For instance, if you wrote that you wanted a guitar, your reason for wanting said guitar might be so that you can learn to play the songs of Metallica (or John Denver or Willie Nelson or whomever else you choose). Try to keep in mind what I mentioned before—that you do not really own anything, but merely have the use of it.

1. _____
2. _____
3. _____
4. _____
5. _____
6. _____
7. _____
8. _____
9. _____
10. _____

The final list is a curious one, and it may be the most confusing. Think about things that *you have but that you do not want*. These are encumbrances—the things, the people, and the obligations that weigh you down. You may find it helpful to refer to list two—the list of things you were encouraged to obtain purely for the sake of convention—a few of which you may already have.

Seven lists, lucky us.

1. _____
2. _____
3. _____
4. _____
5. _____
6. _____
7. _____

8. _____

9. _____

10. _____

All of this list making may have seemed pointless, but it was not.

You now know what you want, why you want these things, what others want for you and why, who is encouraging you to follow the herd, whom you consider to be a true friend, and what you have without which your life would be better.

All of this is obvious. All of this is simple, but a few simple revelations can have a profound impact on your life. You have just put more thought into your goals, possessions, and relationships than many people do in years, decades even.

After you complete this book, go back and review all seven lists. See what, if anything, has changed. Maybe you will have discovered that some of your close friends are not as close as you thought they were. Maybe what you *thought* you wanted for yourself was really the result of going along to get along. Maybe some of the people you placed on the sheeple list should be dropped—they turned out to be something else entirely. These are drafts. That is all. *Be flexible!*

The Rules are all about getting what you want and knowing friend from foe. The better you understand these things, the more successful, the happier, and the freer you will be. The digesting duck couldn't think, but you can.

And that makes all the difference.

3) On Shaming and the Big Three

Beware of shame, lest you be coerced into violating the Rules, the Third Rule—*Always have an exit*—in particular. We will examine this matter in depth, but first, a brief aside about magic tricks.

Shame can be (and is) used to manipulate men so that they act contrary to their welfare, so that they destroy their futures, or so that they kill themselves. The bad news about shaming is that it can be quite effective. The good news is that it is imperfect magic. Once someone explains to you how the trick works—how these little words and gestures are used to control you—the sorcery ceases to be magical. It even ceases to be very interesting.

This chapter will pull back the curtain and will reveal what the magicians are doing and, just as importantly, *why* they are doing it. Once you see these things, you will be all but magic- (and shame-) proof. Think of me as the Wonderful Explain-O—the conjurer who tells all. I get decent crowds, but not many repeat ticket buyers.

I can't imagine why.

The Big Three

Allow me to introduce you to the *Big Three Conventions*—the three things American men are frequently shamed into doing, despite *not* doing them oftentimes being in the best interests of men, in the best interests of the environment, and in the best interests of a great many people around the globe. These three are the buckets of suspicious-something-or-another—maybe liquid LSD, maybe Drano, maybe just flat cola, maybe a mixture of all three—that the folks with wands and capes will try to convince you are wine—and they are:

25

1. Getting married

2. Attending college

3. Buying a home

Shame and the Welfare of a Certain Few

Shame can be magic, but it can just as easily be a dangerous and slow-acting toxin. Succumbing to it makes you weak—a sucker —and you cannot understand its power and effects until you examine it from every angle.

Regarding marriage, let us get straight what heterosexual marriage is and why it exists. Marriage is an agreement in which a man promises money to a woman so that she *may* (and purely at her discretion) have sex with him. The man has an obligation. The woman does not. Marriage is not about friendship.[1] It is about sex. If a man simply wants to be friends with a woman, he has no need to marry her. This text offers the practical, applied definition of marriage. All other definitions are based on theories that have few, if any, real-life applications.

Shame has long been used to restrict sex, sometimes justifiably, sometimes productively, but only recently have the ordinary behaviors and tendencies of heterosexual men been deemed pathological. Traditionally, marriage provided a morally and socially acceptable route for a man to access sex. Now, it provides not even that.

This shift is not entirely the result of feminism.

It is also a product or byproduct of the gradual loss of masculinity in our society that may well be as much technological in its origins as anything else. Physically and psychologically fragile people are more likely to survive now than they were in years past as a result of improved medical care and the less demanding

26

nature of modern work. There is some limited evidence that men are being incrementally effeminized—if not outright chemically castrated—by substances in the food and water supply.[2]

Weak people are more likely to be afraid of all things not feminine or neuter than are those with greater reserves of strength, and this fear is not entirely irrational. Physically and mentally fragile people are more vulnerable than their counterparts of sounder mind and body. One can find quite a few examples of androphobia in academia, which is probably the most lesbian-rich and testosterone-poor corner of American society, and which is rapidly developing an allergy to anything much fiercer than a shapeless bull dyke with a bad dye job and a slightly hairy lip.

But a culture emasculated by high technology, bad chemistry, and easy living is only part of the problem.

There is also the matter of control. Control the range of acceptable sexual outlets available to men, and you have controlled a great many of the men themselves. Artificially restrict men's access to sexual gratification, and you are trapping them. Consider the porn wars—the 1980s push against pornography.[3] The religious right was one of the belligerents—and one can somewhat understand this given traditional views on sex—but, more interestingly, a large segment of the feminist community was as well.

And in this case, the feminists and the religious right were allies, not adversaries.

In theory, all of this handwringing over sex and sexualization was to *protect women*, and it was, but not necessarily in the way a great many feminists have articulated. Many feminists have also fought hard against the legalization of prostitution—something

27

even Amnesty International, which would hardly seem to be a bastion of misogyny, has considered advocating.[4]

How does arresting a prostitute or a porn star—someone who is almost certainly from a poor or working-class background—and giving her a criminal record do said woman any good? More progressive laws, such as those adopted in Sweden, exclusively punish clients.[5] This may be better for the prostitutes, but such is debatable. Does arresting all of a prostitute's clients (and depriving her of a revenue stream) really benefit her? Even a whore has to eat, and unless she is bartering herself for a Whopper (or the Swedish equivalent), she will need money for her victuals. Given that many women who enter the world's oldest profession are probably lacking in the education and marketable skills demanded for *any other* profession, one may reasonably assume that not all prostitutes can simply retire their crotchless panties and reopen their medical practices or resume their careers as petroleum geologists.

An emerging school of feminist thought argues that the sale of sex dolls and sex robots must be restricted to prevent the objectification of women—an odd line of reasoning since the only things at risk of being objectified are *objects*—but such superficial logic is little more than distraction.[6] Unsurprisingly, these groups have yet to advocate for restrictions on women's sexual implements.

In truth, these restrictions and proposed restrictions on sex and simulated sex are largely about price fixing—keeping sex prices high—and pushing men into long-term relationships or marriage, the second and first most expensive forms of prostitution in existence. Although apparently counterintuitive, this dovetails nicely with larger efforts to make marriage and long-term relationships with women as inequitable for the average man as possible. The purpose of all of these things—restrictions on men's sexuality, an emphasis on marriage, and making marriage a joyless and destructive proposition for men—has little to do with sex *per se*, but with using sex to extract resources from men in the most efficient manner, meaning achieving the highest return per sexual encounter.

The economic rationale behind this is well-illuminated by the cold light of aesthetic and sexual market value assessment. The sex-negative feminists (let's call them *the grotesques*) have demonstrated a tendency to treat inanimate objects (books, magazines, websites, sex dolls, et cetera.) as pecuniary threats, and given how horrifically malformed some of these unfortunates are, their fears may be entirely justified.[7] Truly hapless abominations simply cannot compete with even the crudest of sexual substitutes, whereas the sex-positive feminists (*the attractive ones*) have made relatively little fuss about such matters, probably because they are confident in their abilities to outcompete smartphones and rubberized erector sets and thereby extract resources from higher value men—meaning men with more money.

One may encounter a fair number of women who are neither attractive nor threatened by sexual machines or devices. For the most part, such women have found some way to support themselves without entering the sexual marketplace at all. Thus, they do not believe their survival to be imperiled by the growth of alternatives to traditional coitus. The existence of these women does not negate any of what has been argued thus far.

Considering the matter more generally, a great deal of moralizing about the Big Three, regardless of the side of the aisle from which it originates, is engineered to persuade men to surrender their time and money to others—primarily women, but also a great many other people within the legal and economic system—and this is why the Big Three are pushed and pushed hard.

Now, let us turn our attention to schooling. I am only going to cover this topic briefly at present, not because I think it doesn't matter—it does—but because I have given education (of which schooling is merely a small part) a chapter of its own.

Much like marriage and long-term relationships, college is simply one of the most expensive and least efficient ways to obtain that which is readily available far more affordably from other outlets.

Knowledge is everywhere. Online, in books, on your phone, and throughout your community and social network. Anyone with an internet connection has more opportunities to learn and to do so conveniently and cheaply than did any member of any pre-network generation, regardless of wealth or status. Frankly, *not learning* something new every day would seem to be more of a challenge than would be gradually improving yourself through the osmotic absorption of information and skills in a world in which the marginal cost of education is fast approaching zero.

Yet the expense of college, much like that of marriage, keeps rising, and advancements in quality have not kept pace.[8] College traps a man financially and, at least while he is enrolled, ideologically and expressively. Independent and non-academic study do no such things. They liberate the learner, providing him with an opportunity to expand his intellectual and economic horizons.

And we cannot have that, now can we?

Next, home ownership.

Buying a home is not always a bad idea. It *can* work out well enough, but only if done with extreme care and pragmatism, and only for those who understand that a home is *not* an investment (at least not in the income-producing sense) and that the majority of Americans buy *far* more house than they need.[9] A home may be useful, but buying more house than one needs does little more than introduce liability to a financial portfolio. A man must also beware that *good debt* is a notion that makes about as much sense as does that of *good cancer*. A mortgage can easily turn into the worst sort of lease—one from which the man can escape only with considerable difficulty—for anyone who thoughtlessly follows convention or confuses a home with some signifier of his true worth.

Signing With the Lakers Makes Men Taller (and Other Nonsense)

The arguments made in favor of following the Big Three are usually based on confusions of causality. These are on par with the statement that tall people are more likely than short people to sign with the Los Angeles Lakers, so signing with the Lakers will cause a man to grow in stature (in the most literal sense). While some researchers and reporters may be both naive enough and poorly educated enough to be confused by the causal/correlational distinction, stupidity does *not* suffice as an explanation for the majority of these misstatements and misinterpretations of data. Hanlon's razor cuts all the way to the bone, but once we have sliced away all the fat of these arguments, what is left is a skeleton of deception, not well-intentioned idiocy.[10]

Man and Manipulation

If someone must shame or manipulate you into taking a specific course of action, such action must not have much intrinsic appeal. If the Big Three were naturally attractive, there would be no need to shame or manipulate men into following them.

Would I need to *shame* you into going to a good restaurant and having a great meal (assuming you could afford it)? Would I need to *manipulate* you into playing an enjoyable game or pursuing an engaging hobby? Were I in a position to profit from you doing these things—the owner of a restaurant, the designer of a game, or the manufacturer of equipment used in a particular hobby—I might well *advertise*, which is to say I might extol the virtues of whatever I was selling, but I would not need to use shame or manipulation. As far as marketing recipes go, shame makes a weak sauce. Fundraisers may use shame-based marketing strategies from time to time, but they lose their effect relatively quickly.

What of the matter of authentic societal good, of using shame to keep people from doing things that are tremendously harmful to society?

In certain very limited circumstances, shame has legitimate uses, but when this is the case, no great or centralized effort need be made to encourage this application of shame. *Organic shame* is closely bound to a sense of anger and disgust. For instance, child molesters are organically shamed. Even were the government and media to cease to exist, most people would not take kindly to having Lester B. Molester in their neighborhood, and he might well be run out by the citizenry, many of whom would feel *angry* and *disgusted* by the thought of a child molester living next to them.

Shaming from on high is *different* in that it is artificial. I might not want a molester living next door to me, but I would be entirely unconcerned if I lived next door to a man without children, with a vocational (rather than academic) education, and who chose to the rent, rather than buy, a home. The idea of a pederast living nearby naturally disturbs many of us. The idea of a morally upright bachelor electrician living nearby does not.

Here are a few articles designed to shame or manipulate men into following one of the Big Three (in this case, marriage) and the original publisher of each article. Some of these are from the political left, some are from the political right, and some have no obvious political bias. Consider the questionable arguments used in each headline:

1. "Dear Millennial Men, Don't Be Afraid of Marriage and Fatherhood," in *The Blaze*

2. "The Sorry Lives and Confusing Times of Today's Young Men," in *Phillymag*

3. "Men Who Won't Grow Up," in *FamilyLife*

4. "Childish men are to blame for women having kids late in life," in the *New York Post*

5. "Don't be a bachelor: Why married men work harder, smarter, and make more money," in the *Washington Post*

One would be hard-pressed to imagine any reason to publish an article titled "Genocide is Bad, Mmkay" or "Good People Don't Push Toddlers in Front of Speeding Semis, Say Leading Ethicists." That which is obviously immoral or bad is obviously immoral or bad to all and sundry.[11] All but the most demented, damaged, or corrupted of us already know as much.

There would equally little reason to publish articles promoting that which is obviously good or true. "Personal Finance Experts Agree That Making More Money is a Great Way to Get Out of Poverty" and "America's Top Chefs Make Case For Eating Food That Doesn't Taste Like Shit" have never been run as headlines in any U.S. newspaper, at least according what I have found by searching the internet. And you can see why. *Captain Obvious Daily* (originally *Duh-aily*) ceased publication years ago, despite its loyal, if a touch dimwitted, readership.

It is worth mentioning that not *all* articles written on the lack of maturity of younger people focus exclusively on men. Some direct their ridicule at men and women about equally. Additionally, some articles direct their ire towards men who are unemployed and living with their parents—and we can see why a society would not favor supporting those who are simply unwilling to support themselves. However, most of them do *not* address the truly dependent.

Rather, men are shamed (usually by being categorized as being bums or parasites) if they do not actively support others. This is quite distinct from shaming men who are *actual* burdens—disability frauds, et cetera.

And this answers our next question:

Why all this effort to create shame where none need be?

Despite the veneer of concern for men atop some of these articles, beneath the surface, each one describes the difficulties faced by individuals or businesses trying to extract resources from men, who appear less eager than their forebears to be locked into positions of helplessness. *That* is the crux of the matter.

Any other arguments therein are comparatively weak.

Every major element of society that emphasizes and encourages the Big Three stands to financially gain from doing so. This applies every bit as much to home ownership and college as it does to marriage.

Low-initiative women stand to gain from marriage because it enables them to legally extract resources from men. Lawyers, court officials, and various government and social service agencies stand to benefit as well when such marriages end. The buying and selling of homes is big business, and college is a certifiable racket.

From a business perspective, it is in the best interests of almost all of these parties that you practice serial monogamy, serial home buying, and serial retraining. You marry (pay for a wedding, buy a house, et cetera), you divorce (sell the house, pay the lawyers, attempt suicide, go to a mental hospital, end up on fistfuls of psychiatric medications that will cause you to be even crazier than you were before), and you remarry (a sure sign of aforementioned ongoing insanity). Home buying and selling go along almost perfectly with marriage and divorce.

College is a bit different from the other two of the Big Three, but every time your life is shattered by a job loss, a divorce, or a relocation, colleges have an opportunity to jump in and offer you the chance to train for something new. Retraining is great—after all, why *not* learn a new skill—but there are cheaper ways to go about doing so than spending your days roaming ivy-covered halls.

Keep up this cycle of training and retraining, marrying and divorcing, and buying and selling homes, and you will be financially enslaved to so many different masters that you will have a hard time remembering who owes you a beating on a given day. (Short answer: All of them.)

Make no mistake about it, none of the Big Three Conventions are investments. They may be billed as such, but they are not. They are consumer purchases.

College is not really an investment.[12] *Education* may be an investment, but education does not necessarily have anything to do with college. A home is not an investment, and everyone from professors at the Wharton School to writers at the *Forbes* have analyzed the reasons for this. Finally, marriage is most certainly not an investment. It does not even vaguely *resemble* an investment.

Before jumping into any of the Big Three, particularly due to being shamed or due to fear of being shamed, take the time to recognize the brilliance of the strategy behind all of this while seeing it for what it is—*a grand scheme to rob and rape you blind*.

Shame has limits, thank heavens.

The Limits of Shame

Here is the thing to remember about shame: It is a uniquely fragile manipulative strategy. It, much like flattery, only works if you care what those trying to manipulate you think. Appeals to your hedonistic impulses are relatively insensitive to your opinion of the person making them. If I can convince you that something is *fun*, your esteem for me is irrelevant. Skydiving is exciting (I would imagine, although I have yet to try it), motorcycles are fun on the proverbial bun (and I should know, I have motorcycled and scooted around two continents), and the beaches of Thailand are a great place to take a relaxing vacation (or so I have been told). Even if you have no respect for me *at all*, I might well be able to convince you to skydive, buy a motorcycle, or fly to Thailand.

Shame is different.

If you do not respect me, my efforts to shame you will do nothing. I may be able to annoy you, but that is about the extent of it. Additionally, both the attempted *shamer* and the *shamee* must have some values in common. An Aztec priest would have a hard time shaming most of us into attending a human sacrifice, regardless of how much good he claimed it would do our souls, simply because his values are so different from ours that what he considers shameful, we might well consider good or at least neutral.

Cross-values shaming simply does not work.

Once you recognize that almost all Big-Three-related shaming boils down to economics—trying to turn you into a better taxpayer, a better corporate slave, a better consumer of accepted ideologies, or a better tool for women—it loses its effect, in the same way that a charming eBay seller seems far less charismatic once you realize he is only playing nice to get you to buy a used meat grinder—one that was previously owned by Doctor Lecter.

The fastest and most efficient way to inoculate yourself against efforts to shame you is to rid yourself of esteem for those doing the shaming. Once you manage this, you may even grow to find their labors amusing.

Learn to identify the flaws in your attackers, learn to spot their hypocrisy, and above all, learn to follow the money. Do this, and the only people who will be capable of having any effect on your psyche will be those *worthy* of such power—people truly deserving of respect.

Beyond the matter of earthly shaming, there is that done under the color of religion. But rather than attack religion itself, we had better examine a few of the more widespread beliefs so we can at least know what we are up against and if we have any real reason to regard the major faiths as antagonistic to men and the well-being of men.

Religious texts and core philosophies remain relatively consistent over time. The ways in which these texts and philosophies are interpreted do not. Until relatively recently, practice of the largest religion in the United States, Christianity, was at least nominally centered around the control of immorality.

Adultery, drunkenness, and other sins of the flesh were strongly discouraged, and *physical pleasure* was seen as being either deleterious or irrelevant to spiritual development. *Happiness*, regardless of the form it took, was not the end goal.[13] Yet over the last 50 years, most of the fire and brimstone appear to be have been removed from popular Christian thought, so much so that it is difficult to determine exactly what *is* condemned at present, aside from insufficient chivalry—meaning subservience to women.[14]

One of the few things criticized within modern Christianity is a lack of family.

Interestingly, core Christian doctrine does not blindly support marriage or procreation. Consider this quote from the New Testament:

> I say therefore to the unmarried and the widows, it is good for them if they abide even as I. But if they cannot contain, let them marry: for it is better to marry than to burn. (1 Corinthians 7:8-9)[15]

This particular text was written by the Apostle Paul, who was almost certainly unmarried for the duration of his ministry. Different translations even include the words *single*, as in "it is good for them to remain single . . . " and *contain* means *control one's sexual impulses* in this context, so there is little uncertainty as to the meaning of this passage.

Paul categorizes marriage as a poor second to unmarried, chaste status, and his phrasing clearly indicates that he did not believe that all people *burn* with lust or are unable to control themselves. Although abstaining from sex outside of marriage would seem to be appropriate Christian conduct, the idea that Christianity—a pillar of Western philosophy and thinking—is inherently pro-marriage or family simply does not hold water, particularly since there is no evidence of Jesus marrying either.

As far as I have been able to determine from fairly close readings on the matter, choosing to accumulate no wealth or material possessions, choosing to remain unmarried, and choosing to minimize one's economic contributions were not viewed as inherently shameful by early Christians, so long as one did not allow himself to become a burden to others.

If anything, wealth and family appear to have been regarded with indifference by early Christians. Were Christianity strictly followed by a large percentage of the populace, America would be a very different—and almost certainly less materialistic—place than it is today. So why the modern emphasis on family-building in Christianity? No doubt that some of this is a result of legitimate variances in scriptural interpretation. But money—collected by way of filling pews with members and coffers with coins—matters to churches as well.

You can pray to the heavens for a miracle, but someone down here still has to pay the electric bill.

Turning to faiths less common in the United States, one can see that two other major world religions—Buddhism and Daoism—

are no more likely to place marriage and family on a pedestal than does Christianity.

The Buddha was married at a young age, but he *left* his home and family. He also renounced all of his wealth and titles and came to regard both family and most material possessions either neutrally or as *fetters*—bonds that prevent the liberation of the mind.[16]

If legend is to be believed, Laozi, the founder of Daoism, essentially abandoned *everything*, departing into the wilderness to never be heard from or seen again, shortly after he wrote his only known work, the *Dao De Qing*.[17]

Laozi's thoughts on material accumulation and ambition can be summarized in two brief quotes, which are:

This is how the Sage rules:

He empties the people's hearts—leaving only pure void— and fills their bellies,

He weakens their ambitions and strengthens their bones; (3)

and (the second quote)—

There is no greater misfortune than not knowing when you have enough.

There is no failing greater than the lust for success. (46)[18]

In Daoist texts (or at least the ones I have read—the *Dao De Qing* and the *Zhuangzi*, the latter an eponymous foundational work) marriage was never discouraged; however, obsessive pursuit of anything one does not want or need would interfere with adherence to the core Daoist principle of *wu wei* (无为)—which literally means *non-action*, but might also be thought of as *doing*

40

without effort; not forcing things; or even *acting in accordance with the order of the universe, rather than against it.*[19]

All of these beliefs—all of the wisdom traditions, really— emphasize *liberation.* The Big Three and the promotion of the Big Three are about quite the opposite—about binding you, about binding men, to one burdensome thing or another.

If you are religious, about half of what I discuss in this course is likely to offend or annoy you (if not both). But I hope that you have the good sense and maturity to recognize that at least *some* of what I say is both sound and relevant, even if you disagree with me more often than not, and I like to think that you will learn at least one lesson from reading this section: that the Buddha, Jesus, and Laozi—some of history's most revered fonts of wisdom and morality—had no great enthusiasm for the Big Three.

Materialism was not encouraged by these men, nor was marriage, and none of them mentioned formal education or the formally educated in their sermons or texts (unless you count Jesus's less-than-favorable comments towards the scribes and Pharisees), probably because there were no colleges or universities to criticize during their lifetimes. None of these sages were *college boys*, yet I would gladly challenge anyone to find a more significant philosophy written or developed by a member of the academic community.

Look closely, and you may find that the Rules have some similarity to your existing beliefs. They are not identical of course, and in some ways they are radically different, but nothing in the Rules is truly new. The wisdom herein is old, just adapted to modern times.

If anyone operating under the guise of religion pushes you towards the Big Three, ask him this:

If the wise men of the ages saw no shame in modest and simple living, independent learning, and celibacy, why should I?

Other Purposes of Shame

Thus far, I have largely focused on shame and how it is used to encourage you to follow the Big Three, but shame has other uses. It is quite often used to encourage you to sacrifice yourself in some way above and beyond following the Big Three (and following the Big Three Conventions *is* a sacrifice, make no mistake about it.). Be wary of this: Our society is built upon the principle of *male disposability*—the belief that men have little to no intrinsic value, save their ability to serve others.[20] If you really do feel compelled by your conscience to sacrifice yourself for a cause or for another person, act in accordance with your own free will, not the wills or machinations of others.

If you are not so inclined to sacrifice yourself, remember the most important point made in the Introduction to this book: *The world does not owe you a damn thing*, but *you do not owe the world a damn thing either*.

You may have obligations to help specific people, and if so, honor them, but you do not owe society or random strangers even a passing thought.

But you could not survive without society, so you owe your life to it. You may well hear a rebuttal to this effect offered from time to time.

How many of us could survive without the sun?

None of us! Not a one!

Aside from a few animals that live around thermal vents deep in the ocean, no life on this planet would long survive without the light of the sun. We, even the strictest carnivores, are all

42

dependent upon photosynthesis. The meat-eater's food had to eat something, did it not? And that something was probably a plant.

Yet the sun does not shine for our benefit. It shines simply because that is what it does. *The world, civilization, society,* or whatever else we call this grand abstraction of human interaction, does not work for your benefit either. You do not owe the sun worship and sacrifice. You do not owe *society* worship and sacrifice.

The sun will not try to screw you over. People will. Be mindful of that.

Counteracting Shaming Tactics

Now that you can recognize efforts to coerce you into following the Big Three Conventions for what they really are—attempts to extract resources from you—you can resist them. Follow the money, consider the source, and you should be all but immune to the effects of propaganda. Resisting *personal* efforts to entrap you in the Big Three is slightly more complicated. You may well need a rebuttal on hand. Here is the most effective strategy I have been able to devise to address this matter:

1. Consider both who is attempting to persuade you to follow the Big Three and that person's likely motives. Is this someone who actually cares about you, or is it someone who is rationally manipulative? If your parents suggest you go to college, they *may* mean well. If a girlfriend suggests you marry *her*, there is a good chance her objective is straightforward resource extraction. If a boss suggests you marry or buy a house, he may want to see you become so financially tied down that you will have no choice but to work as hard as possible for his benefit, which is why

children, a wife, and a mortgage are sometimes called *golden handcuffs*.[21]

2. Decide how you will respond to these suggestions. Is the best idea to say something sarcastic, to tell a joke, or to provide a serious reply? The most appropriate answer depends on context.

3. Repeat your answer as often as needed and deliver it consistently. Some people learn more slowly than others, and some refuse to learn at all. If you engage in much in the way of petty arguments, you will only frustrate yourself.

4. Remember this: YOU ARE NEVER OBLIGATED TO CARE. NO ONE IS EVER OBLIGATED TO CARE ABOUT ANYTHING OR ANYONE. You need to take the preceding two sentences to heart, which is why I repeat them throughout this book. If you do not care what someone thinks, there is oftentimes little harm in telling them so, directly and without coarseness. If you do not care, shaming attempts have no effect, and if the person who is trying to shame you (the *shamer*) comes to understand that you do not care, he (or she) will eventually abandon what amount to inevitably wasted efforts.[22]

Some people are simply uncomfortable when *anyone* does not do exactly as they do. Such is a sign of insecurity. If everyone *must* agree with you that a certain pizza topping is the best, you have little confidence in your dietary choices. Others may be so bound to convention that anything outside of what they consider to be the norm upsets them terribly. These are pitiable souls. There is nothing to be gained from treating them cruelly.

As for following the Big Three purely of your own accord, there are risks to consider. Any of the Big Three will trap to you a certain extent—psychologically, financially, and in the case of the most hazardous of them—getting married—legally. The last has the potential to be an impossible-to-terminate lifetime expense, whereas once you finish paying off your college loans or you sell your home, the expenses stop.

But your freedom is yours to sell (or not). You need not explain your choices to me.

If you do follow any of the Big Three, for the love of all that is holy, do them for your own sake, not to impress or please others or to avoid their condemnation.

Let your choices be purely your own. They are anyway, though some may try to convince you otherwise.

Next, we will consider *the Evil Five*.

The Thinking Man

(Ten Questions for Review and Consideration)

1. What is the purpose of shame? How does it relate to the individual and free will?

   _____

   _____

   _____

2. Have you ever been shamed into doing something or not doing something? If so, what defined this incident in your mind? In retrospect, do you think this use of shame was reasonable?

   _____

   _____

   _____

3. What is the difference between *organic* and *artificial* shame?

   _____

   _____

   _____

4. Why does our society place so much emphasis on men following the Big Three Conventions?

_____

_____

_____

5. Who stands to benefit the most from your following the Big Three Conventions?

_____

_____

_____

6. Can you think of any men whom you respect who ignored the Big Three Conventions? What do you find most interesting about these men?

_____

_____

_____

7. How can you make yourself more resistant to shame? What steps can you take to counteract attacks on your sense of self worth?

_____

_____

_____

8. What would you say to someone who tries to shame you into following the Big Three Conventions if you thought that person actually cared about you?

_____

_____

_____

9. Do you want any of the Big Three Conventions for your own reasons (independent of fear of shame)? If so, what are these reasons?

_____

_____

_____

10. Does concerning yourself with shame make following the First Rule (*Give as little as possible*), the Second Rule (*Take as much as possible*), or the Fourth Rule (*Enjoy your life to the fullest*) more difficult? If so, how?

_____

_____

_____

4) On the Evil Five

If you only take two lessons away from this book, let them be *the Rules* and *the Evil Five*. With an understanding of these, you will almost certainly live better than you do now.

These are the *Evil Five*—the five habits that consume much of a great many men's time, money, and energy. Beware of them. They are:

1. Alcohol consumption

2. Drug consumption

3. Socializing

4. The pursuit of sex, sex, and the consequences of sex (collectively: *coitus, et cetera*)

5. Status seeking and maintenance (collectively: *status struggle*)

In theory, the Evil Five (Ev5) are fine, but only in moderation. The problem with them is that they, much like salt and sugar, seem to draw upon the immoderate impulses within us. While I am entirely comfortable arguing that the world would be a better place on the balance without alcohol and drugs, this is as much a result of their overconsumption as anything else. Socializing can be beneficial, but not if done in a haphazard or idiotic way. None of the things related to sex, reproduction, and child-rearing (*coitus, et cetera*) are inherently bad either, but they have a tendency to lead to negative outcomes for a great many men due to the dynamics of our culture and the nature of our species.

Granted, the pursuit of sex has always been a dangerous thing for men—it involved competition, frequently violent, for reproductive access—but the object of a man's affections was usually not that much of a threat until recently.[1] Now, coitus, et cetera retains the brutal elements of old, with the added potential of the woman at the nexus being or becoming an enemy. Thus, the modern man may well discover too late that the *war for the womb* is a war fought on all fronts.

Status seeking and maintenance largely relate to coitus, et cetera, with men who are not pursuing sex having relatively little need to establish a high degree of status as it is popularly acquired, largely by accumulating wealth and by signaling that one has access to said wealth.

Status is different from *respect*, with respect being something that quite a few men value and need to a certain extent to maintain their mental health. Status is less important. (This difference will be examined in more depth later in this chapter.)

Of the Ev5, I save *socializing* for last due to the complexity of distinguishing the good variety from its bad counterpart. Making, having, and interacting with friends and allies can be useful ways to spend your time. Much of this constitutes *socializing*, but such is not deleterious. Ideally, socializing should help you build long-term friendships with people who share your interests and passions. It should make you less isolated and give you the confidence of knowing that you are part of a larger community that is willing to help you in your times of trouble (with you being at least somewhat willing to return the favor). Unfortunately, this is less often the case than one might hope. As it is actually practiced, much socializing is an expensive way to pick up destructive habits or to reinforce one's tendencies to pursue the other four of the Ev5 to excess. This does not necessarily need to be the case.

Before digging any deeper into this matter, let us briefly consider how each of the Ev5 has the potential to hurt you, distract you, or make your life more miserable.

Alcohol and Drugs

Rather than focusing on the biological harm of using alcohol or drugs more than infrequently, it is worth considering their psychological and social effects, with one of the worst of these being that using intoxicants makes you more complacent than you would be were you not using them.

The reason that alcohol serves as a *social lubricant* is that it renders tedious interactions seemingly less so. Marijuana also makes much of the sheer awful humdrum of life easier to bear. When used sparingly, this is not a problem; however, at sufficiently high and frequent doses, both work to enervate a man to the point of being willing to bear almost anything. A society without an excess of alcohol or drugs, a society with less of the Ev5 in general, would almost certainly function very differently from the one we have today, for the Ev5 gradually cloud and busy the mind: A room full of clear-minded people is anomalous, wondrous, and at least at first, a bit frightening.[2] A nation in the same condition—a nation all-but devoid of bullshit in general and the Ev5 in particular— would be alight with capability and creativity at rates heretofore unparalleled in all of human history.

Make no mistake about it, alcohol and drug use are heavily encouraged by any number of actors in our society. The drugs that are pushed the hardest are entirely *legal.* Pain pills, sedatives, antidepressants, anti-anxiety medications, and whatever else that happens to be the *snake oil of the moment* are all designed to pacify people—to enable them to tolerate nonsense that would otherwise prove intolerable.

51

The problem with heavy alcohol and drug use is that they, more often than not, amount to self-medication, medication that allows the user to be a better servant. The habitual consumer of intoxicants is taking a treatment to cure what is oftentimes *somebody else's disease.*

Socializing

Chirality is a characteristic of certain types of molecules to have two different forms—a *left-handed one* and a *right-handed one*. Both of these contain the same elements and are, aside from mirroring each other, identical. Given this *nearly* identical nature, left- and right-handed molecules would seem to be equally important, with one being no better than the other, yet such is not the case. We can only process left-handed protein molecules. If you were to consume food containing right-handed proteins, it would do your body no good—the right-handed molecules would prove to be biologically useless.[3] This little change—that of atoms being arranged one way or being arranged in their mirror image—could mean the difference between life and death.

As it is with proteins, so it is with socializing.

Advantageous socializing and disadvantageous socializing systems are chiral.

Consider the differences:

Advantageous Social Networks (ASN)

1. Revelry is minimal or controlled (no one gets maimed, killed, or arrested)

2. Focused primarily on beneficial (or at least non-destructive) social goals

3. Hierarchy serves as *means*, not *ends*—structure exists to keep things running smoothly

4. Aid is mutual—*give something; get something*

Disadvantageous Social Networks (DSN)

1. Revelry rises to excess (injury or death result)

2. Focused primarily on destructive social goals (mayhem for the sake of mayhem)

3. Hierarchy is the *end*, not the *means*—politics and power plays are the norm and conformity is enforced only to subordinate members to the group

4. Aid is never mutual, but destruction sometimes is—either those who give, get nothing good, or mutual sabotage is the order of the day

The key to productive socializing is to see that you land in a group with the correct handedness. This can be surprisingly challenging. About the most concise advice I can give for determining if a social group is good or bad is that you assess said group with a six-question instrument, which asks:

1. Do members of the group generally encourage other members to do harmful or destructive things?

2. Are the members of the group frequently cruel or seriously belittling to each other?

3. Are the majority of the group members sanctimonious or hypocritical?

4. Are the members of the group apparently without any interests or passions aside from alcohol, drugs, sex, or hatred?

5. Does the group lack natural cohesion?

6. Are the members of the group unwilling to help each other?

Answering yes to any of these questions is a good indication that the group under evaluation is a DSN. This is all fairly obvious, but there is something to be said for reading the obvious on the printed page: It reminds you of what you already understand but may occasionally forget.

Next, mating, dating, and all of that headache!

Coitus, Et Cetera

Prior to fairly recently, most mating and dating followed a script—courtship, seeking the blessing of parents, marriage, and then routine married life—and so long as you did not screw up too badly, everything was likely to work about as well as could be expected.[4] Families could be tremendous burdens—such has been the case for millennia—but at least the family was likely to remain intact unless the members were carried away by disease or crushed beneath the hooves of rabid horses, making investing in family a reasonably sound proposition.

Now, such is far less likely to be the case. Once you were settled into a marriage, you pretty much *stayed* in it until either you died from disease or injury or your wife died in childbirth.[5] If the latter happened, you simply got a younger model to replace her.

Go to work, pay the bills, and rely on a fairly predictable family life—that worked up until about the late 1960s.[6] You had responsibilities, but you also had a certain amount of authority. You *still* have responsibilities if you marry, but the authority is gone— an imbalance that makes this particular type of relationship unattractive to a thinking man. Marriage rarely increases your status, and it almost never results in you being treated with more respect—and with this, we should examine the major differences between the two.

Status Versus Respect

Here is the simplest distinction between respect and status: Respect is founded on the notion that *you are what you do*. Status is founded on that of *you are what you have*. One need not be able to lord anything over another to earn respect, but status is a zero-sum game. As peers, we can each consider the other worthy of respect. Respect *may* be hierarchical, but that is not always the case.

Once a group grows to encompass more than about 150 people —which is to say that it exceeds the largest of the Dunbar numbers—relationships become less personal and respect starts to merge with status—it becomes something that is frequently signified by badges, medals, titles, or other officious means. Of course, displays of respect can become hollow as well if overused, used sarcastically, or awarded automatically (meaning that they do not need to be earned). Nonetheless, respect is *less* sensitive to competition than is status. Consider this hypothetical:

You undertake all of the steps necessary to achieve high-status in your neighborhood. You build a 3,500 square foot house and fill it with fancy furniture and the most up-to-the-minute electronics, you buy a BMW *and* a Mercedes, you install a large in-ground pool, and you have an ever-changing cast of 19-year-old large-breasted semi-professional-model girlfriends.

Of course, unless you were born rich, managed to invest your way to astounding wealth, or won the lottery, all of this status maintenance requires quite a bit of work, but that is neither here nor there. You have achieved status in the community. *How* you obtained the markers of status is not really relevant: Status is all about *what* (you have) not *how* (you earned it).

Now imagine that a *new guy* moves into the neighborhood. Even before you meet the guy, you know there is something different about him. You bought three lots (your house would have dwarfed two of them). The new guy bought *six*. Contractors start to lay the foundation for the new guy's house—and it is massive. *What the hell are they building, an aircraft hangar?* you think to yourself.

As construction progresses, truckloads of marble, gold-plated fixtures, and custom tiles direct from Italy roar down the street. You are fairly certain the guy has a pool, at least a crew appeared to be digging one, but you cannot tell much about it, as it is an *indoor pool*, unlike your crappy outdoor model.

After a mere eight months, the framing and exterior work are finished—a feat that was only possible due to the crews working in shifts. Furniture trucks roll up next—most of them bearing fancy European names you are uncertain of how to pronounce, with a few Japanese brands thrown in for good measure.

The guy must have a bit of a fetish—*pretentious weeaboo prick!*—because the landscaping crew appears to be entirely Japanese. They even bring a Buddhist monk to bless the zen rock garden. *Showoff!*

Still, you have never seen *the guy*. You know nothing about him or what he has done with his life. No one else in the neighborhood does either. You see a semi—*IMAX* emblazoned on its trailer—disgorge a team of twenty and what must be several tons of theater equipment, and you look around your house. You realize that your television, all measly 120 inches of it, is now *six-months old*—an ancient throwaway at this point—and you are too embarrassed to donate it to the local orphanage, so you and your Russian *squeeze-of-the-week* break it up with sledgehammers and toss the pieces into a dumpster.

You look outside, and you see a leaf from one of your new neighbor's genetically engineered glow-in-the-dark maples landing in your pool, which now looks more like a *cesspool* to you.

Your lungs tighten. You cannot breathe. Your *little shack* of a house is so claustrophobic that staying in it may well drive you into having a full-blown panic attack. So you step outside, clutching your chest and gasping, and into the shadow of your neighbor's mighty guard tower.

And a Maserati pulls up to the castle beside your drab dungeon of a property. Out steps *the man*—a teenager—followed by a team of strongmen-sized bodyguards who mumble into their sleeves. The *kid*, a fat little tub of scowling ugliness, with skin so rough that Danny Trejo could pass for a boy band member in comparison, glances around, spots your house, curls his lips into a snarl, and spits.

This lousy little town is beneath me, he thinks—you can see it in his eyes. *This*—your pathetic Podunk—is where his father sent him as punishment for his bad behavior (and it *was* pretty bad—three prostitutes died in the fire).

Your girlfriend will leave you for the boy wonder, this oily skinned and rarely washed little psychopath, and without any regret at all. Your status is gone. You lost it, simply because *his was bigger*.

That is status.

Respect can be lost as well. Respect is also fragile, but not as fragile as status. Here is the other relevant point: Status quite often relates to your sexual market value (SMV)—meaning (if you are a heterosexual man) how sexually desirable *women* perceive you to be. Remember, your decency and worth as a human being have almost nothing to do with how often you get laid.[7] If they did, the asshole gene would have died off long ago. Respect has little to do with SMV—meaning (again assuming you are straight) that it is far more likely to relate to how relatively small groups of *men* perceive you.

You would be wise to avoid obsessing over the opinions of anyone, man or woman, but if you *must* concern yourself with the esteem of others, try to focus on the regard of those who are not assessing you sexually. SMV and status are largely external to the man and transient. Respect is far less so. And you will be far happier and healthier if you direct your energies towards making yourself respectable than trying to raise your status. Even if you are quite invisible, you can still build your own worth—making yourself *worthy of respect* (even if much in the way of respect is not given to you), whereas status is purely external: One cannot be *worthy of status* but not actually have it.

Nothing Worth Chasing: The Value of the Ev5

The less a man engages in the Ev5, the greater his opportunities to cultivate peace of mind and strength of spirit.

The blind pursuit of the Ev5 binds one to a cycle of anticipation, consumption, and disappointment: The Ev5 are addictive, even if the particular Evil is an intangible, such as status. In the long term, mindlessly chasing the Ev5 will not make you happy. It will not give you peace. What it will do, is turn you into someone's tool.

The downside of heavily engaging in the Ev5 continues to grow for men, while the upside diminishes. For instance, many of the

58

illegal drugs available today are more dangerous than those commonly found on the market 30 years ago (when really powerful drugs, such as fentanyl, were quite uncommon), and the potential negative legal consequences of being seriously involved with a woman are vastly more severe than they were years ago.[8]

The greatest problem with reducing one's attachment to the Ev5 is that it will lead to an overabundance of free time.

If not pursuing the Ev5, how will you spend your days?

You will certainly need to do less work that does not interest you. You will obsess less over the opinions of others. You will have more resources to spend as you please, as you will no longer need to waste much money or exert much effort to keep up appearances. Your mind will be clearer, and your thinking faster and more efficient.

So what will you do?

What are your other interests?

There are far worse problems than having more time than you know how to spend, but it is a problem nonetheless. You should have already made some effort to determine what you really want and need—after all, the purpose of Chapter 2 ("The Lists") was to help you do just that. Education, not necessarily schooling, can be critical to improving your life and developing your interests. This leads to the next section, in which we will consider both education, how to acquire it, and how it differs from schooling.

The Thinking Man

(Ten Questions for Review and Consideration)

1. Do the Evil Five (Ev5) relate to each other? If so, how?

_____

_____

_____

2. What are some of the drawbacks of intensively pursuing the Ev5?

_____

_____

_____

3. Have you ever seen anyone harmed by pursuing the Ev5? If so, *who* and *how*?

_____

_____

_____

4. Which of the Ev5 is most likely to be harmful *to you*?

_____

_____

_____

5. How much of your time do you think you should spend pursuing the Ev5?

_____

_____

_____

6. What are the differences between *respect* and *status*?

_____

_____

_____

7. Are women more attracted to status or respectability? Why do they value one over the other?

_____

_____

_____

8. If not pursuing the Ev5, how would you spend your time?

_____

_____

_____

9. The first two of the Ev5 obviously relate to addiction. Do the others have any connection to addition? If so, *what* is the connection?

_____

_____

_____

10. Does pursuit of the Ev5 violate the Rules? If so, *which* Rules does it violate? *How* does doing so violate them?

_____

_____

_____

5) On Education

Tell Me What You Want, What You Really, Really Want . . .

The brutal truth is this: Schools want your (frequently borrowed) money. They do not want you, and by *you*, I mean anyone with a penis, unless you have made an appointment to have said penis removed or happen to be a truly remarkable athlete.[1] Yet you are still encouraged to attend college. Getting your (borrowed) money otherwise would be too difficult, and schools, much like those who advocate that men marry, face no repercussions if they willfully misdirect you to the depths of hell.[2]

This is not to suggest that every teacher and every administrator at every college and university in the United States is bound to hate you. A few of them may even care a great deal about how much you gain from your academic experience. Many will not. The concern these people have for you and your education is largely determined by the pride they take in their work and the robustness of their altruistic tendencies. Such traits are fragile, however, and you would be wise to avoid putting much stock in them.

I have been on one side or the other of the teaching/learning experience for quite some time—I taught for four years, mostly college students (although I taught middle school as well)—and I have been in school for far longer than that. Some of my teachers, men and women alike, have helped me. In turn, I have *tried* to help quite a few of my students. I was not always successful, but this was not for lack of effort.

Some teachers and students will not get along, and they might not have any idea as to why. I disliked a few of my students (and I suspect such students disliked me), but I tried to treat all of my students fairly, even if I wanted to strangle them. For the most part, I think I was successful *because I dedicated a lot of energy to being fair.* And being impartial is not always easy. Some people will discriminate against you, and it may have nothing to do with anything that you can control.

I was probably more sympathetic to the plight of boys and young men than most of the teachers you had in school. First, I tried hard to understand my own biases—against the awkward students, against the pushy students, against the sarcastic students, against the students who never smiled and looked as though they wanted to stab themselves in the neck because they would have preferred anything to being in school—and I made a point of double-checking my grades to see that I was being reasonable and consistent.

Did I give that person a "B" because he gave a lousy presentation, or did I give him a "B" because I thought he was an ass? was a question I frequently asked myself. Yet *power corrupts,* and some teachers will downgrade students for being difficult—call it the *little-asshole penalty*—and some will give other students points for likability—the *sweetheart bonus.* I cannot honestly swear that I never did this—my memory is imperfect—but I certainly tried to avoid it.

Second, I am not a woman, and women—more than men—seem to favor their own kind. Think of it as *homophily on steroids.* Oops! I mean *homophily on estrogen.* (Sorry, wrong hormone.) Female teachers generally grade girls' work more favorably than the work of boys—a pattern that is eliminated when test papers are anonymized. And women are about five times more likely to show in-group preference (women favoring women) than are men (men favoring men).[3]

Given that schools are largely dominated by women—in teaching, administration, and policy-making (pretty much everything but the highest levels of leadership)—school is all but guaranteed to be more of a girl and woman-friendly environment than it is to be a boy or man-friendly one.[4]

Teachers and their biases, however, are less a problem than is the nature of school itself.

School is built on the assumption that you need your hand held —that you cannot figure things out for yourself. Much of school requires that you be passive, *really passive,* and that you either have no opinions of your own or that you conceal these opinions and go along with the predetermined way of doing and learning things.[5]

Women's natural passivity is almost certainly one of the reasons that they generally do better in school than do men. Boys and men are harder to teach—at least that is what I have observed. This has nothing to do with a lack of intelligence. It has to do with the fact that they will either try to find their own solutions or (if they cannot do that) simply give up and ignore whatever the teacher is saying. Boys and men expect some sort of *results,* at least from what I observed. They will happily learn when they think that there is something worth learning—something useful or intrinsically interesting—however, they flag when expected to go along to get along for no other reason than that *this is the way things are done.*[6]

As a teacher, I tried to give all of my students—men and women, boys and girls—freedom to think for themselves. I let my students write test questions, I asked what topics they wanted to discuss, and I let them develop alternative assignments if they did not like the ones I had given them. I like to think I was fairly creative in my teaching, but I simply did not have the time to let every student do whatever he (or she) wanted. If I had done that, I would still be trying to wrap up my first class, rather than having finished it years ago.

I also had to pick a level for the material I planned to teach—I usually went for the middle, meaning I selected topics that were neither really hard nor really easy. In theory, this works for everyone. In practice, this means that about 25% of my students found my lessons to be too easy, about 25% found them to be too difficult, and about 50% found them to be just right. *Half of my class* was not getting what they really needed or wanted, and there was not much I could do to solve this problem given my limited time and resources.

School is designed for those who are scattered rather than focused in their interests—gatherers, not hunters. At the lowest levels of education—kindergarten through about fifth grade—this is not much of a problem. Students do switch from one topic to the next, but not so much so that they are left forever bouncing from one subject, room, or teacher to another. In the middle- and high-school grades, this becomes more of a problem. Students run from class to class and shift their attention from subject to subject without really focusing on anything for long.

The problem is most pronounced at the undergraduate college level, where men seem to fare quite poorly.[7]

Consider a typical freshmen schedule at an ordinary (non-vocational) college. Here is how it might look:

Monday—

English Composition

Algebra with Functions

Psychology

Tuesday—

U.S. History—Colonial Period to Civil War

Art Appreciation

Wednesday—

No Classes

Thursday—

A repeat of Tuesday.

Friday—

A repeat of Monday.

This is not a particularly demanding itinerary. It accounts for 15 credit hours per semester and an ordinary range of general education subjects. At first glance, it looks to be outright easy, but there are other things we need to consider.

First, there is a very real chance a student will be working while in college. The majority of college students (meaning 70%) do this for an average of 29 hours per week, with some working quite a bit more. Most of these jobs are not great, and understandably so. After all, most college students have limited skills and can only work somewhat irregular hours.

Quite a few employed students are in customer service, particularly waiting tables, a job at which women, at least the attractive ones, typically make more men than do men (better tips).[8] As I note in Chapter 6 ("On Work"), customer service appears to be generally better suited to women than to men, which is unfortunate due to customer service work being more likely than some other types of work to offer the flexible arrangements that students generally require.

Even if jobs were not an issue, the scattered nature of study in college would be.

It is generally accepted that women multitask better than do men, and there is some research to support this.[9] There are exceptions, of course, and *multitasking* can be defined in more than one way. In the visual multitasking practiced in video games and certain other activities that require high degrees of situational awareness, there may not be much of a difference between men and women; however, the type used in school, which requires switching from one semi-engaging task to the next, does seem to be easier for women.

Assuming that an average class requires four papers or assignments in a semester and that the average student is taking five classes (fairly typical requirements, in my experience), the total number of papers or assignments required per semester should be around 20, and this does not count mandatory online discussion postings, which are sometimes a part of even traditional classroom-based courses. Many of these assignments may be relatively easy, as the standards for an acceptable undergraduate research paper are somewhere between comedically bad and tragically illiterate, but the sheer number of assignments is potentially overwhelming.

The traditional approach to education—many classes at the same time with relatively little attention paid to any one class—favors women and those without really strong interests in one particular field. This teaching method is not a product of feminism. It predates feminism by enough time to rule out that possibility. Rather, it appears to relate strongly to the lack of a clearly defined purpose for college education.

At one point in time, college was designed to train religious workers, independent scholars, or government workers. It then became a sort of finishing school for the upper classes or (in the case of *normal schools*) a training center for schoolteachers.[10] Now, the purpose of college is considerably less certain.

This lack of certainty leads to a smorgasbord approach to education that offers a bit of everything but not that much of anything in particular. Consider some of the popular reasons given for people to attend college:

1. To learn professional skills/to get a better job/to make more money
2. To develop critical thinking skills
3. To develop communications skills
4. To become more responsible and engaged citizens
5. To develop a better understanding of the world[11]

These—the reasons *given* for people to attend college—differ somewhat from the reasons a great many people *actually go*. The latter are addressed within a few pages.

While *liberals arts* in the traditional sense covered seven subjects (grammar, rhetoric, logic, geometry, arithmetic, music, and astronomy), the contemporary usage of the term is somewhat different. A modern liberals arts education—meaning what general education requirements are supposed to provide—entails foreign language, mathematics, literature, social and physical sciences, and history. This is in addition to whatever students are supposed to learn for their given profession.

How in the name of all that is unholy are you supposed to learn all of the subjects mentioned and all of the skills listed *in about four years*?

Consider just one of these fields: foreign language. If you take enough math classes, you may be able to avoid mandatory foreign-language training. Otherwise, two years of study of a language other than English is probably in the cards for you.

Anyone who has ever tried to learn a foreign language in adulthood will understand just how pointless taking a few hours of language classes for several years is. Some adults can learn a foreign language fluently, but most adults will never develop much more than the most rudimentary communications skills in their second tongue.[12] Even if you *can* learn languages with ease, chances are that practicing a couple of hours a week for two years will accomplish little. *Effective* language-learning programs, such as those offered by the Defense Language Institute, vary in length but never exceed 18 months, which would seem to bode well for the college approach to language instruction. However, there are two noteworthy differences: the first is that the Defense Language Institute method relies on *intensive* training, and the second is that the Defense Language Institute is selective about whom it admits.[13]

Focused training for naturally good students—this, not the college way, is how a language is effectively taught to (select) adults.

At its heart, the post-secondary approach to learning encourages half-baked performance. Learning a little about everything is functionally equivalent to learning a whole lot of nothing. I am not the first person to notice this. Entire books have been written arguing that college students derive no intellectual benefit from their studies.[14]

70

To anyone with an engineering background, the problem within the educational system, specifically the higher educational system, should be relatively easy to spot: The design specifications are both impossibly vague and insanely ambitious. Even the best engineer alive (or to have ever lived) would have a difficult time designing an effective food dryer-fusion reactor-rice cooker-rototiller-Blu-ray player with a built-in ice machine and camera. *Someone* might be able to cobble such a machine together, but there is a real chance that the rice would be overcooked, the Blu-rays would be scratched, the ice would melt, and the photos would be blurry. No one and nothing can do all things equally well, unless *equally well* means doing things *very badly*.

College: Because Books Are Expensive?

Think about any of the lectures you have attended. Half of the time the teacher drones on, essentially reciting from a book that you could buy online and study at your convenience. The other half of the time the teacher reads from *notes* that are considerably less organized than those published by CliffsNotes (and devoid of the helpful diagrams). Occasionally, a class may offer a lab or some interesting discussion, but such is the exception rather than the rule.

Why do we (still) do this?

The answer is straightforward, but you need to know a bit of history to make sense of it.

The first university in Europe (University of Bologna) was founded in 1088. Back then, books were expensive. Johannes Gutenberg did not invent the printing press until almost 400 years later, so every book had to be copied by hand.[15] Paying someone to read *from* a book made sense. The entire university was built up around the library—you know what that is: the one place on campus where the majority college students *never go* unless they are planning to have sex or deal drugs between the stacks—because it contained the oh-so-valuable books.

One would think that the growth of low-costing printing would have killed the university, and Gutenberg's invention made books cheap enough for private citizens to own *and read for themselves* after all. Yet it did not.

Since that was not enough to ram a knife into the university's well-fed belly, the growth of public libraries, which first came into being in the 19th century, should have done them in.[16] Yet it did not.

The internet, the e-book reader, the smartphone, free video lectures—with this much competition, the university—fierce zombie that it is—should have eventually met its match. Yet it did not.

Why?

Colleges still have libraries, and some of these libraries contain material that would be difficult to get anywhere else. Libraries are great resources, and I urge anyone who lives near a decent university library to try to obtain a non-student library card—something that can oftentimes be obtained for a very reasonable fee. It is the *rest* of the college system with which I take issue.

The modern college is not centered around the library: It is focused around the textbook and the lecture. The problem with both of these is that they both encourage incredibly rigid deference to authority. In a library, you may find 15 books or articles, each presenting a different opinion or idea on a specific topic or problem. On the internet, you may well find *hundreds* of articles on a given matter—from solid research and writing to outright crackpot material (and everything in between). It is *your* job to assess the strength of the arguments and try to make sense of the material yourself. A good teacher should prepare his students for this—help them develop the skills to spot flaws in evidence and arguments—but helping is distinct from doing: This is the distinction between *aiding and abetting* and wrapping one's hands around the grip, cocking the hammer, and pulling the trigger.

Learning how to assess facts and differing ideas by close reading and careful study is *critical thinking*—one of those things universities claim to teach and which really *is* a tremendously useful skill. In a textbook or lecture, however, you are likely to be presented with exactly *one* opinion—that of the author. And despite the eccentric looks and behavior of certain college teachers, many of whom write textbooks, they *firmly support the status quo* more often than not. There are few people more conventional in their thoughts and actions than professors—not rocking the boat is the surest way to get tenure, and most academics want tenure. Even the most radical of campus radicals has less in common with GG Allin than he does with the kids who shop at Hot Topic.

Bugs within the college system that may have initially resulted from limited access to books or ignorance as to the way humans learn have now become *features*, and the very the *raisons d'être* for the existence of college, which is to *make people as uniform, passive, and unquestioning of accepted norms as possible.*[17]

I should stress this—*the status quo is against you.* In any system that favors blind conformity and a high degree of consistency, women will be more likely to excel. You are not a woman. You will not be favored. This disadvantage is aside and apart from anything related to in-group preferences or feminist theory.

Consistency matters!

Consistency becomes *more*, not less, of an issue the deeper down the educational rabbit hole you go. Women are more nearly uniform than are men in almost every domain: intelligence, height, behavior, degree of loquaciousness or laconism, and willingness (or ability) to successfully complete suicide.[18] This is not to say that men are *better* than are women (with *better* being a meaningless term out of context), only that men are more likely to be unusual. Large-scale industrial processes require uniform input so that they may generate uniform output. School is an industrial system, so school favors the uniform.

My advice to boys and men regarding higher education is simple and has only a few exceptions: *Do not go to college!*

I repeat: **DO NOT GO TO COLLEGE!**

At best, it will turn you into a cynic. At worst, it will break you in body and spirit.

On Being a Hypocrite

I went to college. I went to graduate school. I completed a doctoral degree. That someone who did all of this is telling you to avoid college very well may have set off your bullshit detector. That is fine. Maybe I am a hypocrite, but even hypocrites and bastards are right from time to time.

And think about this: Would you trust me any more if I had *not* gone to college and was telling you not to go? Some people are bound to attack anyone who has not done something and advises against it because *how would he know?*

If I had gone to college and dropped out of it, whatever criticisms I laid against the institution would be dismissed by some as *sour grapes.*

I cannot win this—no matter what I have done or have not done, I cannot escape criticism. What I *can* do is explain my reasons for going to (and staying in) college and how they are unlikely to apply to you.

I started college for the same reason that many people, men and women alike, do—I had no other plans, and I had no independent way of making much of a living. I went to college *because I failed to plan for adulthood.*

I stayed in college because it was relatively easy for me, even though I was not the most enthusiastic of learners, and because I eventually adapted to the environment so thoroughly that surviving in a different one would be quite difficult: This is sometimes called *institutionalization.* In addition to meaning *forced into an institution* (as in *We institutionalized our crazy aunt after she chased little Johnny through the street with a butcher's knife.*), *institutionalization* can also mean the loss of independence that results from spending a long time in an institutional environment.

The extent to which I have become institutionalized is probably somewhat less than is typical for those with my level of formal credentials due to my position at the periphery of the educational system, which is not to say that I am truly free.

My undergraduate degree was a mixture of community college classes, credit by examination, and a once-a-week night-school program for adult students at a religious institution (that, largely for pragmatic and funding reasons, did not attempt to proselytize). My master's degree, while from a state university, was obtained entirely online, and my doctorate was earned through a non-traditional program. Additionally, although I worked for several years as a college teacher, I taught at a small institution in rural China, where I was expected to refrain from criticism of the Chinese Communist

Party but was never expected to show any enthusiasm for its ideals or operation nor expected to toe any particular ideological line or to concern myself with political correctness (in the Western sense). Even my high school diploma was obtained through a correspondence program, which spared me the browbeating and intimidation of female-friendly secondary schoolteachers.

I *do* know how the educational system works—I have learned how to arrange the right words and phrases in the correct order and to think like a native; however, I was not so totally immersed in school that my identity was wholly subsumed into that of the Borg. Thus, I am what one might call *an inside outsider*—someone always connected to school but never entirely in the thick of it.[19]

Had I been absorbed by the greater academic culture, I almost certainly would have become so invested in my academic persona that I would not have been able to write this book.

Exceptions: Few and Far Between

If you have dreamed of being a doctor or a lawyer from the time you were five years old and you can think of nothing else that would make you happy, school may be worth the hassle, but only if you *know*, completely and without doubt, that there is no other work, anywhere on earth, that is suited to you. *If* such is the route you choose to take, **proceed with caution**. Be the one who makes no mistakes.[20] And remember that you are in school to achieve your life's goal, not party, not drink, and most certainly not date. The time for such things, if ever, is later.

Now, to the heart of the matter.

College: Seven Reasons to Avoid It As Though It Were a Plague- infected Rat

What I offer in this section is what I learned from my years in a somewhat unusual position, and what follows are some of the reasons most men should not go to college.

1. College reduces you to a cog.

2. College teaches you to hate yourself.

3. College teaches you to accept the worst deal imaginable (in addition to quite a number of other absurdities).

4. College teaches you to have disdain for anything practical.

5. College teaches you to ignore the value of creative thinking.

6. College teaches you wrong kind of social skills—the kind where you casually feign concern for others but form no real connection with them.

7. College teaches you that learning is boring.

Let us go through these one by one.

Point 1: College reduces you to a cog.

I am not going to analyze this to no end—I think that I have made most of the relevant points already. Rather than viciously flog the bloated carcass of a long-since-departed horse, let me ask you a question:

If school is about learning, why is there so much emphasis on grades, degrees, and certificates?

Let us step back for a moment. *Grading* is not unique to humans. Tobacco is graded. Milk is graded. Eggs and honey are graded. *Why?* The purpose of grading is to allow the uniform assessment and sorting of things, meaning that all Grade A milk should be of the same quality. *It should be interchangeable.* One gallon of Grade A milk, assuming that it is not expired or was improperly stored, is about as good as another. As is the case for grading milk, so is the case for grading students.

Let me anticipate the most obvious counterargument to this, which is that the purpose of grading in school is not to sort people like milk or honey, but to give them *feedback* so that they can more easily correct their mistakes and misunderstandings.

On the face of it, this makes sense. *What cannot be measured cannot be improved.*[21] You *cannot* learn without some feedback as there is no way to know what you should change in order to get better. But *why all the recordkeeping?* I can give you detailed feedback in the form of a small report, some oral comments, or even a smack on the head when you screw up. To varying degrees, all of these can convey the information you need to improve. All of them let you know that you are doing something right or wrong.

But I do not need to keep detailed records *on everything*. The fact of the matter is this: It really does not make much difference to me (or you) how well or poorly you did on something five years ago. You may have forgotten all of the subject material covered in a class in that time. You may have improved greatly. You may have remained exactly where you were.[22] *Long-term recordkeeping of grades is a way to sort people, to grade them on their degree of conformity and as commodities.*

You only need to be graded for two reasons: 1) you plan to work for someone else (and *they* need to be able to quickly categorize and sort you); 2) you plan to work in a highly regulated field, such as medicine, in which the degree is a prerequisite to starting employment.

Generally, I would advise against either of these routes. If you work for someone else, *they* will have the bulk of the power. If you work in a highly regulated field, the board/bar/licensing association can kick you out—meaning that they can render your years of formal schooling and debt *less than worthless:* negative-value encumbrances—millstones around your neck.[23]

Point 2: College teaches you to hate yourself.

Academics are a self-loathing and peculiar bunch—believe me, I am one.

Part of this comes from academics not knowing what they really are. Consider the campus protests around the United States over the last few years. Many of the protesters were mere students. I do not want to be too hard on those still in their salad days—they are still young, dumb, and full of . . . rum (or jelly shots, possibly). I never participated in a protest in my pre-befuddlement years, so I suppose that I could safely cast a stone in this particular direction, but I was not without my transgressions. Fortunately for me, my youth came to an end before the days of smartphones and online videos and their ability to turn every act of foolishness into fodder for the global troll network.

But consider the teachers involved in this overacted street theater.

Most of these teachers are older—at least thirty years old, probably in their *thirties* or later—and they should have sown their wild oats years ago, yet they apparently did not. Nevertheless, they persist.

So what (or *whom*) are they protesting?

1. The privileged
2. The conventional

79

3. The powerful

Let me repeat: *the privileged, the conventional, and the powerful.*

They are protesting themselves, and for the most part, quite earnestly!

College professor may not be the most lucrative job, but it provides a reasonably high degree of economic security, good benefits, time off, and opportunities for advancement. It also provides power—power over students based on the grades assigned to them and the power to be taken more seriously as an *educated person* when discussing just about anything.

This is but a small part of a larger irony—that of the members of the professional class who rail against the rich, the privileged, the underworked, and the overpaid—but *not them*. They mean *those other rich, spoiled guys*. A competent student of human nature could have a field day with this, but I have neither the time nor the inclination to examine at present the matter in depth.

It is true that not all college teachers are *professors*. Those who are not tenured (or at least *tenure-track*, meaning that they are in line to get jobs for life) receive far less in the way of benefits than their tenured peers, but those people are rarely at protests—they are too afraid of being fired.[24]

Those who cannot *do, theorize*. Those who cannot *theorize, mimic*. Those who cannot manage that, *protest* (oftentimes too much)! There are few things in heaven or on earth *less* intellectually demanding than spouting ideology at great length and high volumes.

Do you doubt me?

Try this: Order copies of *The Manifesto of the Communist Party* and *Quotations from Chairman Mao Tse-tung*. Skim them, memorize some of the more interesting phrases about the proletariat, order a beret (basically a glorified sock for your head) and some drab fatigues from those filthy capitalists at Amazon.com, and quit shaving for a week. Now park your posterior in front of the social sciences building at your nearest college campus. Start spouting off your Prussian and Asian rhetoric, throw in a few phrases about *gender oppression*, and wait to be dragged into a classroom! You might be able do something similar by standing outside the college of business and reciting the bon mots of Milton Friedman, but you'd need to buy a suit, lest you look out of place, and that would necessitate spending at least $75.00 in the Walmart menswear section—maybe more—and who has that kind of money?

If protesting *yourself* seems an odd way to spend your free time, that is because it is. Bankers generally do not prattle on about the evils of banking. Lawyers may know a few lawyer jokes, but most would not seriously advocate doing away with their profession. Doctors are not likely to tell you that medicine is all bullfeathers and that physicians should be forced into the countryside to raise pigs.

Yet academics and those who spend an excessive amount of time around them develop this peculiar self-hatred. I suspect this is at least partially the result of *impostor syndrome*, which is the tendency of certain people to consider themselves, deep down, to be frauds.[25]

Unfortunately for a great many academics, these feelings may be at least partially justified. If you can set a broken arm; perform a heart transplant; design or repair an engine; or code a bigger,

81

better, and cooler video game, you know that you *can* do something. Joe Schmo *cannot* do these things, at least not without some training. You will notice that most of the academics in the harder (more substantial) fields—those people who can *make* or *do* something—are not very active in radical campus activism.[26]

There are several reasons for this pattern of protest versus non-protest across the disciplines. One involves the peculiar strain that attempting to achieve professional success in academia places on the psyche.

The professional fate of academics is largely determined by their productivity as authors—meaning the number of books and papers they can get published. Their performance as educators is also assessed, but the value of instruction is difficult to quantify, with the closest thing to an official measure of teaching effectiveness being the result of student evaluations—essentially a measure of how much students like their teachers. Beyond grading gently, there is not much teachers can do to control student evaluations, with some people simply being more likable than others and receiving better evaluations as a result.

The value of academic papers in most fields is somewhat easier to assess, largely based on the *impact factor* of the journal in which they are published.[27] While there is some debate as to the exact numbers, the lion's share of humanities papers are never cited, and about one-third of social science papers fare no better. This means that, at least in some fields, *there is no evidence that anyone anywhere thinks the majority of papers are worth mentioning.*[28]

Imagine this: You spend months hammering out page after page of incomprehensible verbiage. You send your paper to one editor after the next. You finally get your paper accepted. You spend months more on revisions. The paper is finally published, and . . .

That is it.

Nothing.

You never hear from anyone about what you wrote. Except for the fact that you have another line to add to your *curriculum vitae* (that is *academic-eze* for a resume), there is no evidence that your work served any purpose whatsoever. After a while, you grow to wish that someone would even *argue* with you about what you write: Having your ideas attacked is considerably less depressing than having them totally ignored. So you push the envelope, trying to get a rise out of someone. Still, *nothing!* No matter how outlandish your words, no matter how absurd or hateful your sentiments, no matter how provocatively phrased your ideas, all that you deem fit to print is drawn into the singularity of the research database, never to be recalled again, save for by desperate undergraduates whose final papers are short four references (out of a total of five) and were due *last week!*

How would this make *you* feel?

I have been on both sides of this. I have skimmed hundreds of papers and thought to myself *why did they write this?* At the same time, I have written papers—spent far too much time on them—so that others may ask themselves the same question. At best, seeing one's words perform the same disappearing act time and again leads to a gentle ennui. At worse, it has the potential to lead to an existential crisis.

Another obvious reason that these apparently fat-but-unhappy academics rally behind nonsensical political and social theories is that *theories are theories*, and academics *like* theories. Theories are their stock and trade. In some domains, such as physics, most theories are testable. In other fields, such as some of the social sciences and any domain with the word *studies* in it, untestable theories are so common that they barely cause an eyebrow to be raised.

All-encompassing, unfalsifiable theories are essentially religious beliefs for the godless, with the major difference being that most religious beliefs appeal to one's desire to be loved and connected to something great, whereas academic theories appeal to the desire to feel *really, really smart*. In *theory*, social/political theories prove and explain almost all human interaction. In practice, such is not always the case. Yogi Berra, the philosopher-sage of New York, had some interesting things to say about the theory versus practice distinction, but I will leave you to search for his wisdom on your own time.

Marxist theory and the many academic derivatives thereof—feminist theory, intersectionality, and whatever else is in vogue on college and university campuses at the moment—provide an elegant view of the world that makes feeling morally superior easy and that are of low enough viscosity to be easily poured from any technical or epistemological container into any other. What has not been proven to be false *may* be true, which can be good enough if you really need something to believe. Theologians, with their argument for the necessity of a *leap of faith*—the idea that religious beliefs can only be truly accepted if one is willing to forgo demands for empirical evidence—are ahead of the Marxist/social theorist curve by a few hundred years in this regard, so they spend little time trying to prove the unprovable. Academics have yet to catch up. When they do, there will almost certainly be fewer soporific papers written.

The cruel reality of all of this self-protest is that ideologically enraptured academics would lose terribly if they won. Extreme left-wingers—Pol Pot and Mao Zedong, for instance—have proven to have little loyalty to the academic community that supports them *in theory*.[29]

To anyone outside the ivory tower, academics are *the privileged* —the bourgeois, the well-to-do—and the privileged do not fare well in societies that emphasize equality at any price. To the oblivious academic, ending up on the killing fields (and not as the gardener) would come as quite the unwelcome surprise. To the less oblivious, this untimely end would be no more shocking than the rising and the setting of the sun. We must also consider the possibility that many within the academic community are not so lacking in historical awareness as they appear—that they are in grips of a collective castration fantasy or a bout of suicidal ideation.

Imagine an entire career in which you are paid to do something that you suspect has no value at all. This likely leads to either extreme cynicism or extreme insecurity, and insecurity can turn to self-hatred and, somewhat paradoxically, protective arrogance combined with self-destructiveness.

Do you really want to be taught by these people?

Point 3: College teaches you to accept the worst deal imaginable and a number of other absurdities.

Do you have a car? *No?*

What about a motorcycle? *No?*

Scooter? *No?*

Snowmobile? *No?!*

Jet ski? *No!!!*

Nothing? Really?

I hope that you that you have *some* way of getting from point A to point B that is better than walking. If you *are* in such an

85

unenviable position, I hope that your city has a subway. If it does not, consider a unicycle. Laugh all you want, but I know of at least one guy who can do a solid 15 miles per hour on his. And he never has to rotate his tires—that is a bonus.

If you are like most Americans, you have some form of motorized transportation, and there is a very good chance that you financed the purchase of it.[30] Transportation is a big-ticket item, and for that reason, many people have experience obtaining and repaying automotive loans. Even if you have no wheels or always pay in cash, there is a good chance that you have financed *something*, or at least someone you know has financed something, and the point of this section is *finance*, not cars.

Imagine talking to a finance officer and being offered this deal on a car:

1. You, the borrower, agree to start borrowing money now and to keep borrowing money for the next four years. If you do not, *no car for you!*

2. You agree to do anything and everything anyone and everyone at the dealership says you must do for the next four years. If you do not, *no car for you!*

3. You must attend various events at the dealership. If you do not attend these events, again, *no car for you!*

4. You can be kicked off the car lot for any reason (or no reason at all). If this happens, *no car for you!*

5. If you are denied your car, you will receive absolutely no refund. *No car for you!*[31] *And we are keeping your money, dumbass!*

6. You agree to buy the car entirely without warranty. Even if you finally manage to jump through every required hoop

and you are given the keys, the vehicle may not start. *And that is your problem! All sales are final!*

7. None of the debt incurred over these four years shall be dischargeable in bankruptcy. Car or no car, your fault or the dealership's fault—these make no difference. *You are stuck with this debt until you are dead or disabled!*

To summarize: For most people, going to college requires agreeing to the layaway plan from hell. Were this anything other than a college degree—a car, a yacht, a toaster oven—almost anyone would run screaming in the other direction. Yet people borrow money for college and spend years hoping that Satan's salesmen do not do them wrong because:

1. They are young and foolish enough when they start college to agree to almost anything.

2. Almost everyone they know is going to college—and herd instinct is a powerful thing.

3. They do not know what else to do with their lives.

4. They believe that college will be fun.

5. They think that college will help them make more money and lead better lives, which is what the majority of experts suggest to be the case (and said experts have colorful charts to prove it).[32]

Lies, damned lies, and statistics!

As to the first matter, I do not want to be too hard on freshly minted high-school graduates. I do not often blame people for their innocence. I blame those around them who encourage such stupidity. I might not be able to stop a man barely of the age of majority from doing 120 in a 35 miles-per-hour zone, but I would not feel right about encouraging such behavior. *No one* should feel good about encouraging such recklessness.

Regarding the second and third points, I *get* these two—following the herd and not knowing what else to do. Quite a few young men have no clear goals when they graduate high school (I did not) and their parents want rid of them. This leaves the bulk of them with three options:

1. Moving in with friends (which can be tricky to arrange)

2. Joining the military

3. Going to college

The military has considerably higher standards than do most colleges. In fact, about 70% of Americans who are 18 to 24 years of age are not eligible to join the armed forces, whereas about 69% of high school graduates go on to college or other postsecondary schooling.[33] Those numbers are not perfectly comparable—*all* Americans 18 to 24 in one camp versus high school graduates (a subset of the total population) in the other—but they do suggest that Uncle Sam has at least slightly higher standards than do run-of-the-mill state universities and community colleges. Following the herd to college is the natural default. After all, if *everybody* is doing it, how bad can it be?

Next, there is the long-promoted notion that *college is a blast*. I wish I could report that this is correct, but in my experience, such was not the case. Forget *Animal House* and *Van Wilder*, college will be less fun than you could possibly imagine. The old frat-boy tropes are from *years ago*—before mandatory sexual-harassment prevention courses, before the claim that *one-fourth* of women in college have been sexually assaulted.[34]

My college experience was, aside from when I paid tuition or bought an obscenely overpriced textbook, pleasantly violation free, but I may well have benefited from years of terrible dental work and a general disregard for my appearance: I do not, thank God, have a pretty mouth.

And with that happy thought, we segue the next subtopic, that of the alleged value of a college degree (assuming you can finish one).

Much of the research used to back the argument that college is a great investment is based on some rather curious slights of hand, with the most significant one being that the benefits of higher education are frequently overstated, while the drawbacks are understated.

College helps *some people some of the time* in their pursuit of a middle-class lifestyle. But for quite a few people, college will prove to be nothing more than a lifelong burden of debt.[35] Overall, the benefits of college are uncertain. The cost is not. Your father may have been able to pay for college by working summer jobs, but such is likely to be nightmarishly difficult for you. To accept such a deal, a deal requiring that one borrow large sums of money for the most uncertain of returns, is absurd.

Point 4: College teaches you to have disdain for anything practical.

One of the first things you will notice about a great many academics is that they are relatively helpless outside of the classroom. There are some exceptions to this—the writing teacher who philosophizes as he motorcycles across America or the professor of history who builds his own house—but for the most part, you will find that a college professor is more likely to need your help outside of the academy than you are likely to need his.

Then there is the natural tendency to disdain that which makes no sense to us. This is worth exploring.

Academics may argue that said tendency is one reason that they are not better respected—that very few people understand the value of what they do—and they may be right. But this goes both ways. Quite a few academics, like all people, disregard what they cannot understand and ignore the work done by others.

Consider the more extreme gender studies professors as examples. They wake up in houses built *by almost exclusively men*, get in a cars maintained *almost exclusively by men*, drive on roads built *mainly by men*, and spend their working days in offices built and maintained *mainly by men*, exercising their rights to freedom of speech and association—which are rights protected *almost exclusively by men*.[36] They then write papers explaining, at great length, that men are no longer necessary.

I do not know if this qualifies as hypocrisy. Can one be hypocritical without knowing as much? If it is hypocrisy, it is more the result of ignorance than intent. Only the most unknowledgeable can seriously entertain the notion that taming our brutal planet is easy and can disregard the herculean efforts required to prevent our fragile communities from descending into a lawless, unlit, and uninhabitable Gehenna.

The contempt shown by these privileged few is partially the product of a romanticized view of nature—either the somewhat pedestrian (and largely metaphorical) view of the natural environment as Mother Earth or the more literal Neopagan view of the natural environment as being *Gaia*, an actual goddess.[37] Within both of these worldviews is the tacit belief that all of womankind (including the earth herself) could get along just swimmingly were it not for *mankind* and his evil and destructive inventions. This is likely the result of having only seen nature from afar.

As someone who was raised on a farm—45 rolling acres with a fair amount of woodlands—I have a certain respect and appreciation for nature that many of these suburban-born-and-bred *eco-feminist-romantic academics* lack. I spent years in the forest, photographing the natural environment, gardening, and learning about herbal medicine from my grandmother. And I *did* enjoy much of my time wandering the hills and valleys of the surrounding countryside (probably committing trespass more than a few times in the process). I also got one tick-borne illness after the next, was hospitalized more than a few times due to severe allergies and a few more times from infections developed as a result of drinking contaminated water, and learned the value of looking where I stepped or swam, lest I irritate one of the local water moccasins or copperheads, the latter of which would periodically find their way into the family shanty.

Nature can be beautiful, particularly if viewed from the comfort of a lodge or cabin window. It can also be miserable and awesome in its indifference—this is something I also learned to appreciate. Snakes; ticks; sunburn; allergies; rabid raccoons; and poison ivy, oak, and who knows what else—all of these things are every bit as much a part of nature as are Bambi and her family (whose primary pastimes are eating soybeans and jumping in front of cars).

Lest I overstate my credentials as a Natty-Bumppo-grade woodsman, let me make clear that I never tried to live off the fat of the land. Doing so is monstrously difficult—far too much so for a pampered soul as am I—and I have no doubt that the majority of the moon-goddess-adoring, tie-dyed, tree-hugging professoriate would running screaming into the arms of the nearest logger if they had to spend more than a week outside *Naked and Afraid*-style, getting in touch with the cycles and whims of Bitch Mother Earth. Still, peculiarly idealistic notions grow like weeds in the minds of the well-protected, and I cannot much fault those members of the academic community who have only seen the natural world in documentaries for holding certain Disneyfied misconceptions about it.

Yet I fear that this romanticism is likely to be turned against *you*, brutish man that you are, and your desire to interact with the world directly rather than contenting yourself with abstractions, which, in truth, we could not all do even were we so inclined. After all, someone needs to keep the campus lights on and the canteen stocked with quinoa. And the robots can't do everything on their own (yet).

The inability to understand the importance of the labors of others is largely resultant of a lack of imagination. It takes effort to imagine what would happen—to play *what if*. What if A or D or Z simply ceased to exist? And this leads to . . .

Point 5: College teaches you to ignore the value of creative thinking.

Try as a good teacher might to encourage independent thinking, conformity is built into college. There are few processes of creation less creative than the writing of a paper in the American Psychological Association (APA) or Modern Language Association (MLA) formats. Do not misunderstand me—*writing* is a great way to develop your creative capacity—but academic writing has the opposite effect. When writing fiction or non-academic nonfiction, there is some room to develop a *style* of one's own. Just as there is more than one way to skin the proverbial (and unfortunate) cat, so is there more than one way to write an essay, story, or letter. *How* you write this is up to you in most instances. Some editors and readers may hate your style. Some may love it. Oftentimes, the key to getting your work read is finding the right audience—people who want to read what you write *the way you write it.*

In academia, however, creativity is a cardinal sin, and unreadability is considered a virtue. Such has the perverse effect of making you a worse writer while being told you are *getting better.* Given enough time in academia, you will eventually become *wonderful at writing horribly.*

I focus on writing because I have more experience in it than in any other creative domain, but I have no evidence that years of college are more likely to help you become more mentally agile in other areas. I would challenge you to find anyone who left college *more adept* at creative thinking than when he went into it. Mind you, I am not making an absolute statement—*someone somewhere* probably did just that, but the odds of your meeting this person are so low that we can dismiss him (or her) as an anomaly.

Let us not confuse *technical proficiency* in the arts with genuine originality. Being able to perfectly play a song in the most machine-like manner is only proof that one has become a human synthesizer or a well-calibrated metronome.

But even if college encourages you to become an achingly conventional drone, at least you will be a socially adept one. Or will you? How conveniently we transition.

Point 6: College teaches you the wrong kind *of social skills.*

Socialization, socialization, socialization—these are (in no particular order) the three most frequently touted reasons I have heard for sending children and young people to school. And there is some truth to this. School *does* socialize students, but sometimes what a word means is different from what we think it means.

What is socialization, anyway?

According to the experts (meaning sociologists), socialization "refers to the preparation of newcomers to become members of an existing group and to think, feel, and act in ways the group considers appropriate."[38] This is not inherently good, nor is it inherently bad. You can be *socialized* into a community of vegetarian, peace-loving monks, or you can just as easily be socialized into a community of Devil-worshiping, dog-molesting, child-killing cannibals. From a purely technical perspective, both of these forms of socialization are equivalent. They both meet the criteria of teaching conformity to the standards of the group and preparing one to become a member thereof. From a moral perspective, I would suggest that they are not.

To a certain extent, *socialization* is necessary. You very well may have spent your first few years of life smearing your excrement against the walls and trying to eat anything that you could put in your mouth—after all, we should never underestimate how similar young humans are to other non-human primates in their behavior. The fact that you no longer do this (I hope) is a sign that you have been socialized.

With any luck, however, you learned that this sort of behavior is unacceptable at least a few years before you started school, and you almost certainly learned as much before you became old enough to consider college. This suggests that college is not requisite for essential socialization.

So what does the *socialization* of college teach you? What *social skills* are you learning?

First, you are learning to tolerate almost any amount of bureaucracy, to go along with the pencil pushers, educators, and officials to get your sacred sheepskin. Second, you are learning to agree with whatever claptrap is the order of the day—intersectionality (why not?), rape culture (sure!), microaggressions (whatever you say, Teach)—lest you face the wrath of *the group in charge*, whoever that group happens to be at the moment.

If it seems as though I am only picking on left-wing ideas, that is only because it is easier at the moment. Go back a few years in history and consider the 1940s-era emphasis on loyalty oaths for college professors. In a few states (including California, oddly enough), professors are still required to swear that they will defend the state and U.S. constitutions "against all enemies, foreign and domestic."[39]

Consider the sheer meaninglessness of this. What, exactly, would a middle-aged professor of psychology, history, or postmodern literary theory do to protect *anything* from *any* enemies? Throw a book at the berserkers? Talk the invading hordes to death? Assign invading troops a few *really, really* long papers until reinforcements arrive? Yet the vast majority of academics—even those who appear to have no great love of country—sign these documents without complaint. These oaths do not mean much, which makes rationalizing signing them without complaint or protest easy, but apparently, the supposedly free-spirited nonconformity of the academic community does not mean much either, at least not when tenure is on the line.

Given the influence of their less-than-stouthearted teachers, most students do not seem to leave the experience of college much bolder than when they entered it.[40]

What we can establish is that college teaches you to work and live inside a very specific type of box. I speak from experience on this—the longer you stay in college, the more adept you become at in-the-box thinking, and I can assure you that there is little less engaging than bouncing from one corner of the box to the next. This leads to my next assertion, that:

Point 7: College teaches you that learning is boring.

Let me stress a few points: Learning is not inherently boring. Learning is not unnatural. You do not need to be taught *how to learn*.

You learn all of the time. You always have. No one taught you how to do it. There is a very good chance that no one particularly encouraged it.

We are born helpless and pathetic. We can do nothing for ourselves in our first moments. Aside from the instincts to cry and to find a breast upon which can suckle (something a fair number of people never outgrow), almost everything that we—you, me, anybody—can do is learned. If you can speak even *one* language reasonably well, you have demonstrated the ability to achieve mastery of a complex body of knowledge. Aside from some disabled people (and a very few who were raised by wild animals), *almost everyone* learns a language, yet very few of them were *taught* in the formal, classroom sense of the word.[41] My point: to be a normal human is to be able to learn.

If you are the stereotypical slacker (not that there is anything wrong with that), you probably await the newest video games with a certain eagerness. You *do not* want to keep playing the same game over and over—that would be tedious, namely because the thrill (and the challenge) would be gone. Achieving mastery over a new game is a learning task—one that millions of people pursue obsessively, sometimes for days on end, frequently forgoing sleep, food, and sex—and gamers *want to do this*.

Some games *do* teach complex skills, better *visual perceptual template processing* (integral to object recognition) for one.[42] Some other game-acquired skills, such as the ability to fit certain complex three-dimensional objects together in novel ways, become so finely honed in the competent gamer that a small team of them can outperform even the most powerful supercomputers of today.[43]

While many of us might dread a college course called *Advanced Perceptual Template Processing for the Dilettante* or *Supercomputer-level Protein Folding Made Easy*, plenty of people are taking just such a course. But when your teacher is an Xbox, the class is something to enjoy rather than something to dread.

On Real Learning

My criticisms of college may seem blunt to the point of cruelty, and those who conflate *formal education* with *learning* may suggest that I am anti-learning, anti-knowledge, anti-arts, or anti-critical thinking.

Nothing could be further from the truth.

What I *am* suggesting is that you learn according to your own needs, interests, and abilities—that you learn to recognize all of the good teachers around you (most of whom have few, if any, credentials)—that you learn to *feed* your mind, rather than waiting for it to be *fed*.

By doing this, you will make your mind sharper and you will become more adept at learning how to play the only game that matters: *the game of survival*.

Everything else is ultimately decorative. Everything else is of comparatively little importance. Survival requires two fundamental skills: knowing how to make the best use of your environment and knowing how to make the best use of yourself.

School teaches you *katas*—rigid forms that *look like fighting* but that are useless in a real ass-kicking contest.[44] Independent learning teaches you how to kick ass and *keep on kicking it.* Many of my highest-scoring students are still dirt poor. They graduated years ago, yet they have nothing. This may partially be the result of personality and values. Some people value an abundance of free time more than an abundance of money—which is absolutely fine. But not all of my dedicated students seem to be embracing the monastic life with glee, or even equanimity, rather the problem seems to be that what they learned in school was *how to do school.*

On the other hand, some of my *worst* students—the guys who barely showed up to class, were lucky to score in the low 70s on relatively easy tests, and seemed to regard school as little more than a place where they could hang their hats while running side businesses—are already making more money than I ever will.

Occasionally, there is *some* overlap. A few of my most academically inclined students managed to get good jobs at large companies, and they have steadily risen in the ranks these last few years. Even then, I doubt that my *studious students* could easily strike out on their own. They are simply too good at following orders. *Institutions institutionalize. Mixers mix. Carburetors carburate. And independent learners learn independently.* This is what they do.

One Sentence Guide to Learning the Right Way:

Here it is: Get paid to learn (and get paid fairly).

That is it. That is the sentence.

Before you walk away, scratching your head, keep reading.

By *paid to learn* I do not always mean *paid in money*. When you are playing *Grand Theft Auto: Nuclear Ebola Detroit* (my idea!), you are being compensated with the pleasure you derive from the game. Some other activities, such as learning how to write, paint, or build should lead to the creation and sale of *something*, ideally in short order. If you are learning to repair things, start charging others for your time and effort as soon as you are even marginally qualified to do so. If you are teaching yourself an instrument, remember that you do not need to achieve technical excellence to generate some income. If only talented musicians were rewarded for their efforts, grunge would have died even sooner than it did.

This is all quite distinct from paying to get rubber stamped— which is what most formal schooling offers—and which provides you with nothing more than the *approval* of someone in a position of power.

Effectively taking a paid-to-learn approach can be easier said than done, but that makes it no less worthwhile. Remember this: The more someone charges to *educate* you, the more likely he is to treat you as a cash cow, teaching you as little as possible over as long a period of time as possible. Such is a simple matter of maximizing profits while minimizing effort. On the other hand, if someone is *paying* to train you, you can bet good money that he will waste little time and effort when getting the job done.

Flip the script—minimize your labors and expenses while maximizing your return on educational investment. *This* is the essence of the Rules—getting the most of what *you want* out of life as efficiently as possible.

Next, we will consider how to apply the Rules to work.

The Thinking Man

(Ten Questions for Review and Consideration)

1. How is schooling distinct from education?

   _____

   _____

   _____

2. Are colleges still necessary? If so, for what subjects and what types of people?

   _____

   _____

   _____

3. What are some of the unique problems and obstacles that men and boys face in school, particularly in college?

   _____

   _____

   _____

4. Compared to non-academic study, what (if any) are the advantages of learning in school?

   _____

   _____

   _____

5. Compared to learning in school, what are the advantages of non-academic study?

_____

_____

_____

6. Why might professors and schoolteachers discourage practical thinking?

_____

_____

_____

7. Does going to school (particularly college) make you a stronger person, a weaker person, or neither? If it does make you stronger or weaker (meaning it has some effect), why?

_____

_____

_____

8. Under what circumstances does attending a higher educational institution violate the Rules? *Which* Rules are violated? *How* are they violated?

_____

_____

_____

9. Are you satisfied with your level of education? If not, are there any ways you could get paid to learn something new? What is this way/what are these ways?

_____

_____

_____

10. Does college offer you a better or worse deal than marriage? What are the reasons for your answer?

_____

_____

_____

6) On Work

Here is the message you have been told: Follow convention, get an education, get a job, get married, buy a house, and establish yourself as a member of the middle class. Be loyal to your employer, and you will be promoted. Even if that employer fires you, your years of hard work will prove useful to you. Eventually, your efforts will pay off, and you will be the better for it.

Think about your father's life. There is something like a 50% chance, even if he is one of the Boomers—a cohort more prosperous than those that followed—that his life went worse than planned. Maybe he got divorced and lost most of his money. Maybe he was laid off when he was in his later years and he had a difficult time finding something that paid anywhere near as much as did his previous job. Maybe he developed a drug or alcohol addiction.

Maybe he is already dead by his own hand.

Maybe this is not your father. He might have been one of the lucky ones. If so, look at his friends and associates. Odds are that many of them are struggling. Your father's generation, assuming he is a Baby Boomer, has one of the highest middle-aged suicide rates of any cohort on record.[1]

Many cannot live on flower power alone, it seems.

This chapter is not an attack. It is an autopsy. I am not a murderer. I am a pathologist. Both killers and coroners may cut open chests. The difference is that the latter only do so after a person is already dead. There is no harm in that.

Why did this happen? Why did so many of these older men play by the conventional rules only to lose?

They tried to make their way to the middle class and stay there. This brings us to some critical advice:

Do not be middle class. It will kill you. You will not die a happy man.

Being middle class has as much (if not more) to do with mindset, career, and lifestyle as it does with money, but before we examine that point in detail, we consider the relative advantages and disadvantages of wealth and poverty.

Being rich, and by *rich* I mean earning an income that is at or above the 98th percentile or having enough in savings to be able to regard work as purely optional, can be great. Money does not guarantee happiness, but it certainly can help stave off misery.

Being poor also has its advantages—those with nothing to lose, lose nothing. The life of a poor man can be frustrating and frequently miserable, particularly if that man has children or other dependents. However, the poor man has a strength—there is nowhere for him to go but up. The truly poor man is less likely to be sued or legally harassed simply because doing so is not worth anyone's effort. Lawyers, as bad as they may be at times, are in business, and trying to extract blood from a turnip is a terrible business plan. Additionally, women are less likely to try to manipulate men who look to be poor.[2] There are some women who do all that they can do to drive men over the edge, purely as a matter of spite; however, apparently penniless men rarely draw the attention of *anyone* (man or woman), simply because the poor are invisible, even to other poor people. There are far worse things than being a ghost, and the man of modest means who makes no effort to be noticed is just that—an apparition.

Life is most precarious for the members of the middle class. They do have *something* to lose, but their ability to protect these things is limited. Let us only briefly address the matters of women and divorce in this chapter. (We will examine them more thoroughly later.) Rather, it is worth focusing on the issues of economics alone. The poor man needs exactly what he needs— food, a place to live, clothing, and enough enjoyable activities in life to keep him from swan diving from the nearest overpass. The rich man can spend as much or as little as he wants: He has no point to prove that has not already been proven well enough by virtue of his fortune. At worst, the rich man who lives extremely modestly is an eccentric. At best, he is wise for guarding his assets. The poor man has nothing—there is nothing else to it. He can only afford what little he can afford. Status is so clearly out of his reach that he not need be concerned with it.

But to live the middle-class lifestyle, you need *things!*

At least one late model car, a house of a certain size, proper schooling for his children, the right kind of clothes, and a respectable ZIP code—all of these are required of the middle-class man. Rich *and* poor are economic conditions. Middle class is a *way of life*. Do not live the middle-class lifestyle. It is designed to keep the middle-class man beholden, helpless, and fearful. This way of life is almost impossible to maintain on a middle-class income. The average (middle-class) household owes more than $130,000.[3] Most of that money will never be repaid. Debt held by those with nothing to lose is of little relevance. Again, *blood from a turnip!*

However, the middle-class man *does* have things to lose, which is a problem for him. He has a house subject to confiscation, forfeiture, and foreclosure. He has a certain lifestyle vulnerable to economic disruption. If his wife divorces him, she can use the government to extract from him (at gunpoint) amounts of money he cannot reasonably expect to make for any length of time. If his employer terminates him, he will be left scrambling for food, freedom, and dignity. If he or someone in his family requires extensive medical treatment, the resultant bills and loss of wages are likely to drive the middle-class man to bankruptcy.[4] For but a very few, filing for bankruptcy is not fun on the metaphorical bun. Still, it is likely to be less emotionally traumatic and legally complex for the man without assets or middle-class pride than it is to be for the man shackled to the detritus accumulated while trying to keep up with the Joneses. The former man is never far from home—*his home is on his back*. The latter man is one who will have grown psychologically brittle from years of static living and the pursuit of external validation. His home *is breaking* his back.

Middle-class men rarely tear free from the bondage of the wrong kind of debt—the kind one is actually compelled to repay. *This* is slavery.

You may think you can avoid this—that you can work in a middle-class job, save your money, avoid the trap of marriage, and do well. You may.

Do not count on it.

The more entrenched you are in the middle class, the more vulnerable you become. This is largely due to the nature of a great deal of what constitutes *middle-class employment*.

Regardless of social class, chances are that you will need to do something to pay your bills. This can be anything from shoveling manure to designing supercomputers. In the best-case scenario, you are working for yourself—buying and restoring cars, motorcycles, or houses; building websites; or designing software are just a few examples of independent employment suited to the independent man. Your work may be irregular; however, there is no one person or department that can pull the plug and render you without income. The worst jobs are those traditionally held by the middle class, particularly those that involve doing nothing of any apparent value and that provide no opportunity to work independently, such as being a mid-level manager.

Here are the problems with those jobs:

1. *You cannot just* get *them.*

You have no choice but to deal with the gatekeepers. The major gatekeepers are schools and human resources offices, both of which are largely controlled by women, most of whom demonstrate strong in-group biases (meaning that they are likely to give other women preferential treatment over men).[5] Even once you get through the gate, you can be tossed out again in an instant, which leads to our second point.

2. *They are dependent upon a man's reputation.*

By this, I mean that the middle-class man need be concerned with what other people think of him. People are fickle. They change their minds for strange reasons, petty reasons, and sometimes no good reason at all. Say something wrong, do something wrong, even if it has little to do with work, and you may find yourself out in the cold. A manager is extremely vulnerable, particularly in the internet age. And the middle-class man does not need to do anything obviously stupid, such as posting controversial comments online, for the lunatics of the web to single him out for attack.

Cameras and microphones are everywhere—in almost every cellphone made over the last ten years. Get angry and yell at someone, or even get slightly snippy, and your bad moment may go online. People have short attention spans, and a great many of them are overeager to judge others on nothing more than a five-second video clip. Even if you do nothing slightly out of line—you manage to avoid so much as picking your nose on camera—the *hint* of having behaved imperfectly may be enough to hurt anyone employed in a reputation-dependent line of work.[6]

3. *With the exception of doctor, almost all middle-class jobs are bullshit (and everyone knows it).*

Bureaucrats and managers do not do much. What do they make? Whom do they save? Do they put food in anyone's belly? Do they keep on the lights? If all the middle managers stayed home for a month, would anyone notice? Now, what about if all of the trash collectors and plumbers did the same thing? Can you see the difference in effect? Most bullshit workers are vulnerable because *anyone* could replace them, assuming *anyone* was willing to spend a few weeks learning jargon.[7]

4. *They tie you down.*

The poor man can go anywhere his feet can take him—and since he owns nothing and has nothing to move aside from his person, disappearing in the middle of the night is entirely feasible. The rich man can hop on his jet and fly away to any number of exotic countries with beautiful beaches and officials who are easily bribed. The middle-class man is helpless. He has things to lose, but he cannot easily take them with him. Additionally, he cannot easily find a replacement source of income that will allow him to live in the manner to which he has become accustomed. Every city has lousy jobs. You can always find something to do if all you need is enough money to buy beans. On the other hand, if you are truly rich, you can scatter your funds across ten different countries, and in some of these countries, a small fortune will make you into a *big man*.[8]

5. *They make you forget how to be a resourceful person.*

If you are at the margins of society, you will have no choice but to exercise your mind. Odd jobs may be odd, but they can teach you how to think and handle new problems. The rich have the benefit of always wheeling and dealing—this keeps the mind sharp. Go for the middle class, and you will spend all of your days enforcing protocols other people have written. Given enough time, you will forget how to be human—how to solve problems and adapt.

6. *They destroy your organic sense of identity and replace it with your role within an organization.*

The problem with *the organization man*—a term first used by William H. Whyte in the 1950s—is that he is so psychologically invested in his role within the company that he is, for lack of a better word, *codependent.*[9] Much like some children of extraordinarily cruel or distant parents, the company man becomes tremendously dependent on the approval of others. I have seen grown men cry at the prospect of losing their jobs, and some of these men were not even all that financially vulnerable. For these men, work is about more than money. It is the foundation of their sense of self. The party that cares *less* about a given deal or relationship has a huge advantage relative to the party that cares more. You *do not want* to be in the position of vulnerability.

7. *Most of these jobs will be automated out of existence within two decades.*

I have mentioned this before, but it is worth considering at some length. Factory workers have been losing jobs to robots for years. Retail workers are also starting to feel the crush of automation (think of self-checkout lines). Thus far, a great many middle-class jobs have been spared, but this may well soon change. A Japanese company has already started to replace its insurance underwriters with computers enhanced with artificial intelligence, and PricewaterhouseCoopers (a major auditing and consulting firm) predicts that 32% of financial and insurance industry jobs will be automated within a few years, with other experts predicting that teachers, therapists, middle managers, lawyers, and workers in a great many other middle-class lines of work will face significant competition from artificial intelligence.[10] This stands to be good for customers (who will gain access to better, cheaper services), but it will almost certainly *not* be good for those who invested years of their lives into professional desk jockeying.

8. *They all but guarantee that your wallet will be gang raped every tax season.*

More than 40% of Americans pay no income tax.[11] None! The rich may or may not pay more in taxes than do the middle class, but for the sufficiently wealthy, even huge tax bills make little difference in quality of life. For the middle class, tax season can be a time of weeping and gnashing of teeth.

All of these are but some the many pitfalls of middle-class work. Yet you have been told a middle-class existence is what you should desire. Your mother, your father, your teachers—almost all of them think that the middle-class life is ideal, or nearly so. Unless you stand out in some way, most of these people will doubt that you have the ability to be rich. Many of them will hope that you are not forever poor. Becoming a pencil pusher would seem to be only option left, right?

Wrong.

My advice is this: practice moderation in nothing involving money. Learn how to live so cheaply that you have no financial footprint—that there is nothing for anyone (or *nothing that they can find*) to take from you —or go big, try to get so overwhelmingly rich that you can compel anyone who annoys you to take a long walk down a short plank. These are not mutually exclusive: One can be both be rich and appear to have very little.[12] Both of these require that you use your mind and your creativity. *Doing the two at the same time* requires self-discipline as well. Regardless of what anyone has told you, you have plenty of both.

Living cheaply requires creativity. *Getting* rich requires creativity. Neither of them involve passively following orders. Both of them have the potential to earn you admiration from some and scorn from others. Both of them require that you do not give a damn about what anyone thinks. Once you can start doing this—ignoring the naysayers, the nags, and the idiots—you will have effectively started down the path to freedom.

Remember, some of the aforementioned conformists want you to be their slave. The rest are too cowardly to try anything different for themselves and are likely to suffer from the *crabs-in-a-basket* mindset.

I am and will likely remain too poor to tell you how to become rich, but I do know how to survive on almost nothing. You do as well—the will and ability to persevere is baked into all of us—but you may need your memory refreshed. Do not feel bad about this. No matter how ingrained in you something may be, you can get out of practice. Getting back into practice may be difficult, but in this case, it is worth the effort. Probably the worst thing you can do to yourself is underestimate your own flexibility. Apply your mind to the problems of survival. Do so every day.

And here are two more pieces of advice worth heeding:

1. Never become your job.

2. Never allow yourself to become a target.

Never Become Your Job

I realize that I have already covered this somewhat in relation to the middle-class man in list item six, but it is worth reiterating as much to men of *every* social class. It may well be true that *women are what they are* and *men are what they do*, and men, regardless of their culture or their nationality, judge themselves by their accomplishments. One does not *do* anything to be *pretty, beautiful,* or *smart*. One just *is*. On the other hand, boys and men are expected to *achieve* something, and such is how they prove their worth.[13]

The conflation of work and identity is likely greater in the United States and Canada than it is in much of the rest of the world, with our habit of asking "What do you do?" as a conversation starter being less common in some other countries.[14] But I suspect that this is largely innate—a part of how we, as men, instinctively operate. Assessing yourself based on your achievements is fine, but you should not allow this to turn you into a tool for others.

This *seems* to be more of a problem for middle-class men, but it is not entirely restricted to them. *Some jobs* do warrant a certain pride of position. An aircraft mechanic (or pilot) can rightfully take some pride in what he does. These jobs require robust skill sets, attention to detail, and dedication. And if the men in these positions (and yes, I know some commercial pilots are women, but only about 5%) are careless in their performance, *people die!*[15]

This leads to the single best question to determine the importance of your job: If you screw up, how many lives stand to be lost or ruined?

If the answer is *hundreds, thousands, or millions*, by all means, take your job at least somewhat seriously. If the answer is even *one or two*, go ahead and take your job seriously as well. Even the most incompetent doctor cannot kill more than one or two people at a time, but quite a few doctors seem to think highly of themselves. This is somewhat justified. Even then, those who allow themselves to become *the Doctor*—who think of themselves only in terms of their profession—are making themselves far more vulnerable than they have any reason to be.

So how many people stand to die or suffer horribly if *you* screw up today?

For a great many of us, the answer is *zero!*

And yet, I know men in jobs that simply do not matter one way or the other—low-level bureaucrats, retail workers, and quite a few academics in disciplines that even other academics regard as fluff —that take their jobs with a mortal seriousness that would be comical were it not pathetic. From a few of my more devout friends, I have even heard this maxim regarding work: *Whatever you do, do with all your heart.*

Actually, this is a misquotation. Here is the relevant passage, with the most critical text in bold:

> And whatsoever ye do in word or deed, do all in the name of the Lord Jesus, giving thanks to God and the Father by him. Wives, submit yourselves unto your own husbands, as it is fit in the Lord. Husbands, love your wives, and be not bitter against them. Children, obey your parents in all things: for this is well pleasing unto the Lord. Fathers, provoke not your children to anger, lest they be discouraged. Servants, obey in all things your masters according to the flesh; not with eyeservice, as menpleasers; but in singleness of heart, fearing God; **And whatsoever ye do, do it heartily, as to the Lord, and not unto men**; Knowing that of the Lord ye shall receive the reward of

113

the inheritance: for ye serve the Lord Christ. (Colossians 3:17-25)[16]

I am not citing this to proselytize. Rather, I include it to give you an idea of *context* and to establish that the ancients were neither as masochistic or as lacking in wisdom as modern expositors might have you believe.

First, this is from a text written several thousand years ago (when there were almost certainly fewer bullshit jobs). Second, there are *many* instructions therein, for many different groups. Wives, children, servants, mothers, and husbands—all of these groups had quite a few obligations imposed upon them. Implied mutuality is an integral part of the instruction set—*give something; get something*. Third, this quotation is entirely meaningless without a belief in God in general and Jesus in particular.

Yet many men, even those with relatively little in the way of religious beliefs, take this message to heart. Wives now do what they wish, children feel comfortable treating their parents with open contempt, and servants are hard to find unless you are a wealthy Saudi with a Bangladeshi woman locked in your basement.

Thus, a long and intricate passage, one that describes a specific set of ideal social relationships within a larger religious framework, has been reduced to an obligation that only binds one party—*the worker*—and does so without any promise of supernatural reward. For a great many American men work is not done *for God*. Instead, work *is God*. And the reward for all of this superhuman dedication and purity of heart is . . . *what?*

Japanese-style lifetime employment?

(*Nope!*)

Great benefits and opportunities for advancement?

114

(Ha! Ha! Ha!)

An appreciative and respectful family?

(Good luck with that.)

Salaries higher than those earned by our fathers' generation?

(Demonstrably, no.)[17]

So what are *you* getting out of all of this dedication?

There are only two probable reasons to take much pride in your work. The first reason—one that we have already considered—is that your job *really is* a matter of life and death. The second is that you are working for yourself and think that your job will provide you with substantial opportunity over the course of many years. Remember that the only employer not likely to get rid of you at the drop of hat is *you*.

There are almost certainly some exceptions to this last point. Ours is a big world, so absolute statements about billions of employer/employee relationships are unlikely to be entirely true. A *very few* employers will go above and beyond to stand by their employees. Nevertheless, the employer with the greatest vested interest in your well-being is *you*. Loyalty from anyone else is an anomaly.

Never Allow Yourself to Become a Target

Regardless of how much or little money you make, you are well-advised to avoid making yourself into a target. *Flashing cash* (or driving a luxury car or doing anything else to draw attention to yourself) has the same effect as painting a bullseye on your back. Unless you are tired of living, you would be wise to avoid doing as much. And this is what hurts so many middle-class men: They take great pains to establish their social worth. This attracts the worst

115

sort of charlatans. Many of these crooks are women, but there are quite a few men in the mix. To allow your pride—your desire to achieve *status*—to destroy you is terrible, and if you do, you will have no one to blame but yourself.

You may manage to make a middle-class income without working a middle-class job. Plumbers, electricians, and other skilled tradesmen; certain types of technicians; independent artists, writers, and creatives; and those in a few oddball lines of work (professional gamblers, et cetera) may manage to make decent incomes without being bound to the middle-class lifestyle and the attendant reputational fragility. If you can make a mid-level income without getting sucked into the middle-class miasma, know that there are worse fates. But beware of the temptations of pointless competition: They pave the road to perdition.

If you can avoid the muck, you can almost certainly turn your middle-range income into real wealth through careful (diversified) investments, preferably scattered about in such a way that neither governments nor greedy individuals will know how much wealth you have or where you have placed it.

If you are in this position—that of being potentially wealthy without bearing the burden of status—consider yourself lucky. Keep your head down, keep your nose clean, and use your money to give yourself more options and escape routes.

Remember: *Always have an exit.*

Work Friends and False Community

Now, let's consider another reason men stick with their jobs to their detriment—that being the existence of *work friends*.[18]

One of the major reasons that a great many men seem to be deeply attached to their jobs is that their work serves as their only social outlet. This is a problem. Work is not a great place to make friends. It is rife with complex legal situations. Humor, a useful tool for building relationships of any form, is hazardous in the workplace, so much so that only the most innocuous of jokes (preferably vetted by a lawyer beforehand) can be safely used, and fraternization with coworkers and supervisors can lead to claims of discrimination from those kept out of the loop.[19]

Outside of the legal realm, there is the matter of culture. More than almost any other group, Americans have relatively little interaction with their colleagues outside of work—about half as much as do Poles or Indians. Rather than this being purely the result of them fearing legal repercussions, Americans appear to regard any non-professional workplace interaction as contradictory to the Protestant work ethic's emphasis on productivity, so there may not be much in the way of friendships to be had in many workplaces, even for those so inclined to make them.[20]

Given the rather competitive nature of work in the United States, forming clear professional boundaries may not be a bad idea. Additionally, there is the inherent impermanence of workplace friendships. It is not uncommon to lose touch with former colleagues after changing jobs. *Work friends*, while not necessarily harmful, are a poor substitute for authentic friends and allies. Nothing good can come from putting all of your eggs in the single basket of work.

If you *do* function better as part of a large, highly connected social system, you are at a certain disadvantage in America. Nuclear and extended families in a state of collapse, and they may fade away to historical novelty within a generation.[21] Many of the other venues in which men traditionally built their identities have been destroyed—a matter I examines more in Chapter 11 ("On Isolation")—and such compounds an already substantial problem.

During my time as a teacher, I found that reiteration of key points helped student retain them, so I leave you with three bits of critical advice I have already given, but in slightly different words:

1. Do not allow yourself to become enslaved to your employer, the perceptions of others (status), vanity, or pride.

2. Strive to avoid making others jealous of you. *Envy breeds enemies*, and you have enemies enough.

3. And bear in mind that if no one thinks you have anything to take, no one will have designs on what is rightfully yours.

This is how you become more resilient, sane, and resistant to attack.

The Thinking Man

(Ten Questions for Review and Consideration)

1. Why is basing your sense of identity on your job a bad idea?

   _____

   _____

   _____

2. Why might others encourage you to base your sense of identity on your job?

   _____

   _____

   _____

3. What are the defining characteristics of a company man, and what are the major psychological and economic disadvantages of being a company man?

   _____

   _____

   _____

4. What are some advantages and disadvantages of being poor?

   _____

   _____

   _____

5. What are some advantages and disadvantages of being rich?

_____

_____

_____

6. How are middle-class men uniquely vulnerable (compared to rich men and poor men)?

_____

_____

_____

7. What are the defining characteristics of bullshit jobs? What is a good example of one?

_____

_____

_____

8. What is a job that matters? Why does it matter?

_____

_____

_____

9. Is relying exclusively on workplace friends a good idea? Why or why not?

_____

_____

_____

10. Which of the Rules are violated by becoming a company man? *How* are they violated? (Consider the loss of independence that comes from investing too much in your job.)

_____

_____

_____

7) The Mantra

Now that you have gotten this far through the Rules, you should be aware that following them will cause you to break with convention from time to time, not for the sake of being a rebel, but because following convention simply as a matter of course is to surrender your decision-making to the indifferent mass of humanity. You know your life is too important to be administered by everyone in general but no one in particular.

Likewise, by focusing on yourself and your well-being, you are progressing towards liberation, but you may well face attacks from those who weaponize the notions of decency, empathy, and maturity—who forge these concepts into blades and hammers to cut you down or to break you so that you will more readily submit to them and labor for their benefit. I return to a lesson I first mentioned in "On Shaming and the Big Three," this time in the form of a mantra—one to be repeated whenever faced with something you regard as unworthy of your attention. Here it is. Repeat it as often as needed:

I do not care.

I will not care unless I choose to care.

Soon I will be dead. I do not have the time to care about bullshit.

Granted, you may have a duty to *act* when you have willfully assumed responsibility for something or someone, but *you are never obligated to care.* Caring or not caring is your choice. *Caring* is a mental state, and no one else can dictate your mental state to you. It is always yours and yours alone to control. And as for *soon* —*Soon I will be dead*—you likely do not know how much time you have remaining, only that your time is limited. If you have 120 seconds left, that is not long. If you have 120 minutes left, that is not long either. One hundred and twenty days, 120 weeks, 120 months, or 120 trips around the Sun—none of these are long at all. Regardless of your health, age, or luck, you have no time to waste on bullshit.

Say the Mantra calmly. Say it without anger. And learn to say aloud the relevant parts whenever needed and to expand upon the Mantra as necessary.

What about the children? wonders the politician.

Unless they are my children, I do not care.

I will not care unless I choose to care.

What about the women? shrieks the angry feminist.

I do not care.

I will not care unless I choose to care.

What about the Jews, the lizard people, and the Illuminati? inquires the anonymous internet conspiracy theorists.

I do not care.

I will not care unless I choose to care.

What about the trees, the birds, the bees, and the girls with knock-knees? plead the fundraisers, the charlatans, and the social justice warriors.

I do not care.

I will not care unless I choose to care.

And here is the big one:

What about what all and sundry think of me? asks the doubting voice within.

123

I do not care.

I will not care unless I choose to care.

I will only value the opinions of those people whom I consider to be worthy of my respect.

Butter on Toast

Like butter on toast, your energy and your compassion will be of little effect—will leave all that they touch dry and tasteless—if spread too thin. Every minute of your life matters. Every minute is irreplaceable. Do not allow yourself to be shamed or bullied into wasting any of them.

I am not suggesting that you do not and should not care about yourself; your passions; your friends; or your parents, siblings, or offspring. Care if you *choose* to care. If you *choose* to care about the girls with knock-knees, fine. Even wobbly women need love, and they are probably fairly chaste (seeing as they cannot open their legs properly). The point is to *choose* for yourself.

And do not allow your concern for anyone to be turned against you. You should blindly trust and obey no one. Bear in mind that you never really know what anyone is thinking or planning, even those closest to you.

But what if you were the one suffering? asks the supposed bleeding heart.

Well, I would be out of luck. No one would give a damn.

But what if it was your daughter suffering? wonders another.

That would be bad for us, and what if my son was suffering?

So what? Would you care? And if I, my son, and my daughter (assuming I had children) were all suffering, that would be our problem, not yours, unless of course, you were the one to screw us over—to inflict damage upon us—and then you *might* have a responsibility to make us whole.

We can lob scenarios at each other until the heat death of the universe, but there is not much point to it. The facts are what they are, not what we wish them to be.

In a fair world, life would almost certainly be different than it is today, but *fair* is a hypothetical state, and those genuinely concerned about fairness and justice (in the pure, abstract sense) would have more in their rhetorical arsenals than flagrantly emotional appeals, such as those just given.

Rather, they would consider fairness from behind the *veil of ignorance*—a thought experiment and tool developed by philosopher John Rawls to test the objective fairness of a law or a social policy.[1] To use the veil of ignorance effectively, one must consider the effects of a law or policy without knowing what his social station would be when the law or policy is applied. You—the conductor of the thought experiment—do not know if you will be a man or woman; a rich person or a poor one; smart or stupid; or Black, White, Asian, or some other race. Now, knowing nothing of your position in society, ask yourself the critical question: Would you consider a given law or policy to be fair—to provide you with the greatest likelihood of seeing an unbiased outcome?

Ideally, this experiment should force you (or whoever is conducting the experiment) to consider the effects of a policy or law from many different perspectives and to try to achieve the fairest possible outcomes for the greatest number of people.

Very few supposedly fair-minded individuals do this. Instead, *fair* is, for them, another way of saying *whatever is in the best interest of me or my preferred group*. Do not forget this last point.

125

Consider the words of others accordingly when they mention *fairness*.

And keep in mind that, most of the time, you are not obligated to be fair, just as you are never obligated to care.[2]

Without a Care

Without a care in the world—that means happy, or at least untroubled, does it not?

And being *without a care in the world* is about as much a matter of choice and mindset as it is one of circumstances.

Of course, you need food, you need somewhere to live, and you need certain levels of safety, security, and health to put your mind at ease. Beyond these, your peace of mind is your choice.

Here is another tip: Never apologize for the actions of other men, other people of your ethnic group, other people who practice your faith (assuming you have one), other people who drive your preferred brand of car, other members of your political party, your parents, your siblings, or your ancestors. You are not obligated to right the wrongs of the world. Such would be an impossible task. There is no reason for you to share guilt, blame, or pride for that which concerns you not and over which you have no control. Do not get roped into this nonsense.

You are never obligated to care.

Remember that. *Carry* the Mantra with you as sword and shield. The more you discipline and regulate your care—the more you understand that it is yours to dispose of and direct as you wish —the stronger you will become and the more effective and focused your efforts will be. This is the nature of life, battle, and negotiation.

The Mantra is at the heart of the Rules. The Mantra is at the heart of winning.

The Thinking Man

(Four Questions for Review and Consideration)

1. Name at least one thing about which you have been told to care (or pretend to care) that you do not. Why do you think you have been told to care about this thing (or these things)? (Hint: When in doubt, follow the money.)

    _____

    _____

    _____

2. How does pretending to care about things that you do not violate the First Rule (*Give as little as possible*), the Second Rule (*Take as much as possible*), and the Fourth Rule (*Enjoy your life to the fullest*)?

    _____

    _____

    _____

3. Has anyone ever tried to manipulate you into caring (or pretend to care) about something that you do not/did not? If so, how did you respond to this person's efforts? How do you intend to respond to such efforts in the future?

    _____

    _____

    _____

4. How does not caring about irrelevant things, people, and opinions give you an advantage in your dealings with others and in life in general?

_____

_____

_____

8) On Debt and Taxes

This chapter is premised on three facts:

1. An economy built upon debt will usually collapse more quickly than one that is built upon authentic value. Investing in the distorted parts of a market will result in little more than headache and heartache for you.

2. As a man, you get almost nothing for the taxes you pay.

3. You do not own most of what you think you own, and what is worse is that your possessions frequently *own you*.

If you can accept these, all else herein will make perfect sense.

Debt

Think back on your father's life. If he was anything like many men of the era, he accumulated debt to no end—borrowing money, huge sums of money at times—for the privilege of being exploited.[1] The exploiters—the first ex-wife; the second, third, and fourth ex-wives; the girlfriends; the kids; the boss; the government; and society in general—varied somewhat from man to man, but they were exploiters, nonetheless.

Again, if your father was fairly typical, he was fearful that he would not be able to pay this money back because if he could not, he risked losing the privilege of borrowing *even more* so that he could be further used and abused. This is the mindset of a slave who does not want to be free, and one might well argue that a man who is so afflicted suffers from *freedom anxiety*.

This will kill a man, in spirit if not in body, and he will not die a noble or joyful death.

Debt, Doom, and Dastardly Dicks

Easy credit and the collapse of civilization go hand in hand.

Cheap credit has slid its well-lubricated tentacles into every orifice of Western society. No anime schoolgirl has had the poor fortune of being violated as badly. After all, we borrow to buy electronics, musical instruments, housing, clothing, medical care, food, and anything else imaginable.[2] What cannot be put on plastic?

The more we buy with credit, the less our coin is worth, generally speaking. Some items may drop in price, but they are exceptions. Televisions, for instance, are better, bigger, and cheaper than they were 30 years ago, despite the inflationary effects of the lending bubble.[3] This reflects massive technological advances and the outsourcing of labor from first-world countries to far cheaper developing ones.[4] For pretty much anything else—whatever cannot be made less expensively as a result of changes in technology and improvements in manufacturing and labor efficiency—credit increases costs, partially by making people *price insensitive*, which is to say that it encourages them to fork over ever-more obscene amounts of money they have yet to earn for the same goods and services and think nothing of it.[5] Thus, inflation.

This trend does not hurt the borrowers who have no intention of repaying their obligations—they can just keep shaking the money tree until the fruit stops falling—and it harms lenders less than one might suspect.

Banks can, after all, write off relatively large amounts of debt or repackage and sell it in the form of asset-backed securities.[6] Since much of the money they supply is simply being pulled out of their magical cash-creating hats, banks stand to lose relatively little even in the case of borrower default or bankruptcy.

Some people, however, are hurt, and hurt greatly, namely those who want to pay with money for which they have *worked* or *saved*. Anyone who does not wish to accumulate debt gets vicious kicks in the teeth, groin, and buttocks; however, the *money makers* and the *money takers* need do nothing more than tack a few more zeroes onto their account balances and go about their merry, spendthrift ways.

This entire system and its illusion of growth is based on the generation of e-bucks by commercial banks—what is referred to in a 2014 Bank of England report as being *fountain pen money*, meaning that which is created with the flourish of a fountain pen (or, more accurately, the stroke of a computer key).

If the above statement confuses you and you thought *Wait, commercial banks do not create money. Governments do that*, I sympathize. The Bank of England report initially befuddled me as well. So here is the relevant text. Read and interpret it for yourself:

Commercial banks create money, in the form of bank deposits, by making new loans. When a bank makes a loan, for example to someone taking out a mortgage to buy a house, it does not typically do so by giving them thousands of pounds [British currency] worth of banknotes. Instead, it credits their bank account with a bank deposit of the size of the mortgage. **At that moment, new money is created.** For this reason, some economists have referred to bank deposits as 'fountain pen money', created at the stroke of bankers' pens when they approve loans.[7] (emphasis in original; text in brackets, mine)

While British English and American English are hardly identical, they are probably similar enough for this statement to mean about what we—*the Americans*—think it means, and unless my mind is even more worn down from years of schooling than I suspect it is, I read this to mean that *commercial banks*—Bank of America, Wells Fargo, et cetera—*create money out of nothing.* I do not want to distort the good bankers' words. They offer some caveats to this statement: Banks cannot create *unlimited* amounts of money, lest they cause too much inflation to occur.

Still, the power of creating money seems to be very much with the banks. We peons just have the privilege of spending years to compensate the banks for their generously lending us that which costs them nothing to make. *They make the money, and we make the value.*

The doers and the creators—those who really contribute something to society—are almost always at a disadvantage due to their inability to increase their earnings and profits at a rate that matches inflation.

Successfully investing in a warped economy is challenging. The housing market is terribly distorted due to easy credit, as is the higher education industry.[8] Prices of consumer goods and vehicles have also been deformed by access to loans. This hurts everyone except the crooks.

Inflation amounts to a tax on non-bastards. Governments can either take your money outright, or they can promote the dumping of money on the market and reduce the value of the dollars you have. Both have exactly the same effect: They degrade your purchasing power, eventually to zero if left unchecked.

This brings us to the next matters, those of taxes and theft.

Taxes are rape, nothing more.[9] I would call them theft, but that does not convey the brutality of it all. A thief may take your money and leave you alone, but the government will take all that you have, establish dominance over you, and demand that you further

133

submit to it for the nominal privilege of submitting to it. Theft is about gaining control of money or property. Taxes are a repeated invasion of the victim's wallet and soul.

And then there is the matter of *taxes by other means,* such as civil asset forfeiture (a concept already briefly described in Chapter 2), which until very recently, has allowed law enforcement agencies to seize your home, your money, and all of your baubles without charging you with a crime—to essentially *steal* everything that you own and to do so for no particular reason. In a country where civil forfeiture is legal, the police, in effect, own everything. You may not believe that you have few practical rights to your property. After all, the Fourth Amendment of the United States Constitutions establishes that:

> The right of the people to be secure in their persons, houses, papers, and effects, against unreasonable searches and seizures, shall not be violated, and no Warrants shall issue, but upon probable cause, supported by Oath or affirmation, and particularly describing the place to be searched, and the persons or things to be seized.

Many state constitutions contain similar language, reflecting how important the concept of a right to be free from unreasonable search and seizure has been considered in American jurisprudence. Unfortunately, this means less in practice than one might think. If you regard my assertion with skepticism, I direct you to a few articles:

1. "They fought the law. Who won?" (from the *Washington Post*)

2. "Law enforcement took more stuff from people than burglars did last year" (also from the *Washington Post*)

3. "Civil Asset Forfeiture: Good Intentions Gone Awry and the Need for Reform" (from the Heritage Foundation)

4. "Taken" (from the *New Yorker*)

Timbs v. Indiana, a United States Supreme Court case that was decided in 2019, has somewhat limited the power of governments to levy disproportionate and unreasonable fines by way of civil asset forfeiture. Still, it is worth noting that this practice—that of theft under color of law—was widespread for more than *three decades* before the Supreme Court placed restrictions on it. If *justice delayed is justice denied*, one cannot be too impressed by the effectiveness of the Court.

Above and beyond forfeiture, there are the matters of condemnation of property (in which the government takes your property and gives you what it—the buyer—deems fair), loss of property during divorce, the authority of taxing agencies to place liens on your property, and a larger legal and bureaucratic system that makes protecting your wallet difficult.[10]

There is a general theme here—working hard to own or lease a lot of stuff that you do not really want or need is a sucker's game. You do not *own* anything, even if you manage to pay your debts in full. Yet you are still responsible for these encumbrances—these possessions that are, in effect, being lent to you by the government (and at great expense).

Keep that in mind before accumulating anything you cannot use, and use frequently; move out of the country easily; liquidate conveniently; or consume immediately.

A Bad Bargain

As a man, you receive vastly less from the government than do most women. Collectively, women take more from the government

135

than they contribute, whereas men contribute more than they take.[11] Yes, you gain access to roads (largely so that you can expeditiously get to work, thus supplying more wealth to a select a group of men and a great many women) and some government services, but these services may do as much to oppress you as to aid you.

An example of damaging regulations (of which you subsidize the enforcement) can be seen in the form of Title IX enforcement on college campuses, which has made schools far more expulsion-happy than they would otherwise be and that has probably led to the closure of a number of men's collegiate sports programs.[12] As far as I have been able to ascertain, few government programs at the federal level are intended primarily or exclusively for men; however, the number of programs dedicated to women is large and growing.[13]

The point of all of this is not to demonize women or government, but to acknowledge that women derive more benefit from government than do men, with working-class men deriving the least benefit of all. Even supposedly gender-neutral programs —the student loan program, for instance—disproportionately benefit women, and the men who do attempt to take advantage of these programs either receive fewer benefits or have additional obligations placed upon them. In the case of the student loan program, an additional burden placed upon men is that they are required to register for Selective Service before they are awarded grants or loans, yet women are not.[14]

Given that women are better served by the continuation of the Western (feministic) political tradition than are men, if anyone owes the government money, they, not men, do.

So what is to be done?

The odds of your receiving much in the way of government benefits are slim. Trying to extract resources from social welfare programs is almost impossible for a man unless he is a fairly high-ranking and well-connected individual. *Take as much as possible*, sure, but realize that *as much as possible* is unlikely to be much at all *for you*.

What you can do, is *give as little (to the government) as possible*. I am not going to advocate that you do anything illegal, but I would suggest that you keep your income, particularly your *documented* income, low. As for undocumented income, whatever you choose to do or not do, I would discourage you from getting on the wrong side of the Internal Revenue Service, just as I would discourage criminality of any form.

I strongly suggest that you avoid giving donations to public universities (which are already consuming your tax dollars and providing you with negative returns). You are entirely free to do whatever you wish with your money, but you should realize that much in the way of alumni donations goes to support profoundly misandric campus departments, academics, and policies.[15] The *right to hate* is a natural one, one that cannot be extinguished or restricted by any known technology. Efforts to ban hatred—to ban a feeling—are bound to prove futile. We all have the right to loathe, despise, and wish ill upon any person or any group of people for any reason or no reason at all. College professors, theorists, writers, and policymakers can (and do) hate whomever they wish to hate, and in America (at least at present), they have a right to express their hatred. Plumbers, carpenters, roofers, and mechanics do as well. This is fine.

But why should you freely grant your enemies your patronage?

If you are feeling charitable and would like to give less to a government that sees you as a throw-away utility, find a non-profit supporting a worthwhile cause and donate to it. Perhaps you could even found your own. This will lower your tax liability (meaning less money for your oppressors) and will give you a chance to contribute to something you consider worth supporting.

But there is no reason for you to give any money to anyone unless you feel so inclined—and never forget the wisdom of the First Rule (*Give as little as possible*).

One of the greatest lessons to be learned from examining our tax system is that many *supposedly* liberated women are no more independent than women were in generations past. They still require men for labor, with the difference being that the women of earlier eras relied upon a specific man to support them individually, whereas many of the *allegedly* self-sustaining women of today burden men collectively (as taxpayers). Think of this another way: Millions of women share but one husband—Uncle Sam—with all other men being his lowly subordinates.

Of course, some women are authentically capable. They can and do take care of themselves, collect no more from the government than they contribute, and engage in work of genuine value. Not all women are mere chair-warming bureaucrats or promiscuous parasites. Generalizations are fine if applied *generally*.

Many more women could achieve independence if given no alternative. *Starvation is motivation!* The less you contribute to the government coffers, the more motivated those around you will become. Your non-contribution to the government stands to be a major contribution to the national character (not that you need necessarily care). About the only reason you should want to give

138

the government a penny more than is absolutely necessary is if you have a desire to destroy civilization and you find a bit of Nero-style fun irresistible.

But be honest with yourself—the more money the government gets, the better those who long for your blood you will eat and drink, and they are fat (yet discontented) enough already.

An Unfunny Joke

Our economy is a catastrophe. It is an unfunny joke. Our entire way of life rests upon large, unsustainable amounts of debt. Eventually, there will be a reckoning. All foolish things must come to an end.

The current model of home ownership—one made feasible by long-term mortgages—will collapse as well, but only after mutilating the entire residential real estate market to such an extent that lenders will be stuck with billions of dollars of oversized homes that very few people will be able to afford to maintain, much less buy.[16] A significant number of these properties will end up being written off by lenders, abandoned, and eventually demolished, lest they become drug dens. For the clever man, this —the post-bubble era—may well prove a great time to invest. Until then, *caveat emptor*.

Bear in mind that owning a mega-mansion is effectively guaranteeing that you will pay an expensive property-tax bill and potentially substantial maintenance costs. Even if you can shoulder those burdens, the devaluation of other residences *in your neighborhood* can destroy whatever value your property has, leaving you in quite the bind. Real estate is not mobile, and the more you are attached to a specific place, the less likely you will be to *always have an exit*.

The higher education system, with its luxurious and overbuilt facilities, will fare no better than the property market when students become unable to borrow enough money for four (or five or six) years of drunken debauchery and political indoctrination.[17]

The truth will out—no lie can be sustained forever—but such takes time, and there may be tremendous suffering along the way.

Save, Move, Survive

Do not allow yourself to become ensnared in the joy-crushing, middle-class, borrow-and-spend lifestyle. Such is not a place for men. Big toys and big bank accounts make for big targets. Consider bitcoin, precious metals, or other portable assets. Try to move at least some of your money overseas, and if given the opportunity, establish citizenship (or at least legal residency) in a second country, preferably one that is not on overly friendly terms with the United States, and be prepared to walk away from your current life at a moment's notice.[18] All of this may be easier said than done, but much of what is worth doing can only be done with great effort.

Immobility is death.

And remember that while there is little hope for our paper-tiger economy, there may well still be hope for you.

The Thinking Man

(Ten Questions for Review and Consideration)

1. Are you or any of your friends in debt? If so, how much money do you owe? What kind of debt is it (consumer debt, a mortgage, student loan debt, debt from medical expenses)? How much of this debt was incurred simply for the sake of status or image?

_____

_____

_____

2. How does easy consumer credit hurt the economy? Do you think easy credit allows us, as a society, to hide any underlying problems in our way of life? If so, what problems are we hiding?

_____

_____

_____

3. How does the credit system hurt you in particular? Does it affect wages, prices, or anything else related to your life?

_____

_____

_____

4. How much do you pay a year in taxes? (An estimate would be fine.) Do you believe that you are getting a fair value for what you pay? Why or why not?

_____

_____

_____

5. Can you think of any taxpayer-subsidized programs that actively hurt you? If so, what are they? (These could be in the fields of education, law, foreign policy, or anything else.)

_____

_____

_____

6. What are some ways you can reduce your taxes/taxable income? (Try to think of at least five possibilities.)

_____

_____

_____

7. What, if anything, do you own that is more burden than benefit? How could you most wisely go about liberating yourself from this thing/these things?

_____

_____

_____

8. Do you own anything that might attract unwanted attention (from government officials, women, thieves, etc.)? If so, do you think keeping this thing/these things is worth the risk?

_____

_____

_____

9. What steps could you take to make your assets more concealable and portable (meaning that they could be moved out of the country)?

_____

_____

_____

10. Have you ever considered establishing residency/the right to reside/citizenship in another country? If so, which one and why? What steps could you take to make this happen?

_____

_____

_____

9) On Women

The Alien

Imagine an alien, after years of analyzing the complete utterances, written words, actions, thoughts, and feelings of every man alive and to have ever lived, were to touch down in a cornfield and were to meet *a woman*. Never mind the fact that heavy agricultural machinery is far more likely to be operated by men than women. Perhaps the woman is an outlier. Perhaps she is just walking around. Perhaps she is a corn thief. But for whatever reasons, it is a member of the allegedly fairer sex that the little green man first meets.

What would he think?

Books, political theories, websites, videos, lobbying groups, academic departments—with all of this material and all of these institutions dedicated to them, women are probably the most overanalyzed organisms on the planet. Assume that the alien has digested all of this stuff, every last word, and that all is retained with perfect, crystalline clarity in his cryogenically cooled, 50-pound, quantum-computing brain. And so he compares the archetypes within this grand corpus to the flesh-and-blood creature before him. What would he think?

This is it? This is all there is?

That is what our little green friend is likely to think. There is no reason to get into the weeds of elaborate arguments on women: The many debates and theories are not worth the trouble. For a heterosexual man to have a certain interest in women is effectively inevitable. And as a species it is entirely sensible for us to assign women some worth: Without a fair number of them, humanity would become extinct. (Although the necessary ratio is different, the same could be said of men.) Even bearing this great utility in mind, men have frequently given women more attention than they deserve.

The problem is that, particularly in modern times, we have become far too comfortable projecting a great deal onto women—awarding them an excess of credit that is largely free of blame. The argument against this silliness does not establish that women are *always* at fault (an equally irrational error, but one made by a smaller group of men than those who make the former), only that they are not necessarily innocent or ignorant of the consequences of their behaviors. This is reality: The great arc of history has been, is, and will continue to be bent by primarily by men, not women.

So here are the fundamental truths about women that are relevant for our purposes:

1. No civilization of scale has ever been built by women. This is unlikely to change, which is not to say that no woman ever has contributed or will ever contribute.[1]

2. Women are both more averse to risk and more likely to go along to get along than are men.[2]

3. Women may love their children, their pets, their friends, their cars, their siblings, or any number of other things, animals, or people. They *very rarely* love—in the sense *we* (men) think of *love*—their husbands or boyfriends, and even more rarely are they willing to surrender anything, no matter how trivial, for their husbands or boyfriends.

   For reasons to be considered in a few pages, this point makes perfect sense.[3]

4. Most women operate according to the *female imperative*: Maximize access to money and power and minimize accountability. Minimizing accountability—establishing *hypoagency*—is the primary way by which women shield themselves from the negative consequences of their actions.[4] Men go along with this more often than not, which leads to the next point:

5. With few exceptions, men like women vastly more than women like men.[5]

6. Women may find weak men to be useful, but they will almost always despise them.[6]

7. As much as height, status, and penis size (the source of a man's *HSP score*—explored later in this chapter) matter to women, they will sometimes date men for an entirely different reason: to have someone to *blame for everything*.

8. Women make poor deities. Their approval (sexual or otherwise) sanctifies nothing: There is no inherent nobility in bowing before a vagina.

None of these are inherently bad. None of these are the fault of women, but it is important to understand each of them if you wish to avoid great and pointless misery.

Consider the Lilies . . .

The lilies of the field may neither toil nor spin, but we are not lilies, now are we? So *we* or someone on our behalf must work to afford us our raiments (and everything else that protects us from the elements).

Consider every thing and service upon which you rely—all that which makes modern life possible—mechanically farmed food, electricity, running water, digital devices, automobiles, buildings, climate-control systems, garbage collection, law enforcement, border protection, et cetera. Who makes these things? Who performs these services?

Men. With few exceptions, men.

As for the dark, dirty, and dangerous jobs—everything from working as an electrical lineman to maintaining the sewer system —who does all this?

Men. With few exceptions, men.[7]

This may change, but such is unlikely. There appears no great push on the part of women to achieve equal representation in the more hazardous, more fatiguing, and more unsanitary professions, particularly those without much in the way of prestige As for the fonts of innovation—mathematics, engineering, and the hard sciences—the *more* liberated (meaning the more free choice) women have, the *less* likely they are to study them.[8] Some women are perfectly capable of studying demanding subjects, but few seem to be willing to dedicate themselves to doing so unless they have no other economic opportunities.

Innovation is not easy. Attempts at it result in disappointment more often than not, and even those who achieve their desired goals—invent what they want to invent, write what they want to write, discover what they want to discover—may derive little economic or reputational benefit from these endeavors. The history of scientific, technological, artistic, and social innovation is one a great many failures and a comparatively small number of successes.[9]

The world of *real things*—the world of tangible progress, of the material goods and discoveries that allow us to live as *humans*, rather than just animals that talk—is the world of men. As much innate talent and drive matter, a certain derring-do is what oftentimes separates the merely technically competent from the truly innovative. Without this willingness to attempt to defy the odds—to accept the possibility of loss—some things may be maintained but little new can be created. Thus, the world of innovation, culture, and *progress* is the world of risk-takers, of whom there are more men than women. This is not to say that there will not be some bright and shining exceptions—some women whose accomplishments are numerous and significant—however, they will be in the minority in any field requiring leaps of innovation.

This leads to our next point:

Nothing Ventured, Nothing Gained

Men have more testosterone than do women, and testosterone increases tolerance for uncertainty. Even when considering behavioral patterns within the population of men, those with higher testosterone levels are more willing to take chances than those with lower testosterone levels.[10] This affects everything from willingness to get into fights to investment strategies. Putting oneself in the physical or metaphorical path of an angry lion has its disadvantages—it can get a person eaten—but it also has its advantages—the possibility of nice fur to wear and plenty of big-cat burgers. Considering this from a behavioral perspective (rather than from a purely hormonal one), differences in risk-taking strategies reflect a radically different approach to reproduction.

Prior to the advent of legally enforced monogamy, reproductive rates for men and women were radically different. By some measures, about 80% of women had offspring in prehistoric times, whereas only 40% of men did.[11] At different times in human prehistory this 1:2 ratio rose to 1:17, with only one man having surviving offspring for every 17 women with surviving offspring.[12] In both of these measures, reproduction was far more of a feast or famine matter for men than it was for women.

This is at the heart of differences in male and female behavior. Reproductively, caution affords women moderate success, and adventure offers them little extra: No matter how *strong and independent* a woman is (or fancies herself to be), she has no seed to spread far and wide. There was no *Ginger Khan*, and had a women tried to copy Genghis and his hard-riding compatriots copulative charades, she would have quickly ended up too often pregnant to leave her yurt except to yak up her butter and beef. On the other hand, caution nearly guarantees a man's reproductive failure: Boldness has its risks, but also its rewards.

Feminists argue that men have done most of what is bad in the world. This is true. The list of dementedly violent and terrible men is long. What they omit is that men have also done almost all of what is good. Another way of saying this is that men are at the heart of *almost everything* that has been done by humanity, aside from having and caring for children.

Such is a double-edged sword. Most homicidal maniacs are men. Most heroes are men as well. And I would go so far as to argue that the application of the word *hero,* much like the application of the word *monster,* to women is only rarely appropriate. Very few warrant the application of such strong adjectives. Life is much more of a win or lose prospect for men than for women, with men being more likely to be wealthy (or extremely poor to the point of homelessness), powerful (or completely powerless), or extraordinary successes (or abject failures).[13]

149

This is where our poor alien would be confused—we (men) use a great many terms to describe women, but simply stated, they are rarely worth as much of our attention as we give them, aside from when considering their reproductive viability. This is not to say that women are *evil*, nor is it to say that women are *wonderful*, only that we have a tendency to regard women as more complex, more sophisticated, and more engaging than they really are. There are outliers—there are a few women who are sophisticated, intelligent, and highly worthwhile human beings—but exceptions are *exceptional*. Women have no reason to be exceptional. Becoming so only entails dangers that would do nothing to further their ability to pass down their genetic material. Thus, we may assume that the majority of women are *unexceptional*.

Not Love, Actually

One of the greatest problems faced when discussing *love* is that it is poorly defined. Read these sentences with due care:

I love candy.

I love death metal.

I love my dog.

I love my children.

I love Jesus.

I love my wife/girlfriend/boyfriend/designated-person-with-whom-I-engage-in-sexual-congress.

Each of the aforementioned makes sense. There is nothing particularly unusual about any of them, yet *love* means something quite different from one example to the next.

One does not (I hope) love his dog in the same way that he loves a sexual partner. Nor does one *love* candy in the same sense that one might love Jesus/Yahweh/Apollo/Ahura Mazda/Satan.

Given how much we use the word *love*, it is surprising how vague a term it is. Fortunately, the English-language has a long and storied tradition of stealing (uh, *borrowing*) from other languages, which is why we eat *lo mein* (from the Cantonese *lou min*, meaning *stirred noodles*), drink *vodka* (from the Russian word for *water*, predictably enough), and practice *Zen* (from the Japanese, originally Chinese, word for *meditative state*).

So let us borrow once again, this time from the Greeks (primarily) and a Canadian psychologist, who later added to the nomenclature of love. With precise language, precise thought is easier:

Agape: A man's love of God (or *gods*, as the case may be) or God's love of man

Eros: Sexual love and desire

Philia: Love between equals, brotherly love

Pragma: Practical or convenient love, businesslike love. (Not originally considered *love* by the Greeks, *pragma* was later conceptualized as a type of love by John Alan Lee.[14])

Storge: Familial love, typically the love parents feel for children (and vice versa)

And even with these words fail to completely capture the full range of *love*. One may feel *storge* for his homeland (as a homeland can be thought of as an extension of the family), but what love do we feel for french-fried potatoes? Is *love* the right word at all? Would you kill a man to save the *potaters*? What about the mustard and biscuits?[15]

The problem with *love* (as a term) is that *you* likely define it to include some form of sacrifice, maybe not of your life or everything you own, but of at least some small thing. A woman's love *for a man* (to whatever extent she has such a feeling) is usually quite a bit different. She may well bend over backwards for her children, and she may suffer hardships for her religion. (For a woman to become a martyr is rare, but it does occur.) She is unlikely to so much as inconvenience herself for her boyfriend or husband.[16] This illustrates a key difference between *eros* and *pragma*—both of which a woman may feel for a sexual partner—and *agape*, *philia*, and *storge*, all of which a woman is quite unlikely to feel for a man.

Given that *eros* typically fades over time, usually lasting less than four years, and that a woman with whom a man is having sex is unlikely to feel *agape*, *philia*, or *storge* towards him, all that remains is *pragma*, which is to say that a woman will love the utility her sexual partner provides her.[17] Of course, this is entirely fine, fair, and reasonable. Let us recall what I have written several times before—*the world does not owe you a damn thing!* This includes love, and *the world* includes whomever you happen to be plowing on any given day. But . . . *you do not owe the world a damn thing either.*

The key to fully absorbing this truth in context is to learn to think about love and relationships from the woman's perspective. Biologically, a great many sacrifices in design had to be made for the benefit of a woman's complex reproductive system. Historically (and prehistorically), women were tremendously vulnerable. A woman's odds of survival would have been greatly improved by rational assessment of her partner's functionality. She *needed* to know when to cut bait and move on to another man. A sick or weak husband was a liability in a way that a sick or weak wife was not. The decision to abandon another is best made without much in the way of emotional encumbrance. A woman too tightly bound by sentiment would have perished in ancient times, as would have her offspring, quickly removing such tendencies from the gene pool.

Barring a few exceptions, a man can survive on his own more easily than he can while in a relationship with a woman. You *do not* need a woman. Few men ever have, and any man weak enough *believe* that he needs a woman is too weak to be of any use to one for very long at all.

Throughout most of the agrarian era, a woman's use to a man was to provide sex and make babies—little farmhands and workers, in effect. This job of carrying a child to term and giving birth was quite dangerous—this was the great peril of a woman's life.[18] Beyond that, a great many women were little more than extra mouths to feed and perpetually vulnerable persons—large children, in effect—requiring shielding from the elements.

Men's natural tendency to regard women with a certain protective affection is largely what keeps them from killing these easily injured creatures (or simply letting them die). It is this instinct that is partially responsible for keeping the species from going extinct, and it is similar to the one women with developed maternal tendencies have in regards to their children, at least when the children are still babes in arms.

There is no reason for a woman to feel such affection for her partner. What would a woman—a person who likely spent much of her life pregnant, helpless, and with a shrieking feces maker attached to her tit (until the 20th-century invention of chemical

153

birth control)—have been able to do for a man even if she were so inclined? Rather, *pragma* is all that any woman should (and likely does) feel for her sexual partner. And this naturally terminates once the man's utility has been exhausted.

For women to have compassion for men makes about as much sense as Egyptian plovers having sympathy for crocodiles. *What is an Egyptian plover?* It is a bird that flies into a crocodiles mouth and picks food from its teeth. The relationship is a symbiotic one— the bird gets free food and the crocodile gets clean teeth—much like the one in which women received protection and physical labor from men and men received sex and little farmhands from women. Were all the crocodiles to die, Egyptian plovers would be the poorer for it, but the odds of plovers having much sympathy or empathy for crocodiles—obviously stronger and more capable animals—are rather slim.

Thus, it is all but inevitable that caring for a woman is bound to be a thankless task. Up until very recently, women *needed* men, whereas men *wanted* women. Now, women do not need individual men, although women still require the services that men provide at the institutional level—for physical protection, infrastructure construction and maintenance, and creative and technical innovation. There is little reason for even the tenuous bonds of *pragma* to hold sway over women's hearts.

While this might be a bit discouraging to some men with frangible hearts, it is the way of the world. As the bonds of affection shift from the individual man (and his utility) to the collective man (and its utility), women will naturally progress from supporting husbands to supporting a grand *meta-husband*—the state—and that is exactly what they are doing when they advocate for more expansive welfare provisions and even more draconian policies within the family courts.[19] Both of these—welfare and policy—allow women to quite effectively replace the inferior (weaker) individual man with the superior (stronger) meta-man of the state. Status is attractive, and who among us is as high status (and powerful) as Uncle Sam?

Romantic sacrifices by women for men—as exemplified by Romeo-and-Juliet mutual suicides and the like—may make for interesting fiction, but they do little to ensure the survival of one's genetic heritage. Thus, they almost never occur, nor should they.

The closest to this that one may realistically expect to witness in an ordinary lifetime would be *speculation in a man's potential peak-years' status*. From time to time, you may encounter a woman who had the good sense to invest a portion of her prime reproductive years in a man with promise—someone who may not have had much in the way of status when she met him but had the potential to rise professionally. This is not self-sacrifice: It is buying futures in someone's status.[20] And fewer women are likely to use this strategy now than they were in the past, as many a woman expects her target to have already achieved his peak value before she deigns to give him more than a passing glance.[21]

That's the Game: Survive

Women in the developed world rarely make much of value, aside from babies, and are quite possibly some of the most unproductive humans to have ever lived. Perhaps this will change. Perhaps we will all be slaughtered by Terminators.

Women's recent successes in entrenching themselves in bureaucracy—in education and management, among other things —may obscure the fact that much of what women do now is what they have long done: get men to do the hard work for them, while keeping themselves at arm's length from risk and responsibility.[22] Not every woman conducts her life in this manner, and women in the ancient and primitive world almost certainly engaged (and engage) in more labor of value than do the privileged, preening princesses of the West. Even here, some contribute to society in very tangible, nonsexual ways, but that some blessed fool occasionally wins the Mega Millions is not evidence that buying stacks of lottery tickets is a practical retirement strategy.

Thus, women largely sustain themselves by extracting resources from men. From an evolutionary and cultural standpoint, the continued tolerance of this is necessary: Women with functional sexual organs are essential to the species. It is in the best interest of the collective that the majority of women who are reproductively viable not be allowed to starve, even if doing so requires hours upon days upon years of extra labor from men who will never receive sexual access.

Unfortunately, women's high reproductive value, combined with *hypoagency*—the tendency to *not* hold a group of people (usually women) to account for their actions—and significant biases in the legal system, stand to hugely disadvantage men at odds with women, who can easily transmogrify to cumbersome, ill-tempered, misshapen millstones tied to a man's neck by the rope of the state. The baby-making value of women does not render any particular woman less troublesome for any particular man, nor does it necessarily make being heavily taxed for the benefit of the community of women any less annoying for said man.

Those who have yet to see *Deliverance*, from which the title of this section is quoted, should make a point to watch it. The movie has its limitations—it is patently, proudly a product of the 1970s in its aesthetic, dialogue, and cinematography—but this does nothing

156

to diminish a point it makes about the relative helplessness of modern man when facing nature (or even primitive man). It also touches upon the brittleness of civilization itself, and not only from a technological perspective. As fragile as the highly complex technologies upon which we depend may be, even more prone to breakage is the human element—our willingness and ability to remain *civilized*.

Even minor, temporary infrastructure problems can lead humans to behave in relatively uncivilized ways—can cause us to *revert* to our older instinctive behaviors. In *Deliverance*, the protagonists' behavior became comparatively brutal in a matter of days, and the best available contemporary evidence suggests that this timeline is about right.

Five Days at Memorial provides a nearly minute-by-minute account of what happened in a New Orleans hospital during Hurricane Katrina.[23] As one would expect, a great many of the complex mechanical systems in the hospital failed shortly after a several-day-long power outage began. What is more disheartening is how quickly the social order went pear-shaped. Consider that the hospital went from a normal medical institution to a place in which sickly patients were likely euthanized in a grand total of *five days*. This is not an end-of-the-world post-apocalyptic scenario. This is not Cormac McCarthy's *The Road*. This is a relatively brief power and water disruption.

It would be unreasonable to lay all of the blame for Katrina on any one person or group of people. Like most disasters, Katrina was the result of many accumulated errors that happened over a period of years. What it *does demonstrate* is the profoundly corrosive effects of hypoagency run rampant.

In *Five Days at Memorial* hypoagency becomes an institutional problem: No one is held to account and pointing fingers becomes the order of the day. Although one of the most obvious problems in Memorial Hospital was that it was governed by women and in a feminine manner—meaning by way of poorly maintained consensus mixed with bouts of rashness, rather than practical hierarchy—it would be a profound mistake to believe that a great many men would not avail themselves of the benefits of hypoagency if given the chance.

The hypoagency within *Deliverance* had some similarity to that of Memorial Hospital. Disorganization, insufficient leadership, panic, and a lack of the toughness required to interact with a world not made harmless through the application of technology: These are not exclusively the marks of women, but of both the feminine and the effeminate mindsets. These are the results of deficiencies of strength, both real and feigned, that are tolerated rather than annihilated.

Deliverance and our collective response to it, particularly its most memorable scene, is a measure of how differently we react to male and female weakness. "Squeal like a pig," which was said to one of the characters as he was being forcibly sodomized, has become a sort of all-purpose punchline. Contrast this (and the ubiquity of prison-rape jokes) with our treatment of jokes of a similar nature directed towards women, which even the crudest comedian would probably hesitate to use on stage. We instinctively despise weak men. They are liabilities and unproductive consumers of resources, and it is in the best interest of the species that they die. Thus, ridicule and laughter.

Weak women are less of a problem—they are redeemed through their reproductive capacity—so we are protective of them.

158

This is neither good nor bad, but it supports the hypothesis women are weaker partially *because we (both men and women) allow them to be so.* Either way, be it a woman acting in accordance with her undisciplined nature or a man who is *acting like a woman*, no such person is fit to make any decisions of consequence.

Not all cultures facilitate hypoagency (and the female imperative) to the extent done in the West, but there seems to be little hope that we will emulate their more reasonable approach until we are faced with an existential crisis that affords us no alternative. Prior to that, the ever-escalating *nice-guy arms race*— one in which millions of American men compete to see who can be the biggest simp—will continue. All the thoughtful man may do in the meantime is carefully weigh out the costs and benefits of allowing a potential feral despot into his home in exchange for possible, never-guaranteed coitus of uncertain quality.

All for One and One for All Versus F*** You, Buddy!

Men compete often. Women compete occasionally. Neither of these is an absolute statement. *All men* do not compete *all of the time*. And some men compete rarely, if ever: They are not competitive souls. Some women *do* compete, but they are less likely to compete than men, and when they do the competition is *generally* less severe, at least when challenging other women.[24] Some women are tremendously, brutally competitive against their peers, but these women are few and far between.

Collectively, we benefit from men's competitive nature— without it, there would be very little in the way of technological or creative progress. *Individually*, competition is destructive for a great many men. And there are far more losers than winners in every truly competitive endeavor. What is good for the geese—

males fighting over females—is not great for many a gander. Nonetheless, nature cares nothing for our feelings.

When men and women *do* directly compete, women have three natural advantages:

1. They lack sympathy for men, whereas many men have quite a bit of sympathy for women. One side is fighting with gloves on (*I don't want to hurt the little lady*), and the other is fighting with hands wrapped in cloth, soaked in tar, and covered in broken glass (*Why not? Screw that sexist moron pig! He's probably a rapist anyway!*). Even if Mr. Gloves is quite a bit bigger than Ms. Glass, the latter has the *Bloodsport* advantage.[25]

2. Assuming they are reasonably young and of even average attractiveness, women can turn men against *each other*, meaning they can win conflicts without having to lift a finger, which leads to our next point.

3. They have tremendous in-group bias (as already explored).

Useful Idiots . . . Not Just For Commies Anymore

The phrase *useful idiot* has several meanings, depending upon context. For our purposes, it describes *someone who sacrifices himself or his resources for a person or cause, expecting to be rewarded with respect or appreciation, only to receive torment or enmity.* The phrase is frequently attributed to Lenin (hence the title of this section), but the actual originator is unknown. Nevertheless, it is a notion worth knowing.

Sacrificing oneself for the church, for a political party, or for an abstraction may have gone out of fashion, but making a fool of yourself or putting yourself in harm's way for the benefit of a woman (or *women*) seems to be in vogue. You too can join the

160

marching morons on their way to prove their utility to women. Of course, doing this is entirely your choice, but you understand that such sacrifice will only lead to *even more* sacrifice, topped with a healthy dollop of contempt.

Man up and marry a single mother?

Great, you now get to pay child support for someone else's kid.[26]

Save a poor, helpless victim from her psychotic ex-boyfriend?

Get shot by said ex-boyfriend (if he really is insane) or get falsely accused of a violent crime (if *she* is the crazy one).

Mentor a woman at your company?[27]

Get a harassment complaint filed against you, get dragged to the human-resources office, and get terminated with extreme prejudice. Do not forget that the difference between *harassment* and *compliments* can be nothing more than the perceived value of the man making the statement.

It would be inequitable to blame women for not liking useful idiots. Most crooks do not hold their marks in high regard. Most religious charlatans have little use for their idiot flock (which is not to say that everyone involved in religion is a charlatan, only that *some* are). And very few people respect a sucker. *Do you?* Why would women be any different?

Remember this: Bastards (assuming they operate within certain sensible limits) do quite well in this world. Hatred can mature into respect. But contempt is the curse of Cain. Once the curse and mark of contempt are upon a man, he will never be free of them. Water, fire, acid, even death—nothing can wash away, burn off, dissolve, or destroy contempt.[28] It is better to be feared, better to be hated, better to be ignored, better to *be gone* than to be

161

regarded with contempt. And *being gone*—leaving and starting anew, far away from where he is known—is about all a man may do if he does not wish to suffer the curse and mark after they have been put upon him. *Always have an exit!*

Flaccid Failures and Fertility Goddesses

Although Americans are, on average, more religious than the citizens of most other developed countries, their devotion to traditional beliefs is on the decline.[29] This is not to say that Americans have no faith, only that they have moved away from *traditional* beliefs. Looking outside the scope of religion to the broader framework of *belief in something greater than oneself*, Americans are also becoming less patriotic and are losing their faith in a great many social institutions.

So are we becoming nihilists? Or are we simply worshiping something else?

Rather than having no religion, there is compelling evidence that we have simply changed our beliefs and are now worshiping women.

The Church of the Sacred Vagina (CoSV) is everywhere. Read any paper, particularly a left-leaning one—*The Washington Post, The New York Times*—and you will find praise immeasurable of women, every bit as much criticism of men, and very little of the opposite of either.

To a certain extent, this is an amplification of humanity's biological imperative to protect the sex with less reproductive elasticity. But biology only explains some of this worship of women, based as it is on the presumption that women are *always* better than men, rather than simply *more vulnerable* (which would seem to suggest *inferior*, if anything).

To understand this, one must look back at America's historically dominant religion—Christianity. It is true that America was never a *Christian nation*. It was never a theocracy, and non-Christians, including Jews, Muslims, Buddhists, Taoists, believers in American Indian religions, and atheists have long been part of American society.[30] Yet is also equally true that Christianity has long been the most prevalent and influential religion in the United States.

Inherent in Christianity is a respect for mild, vulnerable, and downtrodden—a trait not shared by all faiths.

"Blessed are the meek: for they shall inherit the earth," (Matthew 5:5) quite well summarizes the Christian sentiment. In the King James Version of the New Testament, there are 16 occurrences of *meek* (or a derivative thereof), seven occurrences of *gentle* or *gentleness*, and more than 200 occurrences of *love*. Granted, not all references to *love* are positive: Criticisms of the Pharisees made mention to love in a clearly negative context—accusing them of *loving* their rank and status more than *loving* God. (Luke 11:42-43). Yet the general theme remains. Gentleness, meekness, and love are all emphasized within Christian doctrine, as a certain respect for the poor and disadvantaged, and the notion that the *last shall be first, and the first last.* (Matthew 20:15).

This is all endearingly humane in theory, but a problem arises when one starts to interpret these ideas and phrases to mean that *the unsuccessful are inherently good and the successful are inherently bad.* Applied to women, who have had fewer great successes than have men (but are also less likely to suffer from great failures), one concludes that the *apparently* losing team must be better—spiritually, morally, or mentally—than the team with more wins. A close reading of the New Testament does not

163

support this as a Christian doctrine, yet those who *feel* their way through texts, more than *thinking* their way through them, might come to the conclusion that Jesus wants us all the cheer for the underdog and boo the winner.

Thus, we are left with the notion that women *must* be better because they have achieved less. They *must* be more moral because they have had fewer successes. And men—who have done (and struggled) more—*must* be punished for their inherent, winning badness.

Christian theology does not support the aforementioned. *Logic and reason* do not support this. The notion that the universe is, in effect, *perfectly unjust* is no less absurd than the notion that the universe is *perfectly just*. Nevertheless, men's natural goodwill towards women; combined with Christian charity; combined with liberal notions of rights without duties; combined with the peculiar (and entirely *un-Christian*) notion that women have a *right to be happy*, rather than simply a right to *pursue happiness*; have blended into the most unholy of religions—the CoSV. And in the CoSV, women are above and beyond reproach or accountability.

The other reason the CoSV has so many adherents—it appeals to the weaknesses *of men*. Christianity requires a *leap of faith*. This is hard. Accepting that you are acting *on faith*—that there are some things you simply cannot know (but *choose* to believe)— requires some intentionality. And just as difficult is the polar opposite: accepting that whatever decency, humanity, or integrity you wish to find and possess, must be cultivated within the hearts and minds of men, and with human effort alone. This places great demands upon the individual: If he does not like what he sees in the world, it is up to him to try to change it.

164

But the worship of women provides a half-assed alternative: One needs make no leap of faith to believe in women. They are, after all, relatively easy to find. Nor does one need to look within himself for strength and decency. Rather, a man can excuse himself from the hard work of questioning his goals, values, and beliefs, and can dedicate himself to the comparatively mindless (if largely futile) task of placating a woman, pretending there is some inherent virtue therein. Faith and mental self-examination both require intellectual honesty and effort. Following one's penis to heaven requires neither. And then there's the matter of the *eternal boy*—of the man who forever wants a mother's love, which is itself likely to be temporary and conditional. Respecting one's parents is fine, but eventually any man must learn to put away childish things, and the need for a mother's love is one such thing.

Worship at the Church at your own peril. It offers no way, even in death, for you to be absolved of your sin of being a man. There is no path to redemption.

And it is not the best of sex cults either: The longer you attend, the less likely you are to get laid. So if not worship, what attracts women?

What Women Want

Much has been written about what women look for in men. This fascination is somewhat understandable—one's ability to leave a genetic heritage has depended upon it. Thus, it is worth giving the matter due (but not excessive) attention.

This section begins with two disclaimers: First, not every woman wants or needs to be involved with a man, just as not every man wants to be involved with a woman. Such is fine. Strong, independent, and intelligent women living in reasonably developed nations really *do not* need a husband or boyfriend to survive. I have worked with a few of these women. All of them had real jobs (meaning they did not work in human resources departments or the like), which required authentic and prolonged intellectual effort and study. They all had strong interests that engaged in them during their free time, and none of them appeared to have much interest in men. These women were exceptional, but not so exceptional that I cannot rattle off the names of a half-dozen of them at will.

Second, *no man* should assess his worth as a person based upon his ability to attract women. The purpose of this section is not to establish a set of ideals for you, or any man, to attempt to achieve, but to provide a simple model that codifies and demonstrates *that women's sexual preferences are no less shallow than are those of men*. This is not to say that women's sexual preferences are *inherently bad*, only that (with few exceptions) their assessments of men have little to nothing to do with what any sensible man would consider measures of a worthwhile human being. Reproductive impulses are inherently primitive. What we (as humans) want in a sexual partner has been shaped over many millennia, long before modern society and its concepts of decency, humanity, and civilized behavior existed.

Many of the theories and formulas regarding women's desires are extremely complex, oftentimes to point of near incomprehensibility. Rather than paying much mind to random or culture-specific models, we would be wise to focus on preferences that almost all women have, regardless of nationality, culture, age, or socioeconomic status. Here are the three universal factors that determine a man's ability to attract women:

1. (H)eight   (Taller is better.)
2. (S)tatus   (Higher status is better.)

166

3. (P)enis size   (Bigger is better.)[31]

For the sake of simplicity, we will refer to this as the *HSP formula*. As for any number of things you have been *told* are of interest to women—personality, hair color, hobbies, religious practice, ability to make a meaningful difference in the lives of others—these may matter to *some* women *some* of the time.

How many men do you know able to attract women with their passion for woodworking? Hobbies are great—they can give you structure, purpose, and enjoyment. Helping others (purely to the extent you feel inclined) can be great if that is what appeals to you. But in the mating and dating game, such things are very nearly irrelevant. I also note that *status* and *respectability* are largely independent of one another—a point previously examined. An accomplishment may make one worthy of both, but such is no more likely to be the case than not.

Rather than focusing on individual quirks specific to a few women, let us consider a parsimonious, if imperfect, scoring system for determining a man's sexual desirability. To use this model on yourself, note the relevant metric and the score assigned to it. Write it down. Repeat this process for each factor. Sum all three scores to develop a composite score (your HSP total). Bear in mind that this formula is calibrated for American audiences. Different populations have different average heights and penis sizes, and status does not perfectly correlate with income, particularly outside of North America.

The HSP scoring table can be found at the end of this chapter. Note that the economic versus non-economic scoring systems are mutually exclusive. You should calculate both your economic and non-economic scores and pick the higher of the two. Also note that non-economic factors are non-cumulative. Pick the *one* element that gives you the highest score and use that.

This model should be treated more as a heuristic—as something to stimulate further investigation and discovery—than as an absolute truth. Likewise, the following guidelines are meant as recommendations, rather than as absolute rules offered completely without exception.

Extremely Desirable and *Desirable Men (HSP >2)*—Can largely have their pick of the vaginal litter (a regular clowder of pussies, one might say). If anything, such men should work to avoid being trapped by women in relationships they would rather avoid.

Neutral Men (HSP 0 to 2)—May have some luck with women, but should be aware that such involvement may require considerable expense and lead to being regarded as a useful idiot (revenue and labor source and proxy agent of a woman's whims).

Undesirable and *Extremely Undesirable Men (HSP <0)*— Should either avoid dating or expect to be dumped *as soon as an even marginally better option comes along.* Such men— those without any genetic, economic, or social assets—are likely to be regarded with extreme contempt by women, as carrying the spawn of such a man would stand to be a terrible reproductive fail. Any man with a score of -2 or below would be well-advised to avoid impregnating a woman as she is unlikely to ever forgive him for doing so.

You may have noticed that I make no mention of *personality* in this formula. This is by design. Personality is of limited relevance to reproductive success. The same could be just as easily said for *intellect*.

168

Those who have truly *awful* personalities, which is to say that *no one* can tolerate them, may find themselves at a disadvantage when attempting to find a woman willing to copulate with them, but this is an extreme. Likewise, those who are so *profoundly* stupid that they could not find a vagina with both hands and a trained dog are also unlikely to accumulate many notches on their bedposts. This is just as well, given that such blessed fools would not be able to count more than a few such notches even if accumulated. The point: Do not be *completely* insufferable *all* of the time, and do not be an *absolute* idiot. And if you are either of these things and wish to attract women, *try to avoid saying too much*. Beyond that, personality, charm (or lack thereof), and intellect are relevant only to the extent they relate to status and the accumulation of status.

The other point to realize is that even men who achieve the highest possible score (14) may be bested. Not many men make more than 195,000 dollars a year (about the 99th percentile of earners in 2019); are taller than 6 feet, 2 inches; and have 11-inch penises. Those who do are probably in the NBA. That much said, even those who *break the scale*—the guys who play center for the Los Angeles Lakers, have good money-management skills, and have the ability to dribble a ball with their *third leg*—should know this: There is always the possibility someone better will come along, and expecting loyalty from a woman in such a case is worse than naive, it is counter to all of human development: It is *unnatural*.

Finally, I would stress that the sexual market is like any other in that not every buyer (the woman, in this case) will be interested in every high-value item for sale. Said another way: Those men with high HSP scores will *generally* attract more attention than those with lower ones, which is not to say that *every woman* will be drawn to a particular man, even if his HSP scores is essentially perfect.

Badasses and Little Bitches

There is more than one way to get a high score on the Status section of the HSP formula (*a high S-score*), even in the United States, where income and status closely correlate. The non-economic way to achieve a high S-score is to be a *badass*. One can either be a white-hat (good-guy) badass—a soldier, a law enforcement officer, or a firefighter—or a black-hat (bad-guy) badass—a biker, a criminal, or a hard-partying musician or artist— and achieve a high S-score, even with a limited income. Men in these categories are *fun* for women, particularly the black-hat badasses, who may gain considerable sexual access in exchange for very little beyond being their bad selves. Although there is considerable overlap between *badasses* and *bastards*, they are distinct. Being a badass may be beyond a great many men, but we can all learn to be better bastards—something that has applications far more significant than attracting women—and on which this book has a chapter—14 ("On Being a Bastard").

So how do men with low (<0) HSP scores and little likelihood of advancement) get women?

By volunteering to be treated with hatred and contempt— that's how. They accept blame *for everything*. These men—*little bitches*—pay a high price for infrequent intercourse, and any children they have are bound to pay a terrible price as well. Aside from being saddled with atrocious genetic material, the children of little bitches will almost certainly have the same hatred and contempt heaped upon them by their mothers that their mothers, gorgons that they likely are, heaped upon their fathers. For most

170

men, being treated with hatred and contempt is not enjoyable. For children, it is far more damaging. At best, a youth without love, compassion, or concern will cause a person to develop a thick skin of cynicism and detachment. At worst, it may drive a child, particularly a boy lacking psychological resilience, over the edge— to harming himself or others, sometimes in spectacularly violent ways. *Little bitch man + gorgon woman = active-shooter son* (not always, but far too often)

There are fates far bleaker than never being born, and being born to a little bitch (and the abomination he impregnated) is one of them.

It is great to *be a bastard*, but not too much of one—not so much of one that you live with great regret, and not so much of one that it comes back to bite you—making you a *sore ass* more than a *bad* one. It is one thing to be a bastard, and a proud one. It is another thing entirely to discover that your child has left a trail of dead hookers behind him. Any man with a low HSP score should consider this carefully before inseminating anyone—one of the biggest bastard moves he could possibly make and one that is almost certain to curse both his existence and that of his children.

As for suffering and how much of it should one should bear and inflict upon others, consider a question that has been asked more than once in this text (and that any man should keep in mind whenever considering sex): *How much are you willing to pay—how much life, time, property, dignity, and energy are you willing to give—to get laid?*

So are all men with low HSP scores bound to be little bitches?

No! The key, however, is to understand how brutal the mating and dating market really is. Art, music, culture, ethics, philosophy, human decency, and civilized values—these are all the inventions of men and groups of men. They have only tangential connections to reproduction. Any man who thinks his sexual worth is a reflection of his human worth is terribly, dangerously wrong.

The man with a low HSP score may have plenty of value *as a human being.* He may be loyal, compassionate, intelligent, amusing, thoughtful, or in possession of any number of attributes generally regarded as being *good.* He may be a good friend (*or not* —HSP scores have *no* relation to these traits, not an inverse one). But none of this has any bearing on a man's sexual desirability. The low-HSP man would be well-advised to cultivate his interests and his friendships, not his portfolio of sexual conquests. Efforts at growing the latter may do the low-HSP man more harm than good.

The dating market is not where friends are found. Friends are those with whom a person shares common passions, common goals, common values, or common experiences. Sexual partners are those with whom one has sex. Rarely do the twain meet.

In theory, a man may become friends with a woman, but only he if he treats her *as a friend*, not *as a girlfriend.* This is challenging—the boyfriend/girlfriend dynamic is hard to break, unless the woman involved is old, unattractive, or simply *absolutely not* the man's type. In practice, most men are better served by focusing the bulk of their attention on making friends with other men.

The Alien's Advice

What would the alien, our large-headed and glowing-fingered friend, tell men to do with their lives? What errors would he find in their thinking about women and how would he suggest men correct these mistakes? Our alien, being smart enough to know that people will ultimately decide for themselves what to do (unless he uses his mind control machine, which is in the shop, having its oil changed), would probably advise as follows:

1. Understand that women are (at least) as shallow as are men.

2. Do not assess your worth as a human being by your ability to attract or retain women.

3. Understand that any attachment a woman feels to her husband or boyfriend is, with few exceptions, *temporary, conditional, and utilitarian*.

4. Know that any man with a low HSP score may well face torment, manipulation, and mistreatment if he becomes sexually involved with a woman. His children's fate (assuming the man has any) has the potential to be far worse.

5. Know that there will always be someone out there with a higher HSP score. You may never meet such a man, but if your wife or girlfriend does (and he is available), your days with her are likely to be numbered.

6. Remember that almost all science, technology, art, customs, ethics, and traditions—that which separates us from the lower primates—are the creations of men. Do not confuse women's ability to *birth people* with the ability to build civilizations.

7. Know that women have always been a source of strife, suffering, and death for men. This is not entirely the fault of women. It is as much a product of the nature of the species and of men's and women's differing levels of reproductive elasticity. Nevertheless, strife, suffering, and

death are not glorious things, regardless of who (or what) is to blame.

8.   Never forget the power of the Rules. Never accept responsibility without authority, and remember that *you are never obligated to care*—about anyone's survival, about anyone's satisfaction, or about anyone's happiness. Sometimes, you may be obligated to *act,* but you are *never* obligated to care. The happiness of women (collectively) or of *a woman* (individually) is not your responsibility, just as *your happiness* is not theirs or hers.

9.   Remember this: *If she's crying, she's lying.* Do not trust a woman's dramatics. She may not be as strong as a man, but she is likely less fragile than she would have you believe—feigning helplessness is a skill many women have mastered. The more theatrically she behaves, the more likely she is trying to manipulate you.

Moving On

Now that we have considered women, let us give them no more attention: They have received all they deserve. And you, the reader, have been duly educated, informed, and (where appropriate) warned.

Next, we turn to the matters of children and the good, the bad, and the ugly thereof.

The Thinking Man

(Ten Questions for Review and Consideration)

1. What is the *female imperative*? When and where did you last
    see it in effect? Consider your home, work, and social life
    when answering the question.

    _____

    _____

    _____

2. Consider the different types of love. Is there anyone (or
    anything) for whom or which you feel *agape*? What about
    philia, *pragma*, or *storge*? Do you treat these people, animals,
    things, or ideals different? If so, how?

    _____

    _____

    _____

3. In what ways does the government serve as a husband to
    women? In what ways does it do a better job than an individual
    man could? In what ways (if any) does it do a worse job? Do
    not consider sex in your answer: That can easily be had by
    most unmarried women.

    _____

    _____

    _____

4. Have you ever seen a man demonstrate hypoagency? If so, when, where, and why did this happen? Was his attempt to shirk responsibility successful?

_____

_____

_____

5. Can you think of any recent, personal, or historical incidents in which men were *overly* eager to protect and accommodate women and hurt or killed innocent men as a result? If so, describe the incident. If not, try to find some information about the Groveland Four. What do you think about that case?

_____

_____

_____

6. Have you known any women who pit men against each other? Have you personally observed said woman (or women) doing this? If so, do you know *why* the woman (or women) did this? Was there a practical reason? Was this primarily for the woman's (or women's) amusement?

_____

_____

_____

7. Have you ever served as a woman's *useful idiot*? If so, when and why? If you have done this more than once, when was the time you were most inconvenienced? Were you purely trying to sex, or were you a useful idiot for some other reason?

_____

_____

_____

8. Do you or any of the men you personally know worship at the temple of the Church of the Sacred Vagina (CoSV)? If so, what do you (or the other men) do that indicates as much? Remember, this is not a euphemism for *trying to get laid*. This is about acting as though women are the moral superiors of women.

_____

_____

_____

9. What is your HSP score? Based on it and your personal experiences and observations, how would a woman with whom you are sexually involved be likely to regard and treat you?

_____

_____

_____

10. How can the Rules be applied to interacting with women? Consider that *you are never obligated to care*. How would keeping this in mind affect your interaction with women?

_____

_____

_____

The HSP scoring table is located on the next page.

The HSP Formula—United States Criteria		
Factor	Raw Input/Range	Score
Height	>6 ft. 2 in.	+4
	6 ft. to 6 ft. 2 in. (72-74 in.)	+2
	5 ft. 9 in. to 5 ft. 11 in.	--
	5 ft. 6 in. to 5 ft. 8 in.	-2
	<5 ft. 6 in.	-4
Status (economic)		
	>99th percentile	+6
	95th to 99th percentile	+4
	75th to 94th percentile	+2
	50th to 74th percentile	--
	25th to 49th percentile	-2
	<25th percentile	-4
Status (non-economic)		
Elite military status	Special forces and/or winner	+4
	of higher military honor	
Non-elite military	Active duty or veteran	+2
Musician/artist	Famous	+4
	Regionally known	+2
Good-guy/white-hat badass	Firefighter, police officer, et cetera	+2
Bad-guy/black-hat badass	Convicted violent criminal,	+2
	biker gang member, et cetera	
Otherwise famous	Television star, author, et cetera	+2
None of the above	(Use economic scale)	--
Penis size		
(erect, nearest 1/10th in.)	10 in. to 12 in.	+4
	6.5 in. to 9.9 in.	+2
	5.4 to 6.4 in.	--
	<5.4 in.	-2

179

10) On Children

Life is not an unqualified blessing. For a few, it is great. For many, it is mediocre. For more still, it is terrible—days of trudging through a vale of tears towards a pit of oblivion—and even for the luckiest, there is no joy free from the heavy weight of sorrow. This is not news. The days of yore were not all feasting and battle and indulgence and plowing ever-youthful maidens, only recently supplanted by the soul-raping drudgery of a sterile existence within the narrow confines of cubicles and cages. Valhalla was for the dead, not the living.

Here are two quotes from the ancients:

Now this, oh Bhikkhus [monks], is the noble truth concerning suffering. Birth is attended with pain, decay is painful, disease is painful, death is painful. Union with the unpleasant is painful, painful is separation from the pleasant; and any craving that is unsatisfied, that too is painful. (The First Sermon of the Buddha)[1]

Wherefore I praised the dead which are already dead more than the living which are yet alive. Yea, better is he than both they, which hath not yet been, who hath not seen the evil work that is done under the sun. (Ecclesiastes 4:2-3)

The purpose of including these quotes is not to cause you grief or despair, nor is their purpose to make anyone with children regret having them. You have done what you have done. Regret is pointless. The first point is this: Your children owe you nothing for conceiving them or allowing them to be born. Life is, at best, an experience of mixed and uncertain value.

The second point is, barring sexual assault, children are the result of voluntary actions performed *exclusively for the benefit of those doing the conceiving, not the conceived.* This is not to say that having children *is wrong*, only that there is nothing selfless about it. At least within the modern Western world, rationalizations to the contrary simply do not hold water. In an earlier era, one might have *gone forth and multiplied* with good purpose, but ours is no longer a world in which our species is at imminent risk of extinction, and we no longer have tribal affiliations worthy of the name.

Now that we have established that those who have children are doing so for their own benefit, there is the matter of questioning *how* having children benefits a person (if it does) and to what extent this differs from the *perceived* benefits. Before considering this, we must answer an antecedent question:

Why Do You Want to Have Sex?

As is the case for much of this book, this chapter is useless until you have decided what *you* want out of life. This cannot be done without considering your motives, your behavior, and your capacity to reason. And *this* requires asking some questions for which the answers seem obvious but may be less so than they initially appear.

There is an assumption built into this question—that being that you want to have sex. If you are not so inclined, good for you! I write the last sentence seriously and without sarcasm. Without the perpetually irritating distraction that is a sex drive, you have more time and energy to focus on other things. If you *do* want to have sex, as the evidence suggests the majority of men do, answer the question.

Take a moment. Think it over carefully. Sometimes asking seemingly simple questions can yield surprising answers.

The most obvious answers are that you feel biologically *compelled or driven* to have sex and that you are inclined to *enjoy* sex. Although these two elements often go together, they are not the same.

Think of the difference between eating because you are hungry and eating because you enjoy a particular dish. You can eat for *both* reasons, of course, but they lead to outcomes that can be different in subtle, but significant, ways.

Those eating for pleasure have both the opportunity to be quite picky—to refuse otherwise palatable food—simply because said food does not suit the eater's fancy. At the same time, if the food *does* prove particularly agreeable to the *meticulous masticator* (*someone who chews food carefully*. What else did you think I meant?) eating far beyond what is calorically necessary is a distinct possibility, whereas those eating simply to alleviate the suffering of hunger may eat what they need and no more. Some foods lend themselves to one pattern of behavior or the other. Only a few of us would eat bowl after bowl of rice and unseasoned beans simply for the pleasure of it, yet such a meal may be perfectly appetizing to those who have long fasted.

On the other hand, donuts, cakes, pies, and other such calorie-rich, micronutrient-poor foods are quite enjoyable to eat, but at the same, can leave you feeling quite hungry. Generally, sex becomes more recreation and less compulsion/drive as a man ages, which can be either good or bad news, depending upon how much he regards his sex drive as a part of his identity.

Of course, there are other reasons to want sex. None of the reasons are mutually exclusive.

I have already alluded to one of them: to prove a point about your masculinity. This somewhat makes sense for virgins, with *having sex* being something of a box to be checked (or at least penetrated) for many a young man. However, I would certainly hope that any and every man eventually comes to understand that having sex in an age of loose morals, easy access to birth control, and a number of smartphone apps on which prostitutes market their services (with varying degrees of openness), is not much of an accomplishment.

Another reason is simple boredom. This was probably more a factor during our fathers' youths—from the 1960s to the 1980s—when entertainment and computing were less advanced than they are today.[2]

The final reason is the most complicated—to have children, which itself must be disentangled from the matter of identity.

Maybe (You Do Not Want a) Baby

If you are having sex for any reason other than the last, I would advise you to proceed with caution. Aside from abstinence, there are few totally effective forms of birth control and even fewer effective forms of birth control available to men. As for trusting a woman to use birth control (*It's okay. I'm on the pill*), there are some forms of idiocy so profound that there is little to be said for those who would practice them other than *Good luck with that, dumbass!*

The most effective form of birth control available to men is the vasectomy. Granted, even it is not perfect, and the procedure is rarely covered by insurance. Still, if performed properly (assuming that the person who has the vasectomy waits the appropriate amount of time after the procedure before having sex), the vasectomy failure rate is reasonably low—far lower than that for condoms.[3]

As for the price, even a 2,000-dollar procedure is cheaper than years of child support. There is the possibility of post-vasectomy pain, but I would argue that this is almost certainly less painful than being brutally wallet-raped in family court.

The process of obtaining a vasectomy may be complicated for any man under 30. Some doctors may hesitate to perform a vasectomy on a younger man. Many times, a doctor may ask if a vasectomy candidate has children. The doctor is almost certainly wanting to hear *yes* as a reply to this question, and the probability of him checking into the matter further is relatively slim.

The logic behind this line of questioning is, for lack of a better word, *questionable*. For whatever reasons, a great many otherwise seemingly intelligent people seem to take for granted that it is better *to have children and not want them* than it is *to want children and not have them*. Assuming that one sets out with the goal of creating no more misery than necessary, this is wrong. A person who wants children he does not have may suffer in some small way. A person who has children he does not want will suffer at least as much, and the children are likely to suffer as well, possibly far more than the parent. Thus, we are comparing a relatively small amount of misery for one person versus greater misery for many.[4]

You should always remember the Rules, particularly *enjoy life to the fullest*. Having children *may* be a part this (although there is little data to support such an assertion for most men), but you should distinguish between being a *ruthless bastard* and being an *actively malevolent* one.[5] Inflicting misery simply for the sake of hearing weeping and gnashing of teeth stands to do little to make

184

your life better: Pol Pot died in the jungle, probably by suicide, and the Marquis de Sade passed his last days in an asylum.[6]

This is all rational enough, but it does not counter one of the most obvious arguments for having children. For that, we turn to a man whose stature far exceeded his height.

Khan!

In an era in which the role of God and faith are quickly diminishing and philosophy is regarded with considerable suspicion, the question of *What is the purpose of life?* is difficult to answer. One of the simplest arguments is that the ultimate goal of any living thing is to reproduce. While biologically rational, what is most interesting about this argument is that a great many people who make it do a poor job of practicing it.

With 0.5% of men globally having a Y-chromosome lineage traceable back to him, Genghis Khan proved one of history's best impregnators. As one might expect, the kin of Khan are not evenly distributed throughout the globe—about 8% of tested Asian men appear to have Genghis Khan as a distant grandfather, with the percentage being much lower elsewhere in the world—but even in Eastern Europe, Khan or his descendants seem to have done surprisingly well.[7]

If you believe that keeping your genetic lineage going is *good* because such a strategy is evolutionarily favored, you could do worse than to emulate the ruler originally known as Temujin. And there are lessons to be learned from his strategies for seduction. Part of what almost certainly drew women to Genghis was his power. Although Genghis was probably not a particularly tall man (giving him a low H-score), he more than made up for it by building one of the largest land empires the world has ever known, meaning his S-score was almost incalculably high.

And the final part of the winning strategy of *Asia's Greatest Lover* is that the women involved had little choice in the matter. Raiding villages has historically proven to be a great way to pick up women, particularly if you do not mind throwing them over your steed and carrying them back to camp.

Let us keep in mind, however, that the dating game has developed a certain annoying subtlety that it lacked centuries ago, and raping and pillaging (or even just raping) your way across any continent may not endear you to the locals.[8] This was not much of a problem for Genghis, partially due to different cultural norms, partially because he took an army with him wherever he went. Bearing the substantial changes in law and culture in mind, we should not hold Genghis to the standards of today. In some ways, such as his tolerance for diverse religious practices in the territories he conquered, Genghis was quite progressive.[9] Nor should one forget these changes when considering the best approach for ensuring the continuity of his germ line. Assuming that you wish to stay on the right side of the law, your plans for broadcasting your DNA with great velocity are unlikely to start with learning to shoot arrows (of flint, steel, *or love*) from the back of a moving horse.

Still, there are a great many lessons to be learned from the *Great-Great-Granddaddy of All Baby Daddies*. First is that thousands of women can bear more offspring than can a single woman. It is logically better to have sex with 1,000 women one-time each than it is to have sex with one woman 1,000 times. Not only is this likely to yield a great number of offspring, it allows for greater genetic diversity for one's offspring. A given man and a given woman may share recessive (and potentially damaging) genes. The odds of this happening with 1,000 *different* women, or of all of these women carrying the *same* undesirable genes, are low.

Second is that it is better to spread your seed across a wide geographical domain than to concentrate it in a small area. One village may be destroyed, but many villages many thousands of miles apart are exponentially less likely to be, and if such *does* happen, there is a distinct possibility that *no one's* gene carriers will live to die another day. The predominant, lawful, and conventional approach to reproduction—having a small number of children with one or two women—is a poor substitute for the winning strategy of Genghis, or even the considerably less aggressive strategies of any number of men working and living in America today, such as Desmond Hatchett, whose behavior is examined later in this chapter.

This illustrates where a great many who treat biology or evolution as ethical imperatives make a critical error: They try to impose a biological imperative onto a modern, pro-social behavioral values system and demonstrate little fidelity to either. Through certain intersections, biology and social norms cannot simultaneously pass. One must have right-of-way over the other. To deny this—to insist on some impossible compromise—is to embrace the inevitability of a crash.

As for the actual reason Genghis deflowered one maiden after the next, it is doubtful that he was intent leaving a large brood so much as he was simply enjoying the fruits of his conquests. Either way, Genghis's strategies proved effective militarily, reproductively, and recreationally, proving that one can, at least occasionally, do what he loves and the money (and success) will follow.

Who's Your Daddy?

Here is a fundamental truth to know: **Fatherhood is dead.**

It is not merely weakened. It will not recover from what ails it, and decades from now, it will be no less dead than it is today. What we call *fatherhood* is a title without power, without respectability, and without utility. Being *a father* in our society means about as much as being a self-appointed colonel in the Confederate States Army. Such an officer (and gentleman, we will assume) may be able to buy or otherwise assemble a well-made, historically accurate uniform; a chest covered with medals; and an easily rattled saber, but unless the South really does rise again, said officer is little more than a cosplayer, a Civil War reenactor, or someone who is clinically befuddled. Much like our beloved colonel, fathers are quite without power. From time to time, some raggedy troop may follow our colonel, but only so far as its members' curiosity and natural inclinations take them.

If you doubt this—if you think this comparison is an example of hyperbole—*try* to exercise your authority as a father (assuming you have children), in even the slightest way. Try to win a custody case. See how long it takes for police, social workers, and gin-swilling feminists to descend upon you like vultures drawn to the heavy odor of sun-drenched carrion. I would strongly recommend you go ahead and add a lawyer to your phone's speed dial. Perhaps a suicide helpline (one where they actually *help* you to commit suicide) should be stored in memory as well.

Paternity is alive and well, and the technology for determining it is the best it has ever been. The role of *child-support payer* is popular as well. There is much *paternity* to be had, and there are many *payers* to be found, but being a *pater* is no longer a viable option. All that is left is responsibility without authority—a bad deal by any measure.

188

What will replace *family* as it has been defined for several thousand years of agrarian civilization is impossible to predict with total confidence. The safest bet is that of large groups of women (*gaggles* is my preferred term) raising children collectively, with little, if any, input from any man.[10]

This may work well enough for girls so raised and for boys until they reach puberty. However, adolescence throws a wrench into the gears. Women can raise girls into women, but helping boys to make the transition to manhood is beyond the competence and ken of the vast majority of the allegedly fairer sex. In communities where men are largely absent from the home, problems with teenage boys are common.[11] Most women simply do not know what to do with boys of a certain age, aside from either accommodating them—one popular strategy—or tormenting them as though they are ersatz husbands—the other, possibly *more* popular strategy.

Who began destroying the family is an interesting forensic question, but it is otherwise irrelevant. *No one* may really be at fault. There is no reason to assume our complex social and family structures are organic or that they can be maintained without tremendous cultural and economic pressure. Minimal paternal involvement is as least as likely as not to be the natural order. What we have long taken as a given—the conventional two-parent household (CTPH)—is proving ill-adapted to modern times.

Educating the young, caring for the elderly, and maintaining a stable system of agricultural production—some of the most significant traditional functions of the CTPH—have been assumed by schools, nursing homes, and agribusinesses. And although the CTPH still has *some* value, it appears to no longer have sufficient utility to outweigh the psychological and sexual opportunity costs of maintaining it.

189

One can also consider the decline of the CTPH as a struggle between two men—the weak man (the biological father) and the strong man (Uncle Sam)—for control of the family. As one would expect, the better-armed and wealthier man won. The destruction of the CTPH has only a little to do with left-wing versus right-wing politics or traditionalism versus feminism, and much to do with consolidation of power—a trend that has been ongoing since the development of the city-state and its incremental efforts to achieve a monopoly on violence, culture, thought, and moral authority.[12] Thus, the woman who has the biological father of her children removed from her life and her children's lives can be said to be upgrading partners—marrying the state, in effect. Given the profound economic and moral supremacy the state has over the individual man, this may well be a sensible choice.

You may be able to pass down your genes. You may financially contribute to the survival of your children, but anything beyond those two will occur only to the extent that the mother *chooses* to let you do so. This privilege is granted to you conditionally and can be revoked at any time for any reason. If you do not much care to be involved in the lives of your offspring, the possibility of your instantaneous eviction from the family is quite irrelevant. Most children do not die, regardless of the competence, or lack thereof, of the mother and regardless of the intelligence (or lack thereof) of the child. Such is irrefutable evidence of our ability to make a naturally dangerous planet relatively safe. Given the tremendous genius a great many of the intelligence challenged demonstrate in the art of self-destruction, idiot-proofing a civilization sustained with heavy machinery, gasoline, and high-voltage currents is an accomplishment for the ages.

Arguments that fatherhood, be it of the active avocado-toast new-agey type, the never-present Japanese-salaryman type, or the angry Old-Testament type (smashed Commandments included), is beneficial to the father are suspect at best. There is some *limited* evidence that serving in the role of father may prove *somewhat* more fulfilling than not, in certain specific circumstances, but this is with a great many caveats and is dependent upon the assumption that almost everything in the parent-child and mother-father relationship goes smoothly. On the other hand, there is a growing body of research that suggests that people without children are at least as happy as those with them.[13]

This possible sense of fulfillment is also contingent on you not being too aware of (or bothered by) who pulls the strings—the mother—lest you realize how much *fathering* you pretend is little more than performative and done only according to the mother's pleasure.

As for the idea of a *duty* to have children, I hope that you have already been liberated from the notion of a non-reciprocal duty/obligation. *Give something; get something.* If you receive nothing, you owe nothing. Unless you practice ancestor worship and believe that you owe your forebears continuity of their good name, the notion of a duty to have children is absurd. *To whom would you owe this duty?*

Nevertheless, some men are determined to spread their seed and *breed, breed, breed*. Perhaps this is an irresistible biological imperative (although I have found absolutely no evidence of the *irresistible* nature of this), perhaps it is a hobby of sorts, or perhaps it comes from some deeply rooted sense of confidence or lack thereof. If one does feel so compelled, there are far better strategies to continue one's bloodline than the traditional model.

191

History and science show us what these are and for whom they will work.

Everything Old is New Again

Men and women are not equally likely to have children. The rates, already discussed in the previous chapter, were historically somewhere between 1:2 (only one man reproducing for every two women) to 1:17.[14] Although we may never see such a tremendous imbalance in reproductive success as existed in the preliterate era, there exists the distinct possibility that future rutting ratios will be even more unfavorable to most men than they were in the Stone and Bronze Ages. The Western world is already moving in that direction, at least ever so slightly.

In Norway, a country with a level of development quite similar to that of the United States, 14% of men and 10% of women who had reached 45 years of age were childless as of 1985. By 2013, these percentages had risen to 23% and 13%, respectively. The age of 45 is relevant in that it is at the upper end of when most people have children. Those childless at 45 will probably remain so for the rest of their lives.[15] There are exceptions, more so for men than for women, but the fact of the matter is that men in their twilight years rarely attract and impregnate women in their prime fertility windows. Although the rates of childlessness increased for men and women, the rate increased more for men. This should surprise no one.

To a great extent, a man's desirability is a product of his status, hence the "S" in the HSP Formula. Until recently, status and income were restricted by limitations in available wealth—the maximum output of wealth that a community could produce given its geographical and technological restrictions—and the limits of *reputational communications*—the capacity of a society to transmit information about a member's reputation across time and distance. Economies of scale, transportation, and modern communications and media potentially increase inequality and allow for a select number of men to achieve *globally* high status, which is to say that their exceptionally high-status levels are known to billions of people around the planet. It is quite possible that a great many of these men may be able to take the Wilt Chamberlain, Gene Simmons, or Genghis Khan approach to reproduction—thousands of sexual partners across every continent but Antarctica (and maybe a few lady penguins there).[16] Of course, many of these liaisons will not result in offspring, but some of them almost certainly will.

Some other men may be able to achieve elevated levels of reproductive success by frequently donating to sperm banks or by following the more daring path of Desmond Hatchett. Mr. Hatchett, a resident of Knox County, Tennessee, has managed to sire at least 21 children by 11 women, with most of his harem and offspring residing in that county. Despite being only marginally employed, Mr. Hatchett has a reasonably high HSP score. First, he is a convicted felon who has spent several years in prison for violent offenses (S-score of +2). Second, according to the scale in his most recent mugshot, he appears to be at least six feet tall, making his H-score +1. Unfortunately, his P-score cannot be determined from the public record (although it would be convenient if such information were available), but even without that part of the equation, Mr. Hatchett's HSP score is at least +3, putting him in the *desirable* category. And his score may be *much* higher, depending upon how much wood Mr. Hatchet (er . . . *Hatchett*) has at his disposal.[17]

Given that most of us are unlikely to achieve billionaire/movie-star/rock-star/athlete money, fame, or status and that a great many would prefer to avoid Mr. Hatchett's approach to getting his handle waxed, there is the distinct possibility that a number of men will be left out in the reproductive cold—a frigid environment indeed.

And America only emerged from the agrarian era within the last 70 years. It is easy to forget how recently we broke free from the bonds of toil and soil. We—those of us under 40—are the first generation, even in a developed nation such as is the United States, to have almost no connection to the agrarian lifestyle. Our collective ideas about family, specifically the role of the father— ideas that were developed and culturally reinforced over thousands of years—have radically changed in under a century. The traditional, monogamous approach to relationships is not built upon the rock of our natures, but the sands of cultural and economic factors.

When predicting social shifts, one of the more serious errors is to assume that they happen linearly. This is not the case. Rather, customs and traditions carry on with little interruption until about 10% of the population develops the steadfast belief that *the old ways must go*. This is the tipping point, and once it is reached, transformation occurs at lightning speed.[18] Certain subsets of the American population, such as the African-American community, appear to have already made the switch from the belief that the CTPH is necessary to the belief that it is either extraneous or impossible.[19] The rest of America cannot be far behind.

Great change is easier for some than others, with certain members of the older generations, particularly the Baby Boomers, clinging to the ancient ways long past the point of practicality. This may partially explain the peculiar Boomer habit of marrying multiple times. It is true that serial monogamy—four, five, or six husbands or wives in sequence—has not been unheard of throughout human history, but this was frequently the result of the *death* of one's spouse(s), not recreational divorce.

Matrimonial hobbyists may seem an insane lot. Other than having one's limbs removed with a dulled butter knife, there would seem to be few activities less enjoyable than being dragged through the family courts time and again. Yet Boomer men would do just that—marry, divorce, and remarry—and then pretend that a *blended family* has any great strength or meaning. Rather than seeing this as a sign of psychosis, I propose a metaphor and offer my family as an example.

My grandparents, both paternal and maternal, were born and raised on farms in Kentucky. Their early life experiences were probably quite similar to those of their forebears. Other than increased access to information and merchandise from the outside world by way of Rural Free Delivery of mail, they were relatively isolated, so much so that many of their birth families were completely spared the misery of the 1918 influenza pandemic. Yet none of my grandparents spent their adult lives as farmers. Teacher, factory worker, suburban housewife, and bureaucrat—their adult jobs were not so different than those modern Americans. All were dependent on complex governmental and industrial systems that transformed agricultural products into commodities and made the natural environment largely abstract for *their children*—my parents.

My grandparents were *immigrants*, not to the United States, but to the industrialized world and economy, with their homeland being the world of agriculture—all humanity knew since the advent of the written word. This would make me (and my generation) the grandchildren of immigrants.

Carrying this metaphor a bit further, one can see that immigrants oftentimes limp along in their new homes, retaining many of the traditions of the *old country*, but otherwise causing few problems. Their grandchildren are typically fully integrated into the new nation, with their connection to their grandparents' countries being more one of curiosity (and a bit of ethnic pride) than anything else. It is the children of immigrants—the first-generation native-born—who sometimes struggle. At home, they are exposed to one culture. At school and work, they are exposed to another. The language, mores, and taboos of home and community can vary hugely. Some children of immigrants turn this into an advantage—a fluency in two cultures that doubles their options and opportunities and allows them to serve as liaisons and translators between dissimilar groups. Others struggle, feeling not entirely at ease with the practices of their parents or the modern habits of their peers.[20]

Occasionally, this leads to radicalization, but it more often leads to a peculiar sort of vacillation, in which the child of immigrants, trying to walk the line between two cultures, trips and lands on one side only to get back up again and trip and land on the other.[21]

So it was with Boomers and marriage. One generation—that of the grandparents, who had survived the Great Depression and the Second World War—demonstrated pragmatism, a willingness to engage in hard work, and comparatively low expectations for personal fulfillment (much as do many immigrants). The other— the grandchildren—born into the brave new world of post-agrarian modernity and acclimated and trained in the ways of high technology and personalized (if occasionally impersonal) marketing and identity building, are reasonably comfortable with fewer meatspace connections. Through no fault of their own, Boomers got stuck in middle. And there is the rub.

Both the old world and the brave new world provide a distinct model for family life (or the lack thereof), and although each is workable in isolation, they are singularly incompatible. Marry, divorce, remarry. *Wash, rinse, repeat!* This is the behavior of a people unable to decide on whether they prefer a world of atomized, fiber-optic individualism or comparatively restrictive, telegraph-line CTPH traditionalism. Splitting the difference—trying to use marriage as a vehicle on the road to self-discovery—was an abject and expensive failure, as ill-devised compromises often are.

Fortunately, *we*—men under 40—have the benefit of knowledge gleaned from our fathers' mistakes. We can see that the old world is dead, and the big, bad patriarchy (if there ever was one) with it. We have learned to expect less care and concern. We are less predisposed to take the kamikaze flight and final dive into the crushing depths of householder misery. We are stronger. We are stronger because we are better at being alone. And those who have learned to be alone can more easily learn the Mantra—can fully realize the great power of not caring unless they choose to care.

The Father of All Suffering—Children and Happiness

No arguments made thus far establishes that you *should not* have children, only that you (as a man) will have little to no control of how they are raised, that you have no *duty to have* them (although you will have some *duties to them* if you have them), and that having them is unlikely to make you happier and may make you more miserable than you would be without them. I would unreservedly warn only two groups of men against having children. The first are those with low HSP scores—meaning scores of less than zero—as the spawn of such men are, with few exceptions, despised by their mothers, their peers, their communities, and the world at large. The second are those with serious addictive disorders. I address the reasons for this latter caution in Chapter 13 ("On Addiction").

For men with HSP scores below the cutoff, to have children is sadistic. But a great many men have scores far higher than that. Such children may be loved by their mothers and not hated by all and sundry. What about these men? There is nothing inherently *wrong* with such men having children, just as there is nothing inherently *right* about them having children. The decision is personal and morally neutral. The problem with a great many men (regardless of HSP score) having children is that they enter into a potentially soul-destroying arrangement without any forethought at all. As of 2010, about 37% of children born in the United States are the products of *accidents*—a term which I use with some reservation, as I have yet to accidentally land in an open vagina, penis first.[22] *Unplanned* might be a better term might be a better descriptor for such births and children, but I would suggest that the best is *children of carelessness* (CoC). And having a brood of CoC is an almost surefire way to end up resenting every day of one's truncated and miserable existence.

Until science offers us a pill that turns screaming, constantly defecating children into independent adults at a greatly accelerated rate (an invention for which the developers would almost certainly receive a Nobel Prize), raising children will be as slow as it is tedious. Childhood is long, dangerous, and difficult for children. There is no guarantee that the experience will be any better for the parents.

Evidence as to the number of men who *regret* having children is difficult to find. At least partially for social reasons, some may hesitate to admit that they wish their children had never been born, even though this is not the same as admitting that one personally dislikes his children. Common complaints include a total lack of free time; being stuck in a dead-end job for economic reasons; being attached to the child's mother, even when *not* being attached to her would be far preferable; and realizing that one's children are losers and that there is nothing to be done to rectify the matter.[23] Women sometimes express similar sentiments, with a few of them even writing books about them, and what information is available suggests that regret of having children is not particular to any one place, people, level of education, or sex.[24]

Rather than trying to summarize pages upon pages of internet content, I offer an edited, condensed statement that one man (Mr. X) made about his life with children:

Being a father is a miserable experience. It will not make you happier. You will not enjoy it. The men who tell you otherwise —who argue that children are a great blessing—have usually not had to deal with them for any length of time. You will love your children. You will worry about them. I love mine, and I worry about mine. Very occasionally, there will be a light or happy moment, but these are few and far between. Your children will annoy you, possibly every minute you are in their presence. Love keeps you from throwing them out of a window. It does not keep you from getting irritated. Nothing could keep you from getting irritated.

Unlike my father did, I do not get the privilege of going to work and only having to put up with the kids for an hour or two a day—just long enough for them to be cute. Chances are that you will not be so lucky either. Instead, you will get to play the role of both parents—mother and father—and let me assure you that there is nothing quite so odd and unnatural as taking care of small children if you are an even somewhat normal man. Expect no help from your wife or girlfriend. She will have no idea of how to raise a child. Her maternal instinct was never cultivated. She may be even worse with the children than you are. You will be lucky if she does not try to eat them, and she will resent having to tolerate them.

For all of this effort, you will get even more worry—nothing else. There will be no appreciation, and despite your doing at least half of the parenting, you will be regarded as little more than a sperm donor by your in-laws and the government.

For the love of God, think carefully before having children. It is not a matter to be taken lightly.

It is important that one not universalize from a sample size of one. Mr. X's experiences are unique to him to a certain extent: No two lives, even if similar, are identical. Yet his words echo, if somewhat more concisely, quite a bit of what is said by other men.

The unpleasantness of the truths within this chapter makes them no less true. On the other hand, it is entirely possible that one will not regret having children at all. Every Picasso has a father, as does every Beethoven and Galileo, but every Hitler, every Idi Amin, and every John Wayne Gacy does as well. Who your children end up becoming is largely out of your control. This is not *fair* nor is it *just*, but little is. *Fairness* and *justice* matter little in work, less in life, and in the courts, not at all. *Truth* matters here

—between the covers of this book—and it should matter to *you*, so far as you learn to be honest with yourself about all things, including the limitations of your powers and your lineage.

Now, let us have no more talk of justice, but turn to the last concern.

The Hotel California

Someday you will die.

Gasp!

Let us take a moment to let that sink in thoroughly.

Most of the arguments in favor of having children relate to this idea in some way, if only obliquely. Passing down genetic material, leaving a family name or legacy, being remembered by your children and grandchildren—these are attempts to cheat death, if only briefly. There is one more argument that deals not with death, but with the process of getting there. Like so many other arguments, it is phrased as a question: *Without children, who will take care of you when you get old?* Sometimes, it is phrased more angrily: *If you do not have children, who will pay into Social Security so that you can have a pension?! My children?!*

First, let me point out that you may *not* get old. There is no guarantee you will survive to old age. Many people do not. If you die before entering your golden years, all other arguments surrounding this point are moot. Second, contrary to the implied assumptions in both of these arguments, not all children help their aging parents and not all people contribute much (if anything) to Social Security. Every welfare and disability cheat alive today had a biological mother and a biological father. In such cases, having children was *not* a net contribution to the social welfare system.

201

Children do not necessarily want their aging parents to live. You are being unduly optimistic if you have not taken into account the possibility that little Johnny or Janie (or Xiaolong and Meimei, Chanchai and Chailai, or even Vladimir and Sasha, depending upon how far and wide you sow your oats) will be troubled by your demise. Remember, no one has any obligation to *care* about anyone, including their parents. You *may* be able to extract money from your children, but such is not guaranteed. Conversely, they may extract money from you. You may also be able to obtain non-monetary assistance (transportation, labor of various forms, et cetera) from them, but these can only be readily arranged if your children live in moderately close proximity to you. If your children live in Alaska, Texas, and Hawaii, whereas you live in Maine, there will be relatively little that they can do for you in person, even if they *are* much inclined to help Dear Old Dad.

If your children leave the country, this problem grows exponentially larger—flying back from an oil rig in the Persian Gulf cannot be done at the drop of a hat, even if the particular hat dropping is your imminent death. And all of the aforementioned hypotheticals assume a nearly *best-case* scenario—one in which you have a relationship with your children. If you are estranged from your children (a prospect no man should ignore), they might live only a dozen miles away and want nothing to do with you, regardless of how much or little effort you put into trying to be a father.

For some of us, there may be an underlying psychological appeal to being missed when we are gone. Rationally, this does not matter. The dead neither know nor care what anyone thinks of them. What we really mean when we discuss being missed is that *while living, some of us like to entertain the notion that others will be saddened when we cease to be living.* You may have children. They may even remember you (assuming their mother does not run off with them and claim you abandoned/molested/hated them), but even if both of these conditions are met, there is still no reason to believe that they will be unduly upset by your demise.

As for people *not* missing their parents, here are some interesting articles on the matter:

1. "My mother is dead—and it's the best news I've ever had" (*Daily Mail Online*)

2. "My father died and I couldn't be happier" (*MDJunction*)

3. "I'm glad my parents died young" (*Daily Mail Online*)

4. "Finding Joy in My Father's Death" (*New York Times*)

5. "Mom, I Love You. I Also Wish You Were Dead. And Expect You Do, Too" (*New York Magazine*)

6. "Why You May Secretly Want Your Elderly Parents to Die" (*AgingCare.com*)

7. "Why Sandra Tsing Loh Wants Her Father To Die" (*WBUR*)

8. "Let elderly people 'hurry up and die,' says Japanese minister" (*The Guardian*)

There is nothing inherently wrong with wanting *anyone* to die. There is no obligation to *care* about anyone. There is no obligation to feel or to not feel anything. That much said, reviewing articles on this topic, including those above, is instructive. There appear to be two major reasons that children want their parents to die: One is that they personally dislike their parents—sometimes for reasons that almost anyone would find understandable and sometimes for reasons that would make sense only to themselves. Another is that their parents are living too long and taking up a disproportionate amount of resources. The last two articles listed are interesting in that one of them was written by an American of 50% Chinese descent. The other was written about statements made by a Japanese official. This suggests that even those strongly influenced by the Confucian/Shinto traditions of *filial piety* get tired of caring for the aged. Paying respect for one's ancestors is far easier if said ancestors have had the good grace to die in a timely manner. Remember that most of us end up orphans eventually, and the better part of us are not all that bothered by it.

Why would your children be any different?

Death is a big issue, which is why it has its own chapter. I have only touched on the narrowest aspects of it here. Many impractical, misery-inducing, and self-destructive things are done as a result of us either denying it or panicking in response to it. Death is also a great motivator. Understanding how it shapes our thinking for the *worse* and *can* shape our thinking for the *better* is critical living by the Rules.

This is life: We can check out whenever we are so inclined, but we cannot leave. There is nowhere else to go.

Playing an Unwinnable Game

There is a high probability that you will not win at fatherhood, which is not to say that you cannot win at the paternity and sexual games. This distinction is irrelevant to you if you would rather have little to no involvement with your children.

As for those men inclined to care about the survival of their children, no matter how much effort they put into being the type of father they think they should be (or that they are told that they should be), they are singularly at the mercy of others. Legally, they are without rights. From the perspective of society, fathers have little to no value beyond the economic. What we call the *traditional* model—really, the *agrarian model*—of fatherhood is untenable. A careful consideration of reality leaves the sensible man with two viable options

1. Do not have children.

2. *Khan!* (or *Hatchett!* if you prefer)

By this, I mean that you have the option of either not playing the reproductive game or playing it to win. *Go big or go home!* Even had none of the politics of feminism ever developed, there is a very real possibility that we, as a species, would have returned to our natural reproductive imbalance—the same imbalance that skewed male versus female reproductive rates and resulted in a lack of Y-chromosomal diversity for tens of thousands of years.

To reiterate a point from another chapter (and slightly expand on it):

DO NOT BE MIDDLE CLASS!

DO NOT GO FOR THE MIDDLE!

The middle class is for women. The *middle* is for women. Middle management, middle earnings, middling levels of engagement (rather than having strong preferences for one thing over another), middle levels of almost every personality trait. You *cannot* sit as comfortably in the middle as can a woman—they are made for it. A woman may have no problem straddling a fence, but a man will find his testicles to be less than pleased about the matter. Family is decidedly middle class, meaning that it is dominated by women and best suited to women. Men who try to stay in the middle are forever in a precarious position and regarded with a certain instinctively justifiable contempt. This is why *suits* must be so careful of what they say and do: We, as a society, are happy to dispose of them. The loyal company man, much like the father who appears to want or need a family, is not seen as much of a man at all. They are both a bit too much like women for the comfort of most.

Either have no children at all, or have them and expect to have no involvement with them. Given the relatively low levels of infant and childhood mortality, offspring, regardless of the level of paternal involvement, are more likely than not to survive long enough to have children of their own. If you are really intent on passing on your glorious genes, the logical option would be to have several by several different women, preferably across several different continents. On a moral level, you may or may not feel comfortable with this approach. Live according to your conscience, but do not bet on ever being more than a source of sperm and child support.

As far as spreading their *precious bodily fluids* goes, Mr. Hatchett and Genghis both proved successful, but the costs of their strategies need be considered. The *productive papa* may spend years upon in and out of family court and is unlikely to have much pleasure in life that lasts more than five minutes at a time. His children will not spend their lives in a land of rainbows and free cotton candy either. As for *really* winning the sexual and reproductive games, perhaps you should follow the trail of the Greatest of Khans and try Asia.

There are worse things than a life lived Genghis style. Just bear in mind that such is easier done if you have a horse or two.

The Thinking Man

(Ten Questions for Review and Consideration)

1. Do you want children? If so, why? If not, why not?

_____

_____

_____

2. Is there any pressure on men in America (or the West in general) to have children? If so, what is the source of this pressure? Does anyone (aside from you) care if you have children?

_____

_____

_____

3. What is the difference between fatherhood and paternity? Is there a difference now?

_____

_____

_____

4. Do you care to leave a legacy? If so, would children be a good way *for you* to leave a legacy? Can you think of any ways that would be better?

    _____

    _____

    _____

5. Why has Uncle Sam (the government) worked as hard as has to supplant the role of the father? Is this purely the result of women voting for more government money and involvement at the expense of fathers, or is there some other reason that the government has repeatedly strengthened its hold over the family?

    _____

    _____

    _____

6. Considering your HSP score, how do you think a woman is likely to treat any children resulting from your having sex with her? Would she love, loathe, or be indifferent to them?

    _____

    _____

    _____

208

7. What are some of the *disadvantages* of having children versus not having them?

_____

_____

_____

8. If you know your father, is he elderly or in need of help? If so, do you feel inclined to help him? If not, do you think that you would be given to help him were he to become infirm?

_____

_____

_____

9. Are your parents dead? If so, how did you respond to their deaths? Do you know anyone who was indifferent/relieved/ overjoyed that his parents died? Do you know why that person felt as he did? Do you think your children will feel the same?

_____

_____

_____

10. Trying to be a father in the United States violates several of the Rules. *Which* of the Rules does it violate? *How* does it violate them?

_____

_____

_____

11) On Isolation, Faith, and Dark Forests

Let us start with the bad news. You have read most of it before, but it bears repeating:

1. Fatherhood is dead.

2. *Family* no longer means what you think it means. It means collectives of women, backed by the Biggest, Baddest, and Meanest Alpha Male—Uncle Sam.

3. Companies have even less loyalty to employees now than they did in years past. The worker has been reduced to a mindless, worthless cog, to be replaced by a part-timer, a contract employee, somebody in another country, or a machine, as soon as doing so is cost-effective.

Much of this is a return to the mean—a shift away from a brief period of stability for the dedicated salaryman, sucker, and schlub —back to the natural order, an order in which *go-along-to-get-along* men get gone over again and again until there is nothing left to get.

This is fine. This is the way of the world. The era of reasonably durable family relationships, in which the father was at the helm, was a relatively short one in the existence of the species. The era in which one could simply show up, follow orders, and expect to make enough money to survive without much in the way of difficulty and to support a family in a moderate degree of comfort was even shorter. And for the brief period of time during which this was more than fantasy, it was not the global norm.

American men of the 1950s and 1960s benefited from an improbable confluence of circumstances unlikely to happen again

211

within the next few centuries: The United States managed to exit the Second World War with an *excess* of industrial capacity, whereas most of the world had serious deficiencies thereof.[1]

As examined in the previous chapter, the families of the 1950s were unique in that they consisted largely of adults raised in an agrarian era and living in an industrial one. They may not have moved from one nation to another, but the nation moved around them. As is oftentimes the case with immigrants, the men and women of the 1950s lived somewhat conservatively, not wanting to test their luck too much in a new, frightening, and exciting place.

The changes of the last 50 years are not the problem. Change is inevitable. The problem is how poorly millions of men have attempted to adjust to the new system, with some of the adaptations made being so *maladaptive* that one would do better by not changing at all. At least total denial of reality would provide some consistency. Instead, Western men have continued to follow the old customs where maximally *inconvenient* and have begun to follow new customs where maximally *damaging*. The modern man switches between the one set of expectations and the other in such a way that he is always at the greatest disadvantage. Consider these:

1. The Western man demonstrates loyalty to his employer (an old custom) while actively helping the company to rationalize and eliminate his job (the new custom).

2. The Western man assumes considerable legal liability when marrying (the old custom) while expecting the wife to assume none (the new custom).

3. The Western man holds himself to concepts of decorum and independence that are restrictive and severe (an old custom) while actively encouraging women, children, and

212

foreigners to do as they please, without shame or fear of repercussions (a new custom).

4. The Western man strives for impartiality in word and deed (an old custom) while all but begging others to embrace favoritism and group identity (actually a *very old* tribal custom, but one that is new again).

Were someone to set out to screw himself as badly as possible, this would be the way to do it—always grab the short end of the stick and offer others the long.

The old customs were fine. The new customs are what they are. However, problems arise when one tries to combine the two without due thought and care. And this is further exacerbated when certain Western traditions, particularly those they emphasize independence, are driven past their terminus, beyond the last foot of railroad track, to the point of derailment, derangement, destruction, and death.

The Western (in both the *occidental* and the *cowboy* sense of the word) fable centers around an ahistorical character—the radically, totally self-supporting man—someone who may give much, but who needs nothing but that which is contained within himself. One of the few widely accepted additions to the strong, silent, lantern-jawed-hero set pieces (at least in film) is that of a nearly indestructible bond between the strong man and the equally strong, every-bit-as-good-as-a-feller-if-not-better woman.[2]

The incongruity of this addition and the core story has never been entirely resolved.

Presumably, *our Western hero* is so iron-willed, so achingly alpha, that were he and another man in the same room for more than two minutes, the pungent aroma of testosterone would be sufficient to render gay frogs straight (or at least Spartan gay, rather than San Francisco gay), turn cows into bulls, and possibly lead to a fission reaction so explosive that mile upon mile of prairie would burn and the land would be rendered uninhabitable for generations, save by murderous amphibians and their nunchaku-wielding turtle adversaries.

Of course, this explains why Mr. T(estosterone) cannot keep the company of other men, but it does little to explain why he needs the company of *anyone*, man or woman. Sex would seem to be the most obvious explanation. But it is difficult to imagine any one woman being able to satisfy such a demigod of the frontier—someone with an HSP score high enough to burst through one cloud (and hymen) after the next—without being split up the middle, from crotch to pate. Perhaps she lives only to spell the horses or to charm them with her wise-ass humor as she applies unguents to their hemorrhoids.

All of this—extreme independence, Rawlsian impartiality (or *nearly Rawlsian* impartiality: One must always go easy on the womenfolk), and loyalty without reward—requires that the man alternate between being perfectly without needs and being a perfectly useful tool that cares nothing for how it used, only that *it is* used, and frequently. Put another way: When the shovel is not moving dirt, snow, or coal to-and-fro, it should put itself back in the shed.

For the shoveler, this is a great bargain: a tool that costs nothing, requires no maintenance, and takes itself out and puts itself away without even being asked. It should also be able to anticipate all of the wants and needs of its gardener, gravedigger, coal miner, or freedom-loving prisoner-of-war owner, levitate its way to the worksite, and do all labor unaided by human hands.

Who wouldn't want a super-shovel of this sort? *I would*, and even more if it paid me *for the privilege of toiling on my behalf.*

But I ask you this, my fellow tools: *How does this arrangement benefit the implement?*

The sheer badness of this deal (from the shovel's perspective) is not difficult to see. One of the few ways it remains functional is through the creation or manipulation of a *need* or *want* on the part of the tool.

And this is where the contradictions in our campfire stories, our biology, our culture, and our history become critical.

The totally independent man is closer to an aspirational archetype than he is to reality. The notion that capable men worked in nearly total isolation, except for contact with their wives and children, is not much better grounded. And the lonesome cowboy, riding into town with nothing more than his horse and his gun, singlehandedly eliminating the bad guys, restoring order, and disappearing into the sunset, is a Hollywood creation.[3] This belief —that the real man needs no one but himself (and a woman, perhaps)—is aggressively promulgated by our entertainment industry, by our government, and by the enforcers of social norms. At its most extreme, the belief becomes something else—the presentation of *(real) man as either superhero or supervillain.*

This can certainly make for clean, easy-to-follow narratives, which is one of the reasons screenwriters favor it as much as they do. Light versus darkness, with the rest of the population serving as little more than chess pieces to be moved by the *Übermensch*, or helpless victims to be saved or destroyed by the wills of greater beings—even an illiterate child can understand. And this is instinctively appealing. Those of a more passive disposition can sit back and wait for the sacred and satanic forces to do what they

215

will, thinking *all we can do is cheer and groan and plead and hope the best (or worst, if frustrated by our lives)*. Others, with more active imaginations, can dress themselves in the hero's cape or hide themselves in the antihero's lair and entertain dreams of becoming masters of the universe.[4]

What might appear a problem with either of these fantasies—the fantasy of being the savior (or destroyer) or the fantasy of being one of the saved—but is really a strength in disguise, is that both lead their adherents down the roads of inaction and ineffectualness. Victims are, well, victims, capable of little more than suffering, and most wannabe John Rambos achieve little but getting themselves killed or captured.

History has but rarely been shaped by a lone great man laboring in the jungle or the desert, but by groups of dedicated men working together. Few, if any, great causes have been successfully prosecuted by one person. The shapers of history have not worked in isolation (although they sometimes took credit deserved by the many), and few of them have achieved total control of any group of people, unencumbered by the wills of peers and lieutenants.

These truths are neither communistic nor are they incompatible with sensible individualism, and accepting them requires no faith in the abstraction that is *the people*. Rather, they serve as good foundation for the argument that men should build effective organizations to supplant (if not replace) increasingly hollowed-out and highly regulated family and business relationships. Acknowledging this reality should also help all with eyes to see and ears to hear to recognize that the man who has no connections of consequence outside of his work and his relationship with his wife or girlfriend is vulnerable to attack from any and every angle and is quite incapable of doing much for anyone, including himself. After accepting the facts, there are questions, some more relevant than others.

These are the ones that this chapter was written to answer:

1. Who benefits from all of this? Who is working to promote the extreme isolation of men?

2. Aside from the aforementioned entertainment and media influence, how is isolation in men encouraged in our society?

3. What can you do about this? What can you do to make yourself less isolated and vulnerable?

First, an examination of human instincts and how they are manipulated to achieve our present state of learned social helplessness.

In the Good Company of Solitude or Alone in the Crowd?

A man who cannot bear his own company and his company alone is likely no more tolerable to the rest of humanity. An appreciation for the joys of contemplative solitude—for having only one's thoughts as companions—is an essential element of cultivated maturity.

This knowledge is specific to no time, no place, and no people. From the Desert Fathers of early Christianity; to the Buddha; to (according to most accounts) Laozi; to more modern figures, such as Ajaan Mun Bhuridatto; to the occasional wild man of the American West, men who practiced *eremitism*—living as a hermit—have been a part of (if somewhat *apart from*) both Western and Eastern cultures for generations. This independence of mind and person, with its accompanying resilience, is quite different from the isolation promoted today.[5]

The hermit is not bound to be inevitably alone in all ways for all time. Some spend a period of years living by themselves and then return to the world to teach, making friends and allies in the process. Some have careful, but meaningful, interaction with select groups of travelers. Some are truly removed from the rest of humanity, but at least they have the benefit of being unburdened by the load of politics, appearances, and trendy notions.

All of these hermits have a strength that is both loathed and feared by those who would have every man dragged along by the bucking stallions of the sensibilities and fashions of the day and the plodding, sour-tempered mares of the reigning ideologies.

The traits promoted by ordinary society are quite different from those cultivated by the hermit. The ordinary man is, more often than not, deserted in the crowd, too timid and lifeless to offer those around him more than empty pleasantries and too uncertain of his of mettle and too undisciplined to choose a path for himself. *This man* is the man most easily controlled, and he is often far more starved for connection than the hermit could ever be. The hermit at least knows himself and has himself for company. The ordinary man will surge when the crowds surge, boo when it boos, applaud along with others, and have no will of his own worth mentioning. His feet, his hands, his mouth, and his mind serve only to imitate everyone around him and no one in particular.

By all means, learn from the hermit, learn to be alone, learn to examine your thoughts and biases undistracted by the nonsense that keeps minds running madly in place. This will only do you good. It will set you miles apart from those so desperate for connection that they will do the bidding of anyone who bothers to look in their direction.

The Dark Forest: Recognizing the Naturalness of Misandry and Misanthropy

Let us be clear on a fundamental point: there is no natural imperative to feel love or compassion for very much of humanity. From a biological perspective, this makes sense. *The Mantra* (Chapter 7) serves to remind a man of biological truths and sensibilities that are socially repressed.

Up until very recently, anyone who was not related to you was probably a threat or a resource, but not a *human* in the fullest sense of the word as far as you were concerned. Societies started small—largely with extended family groups—and only gradually grew beyond that. Regarding outsiders with suspicion was a sensible approach. One way to think about this is by considering *dark forest theory*—an idea developed by science-fiction author Cixin Liu.[6]

Liu developed dark forest theory as a metaphor to explain how spacefaring civilizations would interact with each other. Our focus is narrower—the realm of human interaction. Still, the theory works wonderfully when applied to this domain. Lets us summarize what is known about the lives of our distant ancestors and see how conveniently it dovetails with dark forest theory and the dark forest approach to interaction:

1. Our ancestors lived in a rough and tumble world, one where resources were limited and different groups had to compete to survive. This was a dark and frightening place, filled with terrible things.

2. They had no way of knowing the intentions of any outside group. Any people outside of the clan/tribe/extended family might be friend, but they might as likely be foe.

3. The potential downside of a negative interaction—death for all men, rape for all women, and slavery for all children —was quite a bit larger than the potential upside for any positive interaction. Interacting with those outside your group might (at best) have provided your clan with a bit of friendly commerce. At worst, it would have lead to the group's annihilation.

4. Within these parameters, the best strategy was to avoid being seen by any potential threats—to lay low and to run and hide whenever possible—and to kill *any group* you saw first, before they saw you.

5. The ancients could safely assume other groups had figured out as much as well, which means that the odds of positive interactions were even lower than they would be were the species involved (*human* in this case) incapable of strategic thinking.

This is the terrible place in which we developed. This is how we came into being. Hating and fearing everyone outside of our group is the natural order. It is an emotional manifestation of a survival strategy that is perfectly rational on a small scale. There is a reason that computers have quickly surpassed us in the realm of perfect-information games: Perfect-information games are nearly the total opposite of the *game of survival* as played by our ancestors—the game we developed to play—which was one of extraordinarily limited information.[7]

We, as a species, have managed to tame our extreme xenophobia through gradually and cautious learning and interaction, through intermarriage between ethnically distinct groups (thus creating the bond of family), and the application of tyranny.[8] Sometimes, we learned to work together for the sake of business and trade, and sometimes tyrants *forced* men to work together, either to do the tyrants' bidding or to band together and overthrow said tyrants. Nevertheless, our practical paranoia has yet to be put out to the Panglossian pasture of perfect peace and prosperity (the *Great P5* we shall call it). The old creature still has its uses.

How does this relate to misanthropy—hatred of everyone—and misandry—hatred of men?

Simple.

We instinctively regard those not part of our tribe with suspicion. This applies to men and women alike to a certain extent, but more to men, not because they are inherently *worse* than women, but because they have the physical capacity to do more harm (or *they did* prior to the age of modern weaponry, which has somewhat leveled the playing field). In a society in which men are taught to keep their distance from other men to the greatest extent possible, a paranoid culture will prevail as an inevitable result of instinct amplified by induced isolation.

People do not naturally fear *all* men so much as they fear *outsider men*. The problem is that *we are all outsiders now*, avoiding isolation requires learning to relate to others as adult men —no small feat. Our forefathers somewhat benefited from childhood friends and long-term relationships with extended family that continued throughout life. We, however, must improvise. Successful men require connections to a community or tribe. This requires trust, and trust is hard to build after the old framework has been torn down.

Cui Bono?

The atomization of society, which entails the breaking down of community into smaller and smaller units until eventually there is only the individual, is useful from an economic, social engineering, and marketing perspective.

Economically, people who exist only as fungible sources of labor can be moved around for the convenience of industry more readily than those who exist as part of larger webs of relationships. This enables the more rational exploitation of labor.

Such isolated people are also more readily manipulated by social engineers. The destruction of established relationships is requisite to the process of building something entirely different. As it is not the nature of most men to exist totally isolated and alone, gaining control of their social connections and sense of community makes them easier to forge into whatever sort of New Man devised in the institutes and centers of the day. This—the nearly complete vaporization of unmanaged social structures and their replacement with closely managed ones—is a goal the social engineers have already achieved. It was their ambition for generations. That they eventually achieved it should come as no surprise: Centuries of hard work can accomplish a great deal.[9]

Where there was once community (more or less), now there is little more than an abstracted and virtual *Commonwealth of Nowhere*, specific to no people, no time, and no place, and defined only by the machinations and momentary whims of the makers. It is everywhere—as close as the nearest smartphone—and nowhere at once.

The Commonwealth is Utopia (in the original sense, as defined by Sir Thomas More), for marketers most of all. It is a surreal place, one in which the world can be viewed without scale,

222

where physics and perspective are optional; where the richest, the poorest, and everyone in between can simultaneously present select views of their lives to each other, completely without context.[10] We are all amateur marketers here, with each man or woman serving as his or her own brand and own brand ambassador. For those who assess the quality of their existences *relatively* (rather than by rational measures of plenitude or deprivation) this can be distressing indeed. For *professional* marketers, this distress is a source of nearly limitless opportunity: Every social anxiety can be made to reverberate down the long and gossip-filled halls of the Commonwealth's virtual high school, from which many will never graduate.

So *cui bono* (*who benefits*)? The answer is anyone who wants centralized control of society in general and men in particular.

When a Man's Best Friend Is His Wife, His Wife Has Problems[11]

Objectively, widespread isolation is good for very few of members of society, save the engineers, who like their metal easily worked, their machined parts interchangeable, and their tools of good and proper function. Marketers, who are effectively *social technicians*—less grand theory, more direct practice—benefit as well. Both of these groups may find their designs confounded by the alloying of personal and collective goals that occurs when people are less than perfectly separated from each other. Yet total isolation and control of each person is more than the engineers and technicians are capable of achieving with current levels of technology, partially because men completely adrift are notoriously difficult to control. So the engineers and the technicians have fabricated the nearest suitable replacement: a newfangled, manufactured religion that is an inelegant, morally hollow, and deliberately unsatisfying product of romanticism, meritocracy, and protestant work ethic. The three major tenets of this belief system —the Cult of the American Dream (CAD)—are:

1. Romantic love is a spiritual necessity, is the basis for the most important relationships in one's life, and is the fastest path to communion with the grand forces of the universe. Romantic love is salvation. Absolute belief in this axiom is also critical to the *Church of the Sacred Vagina* (CoSV), which was already described in Chapter 9.[12]

2. America is fundamentally meritocratic. A lack of success is proof positive of a lack of virtue.[13]

3. All work is good work. Working even when doing so provides one with little or no benefits is inherently virtuous. Hard work will be rewarded, and even if it is not, hard work is its own reward. And above all, busyness is good.[14]

The first pylon of this constructed faith, one that many take as a natural law without recognizing it as man-made, is the notion that a man should view his wife or girlfriend as his *best friend and partner*. This absurdity leads to disability. Few people, man or woman, are totally loyal to anyone, but a woman's dedication to her husband or boyfriend is uniquely fickle. One would be hard-pressed to find any other relationship of less durability, based on more temperamental affections.

A man so kept mentally upright by little more than the support of a woman is certainly unbalanced, probably miserable, and possibly dangerous (to himself, to the public, and to the woman). Some women may *think* that such vulnerable men are ideal, or at least more easily manipulated. But the better part of womankind instinctively, if not necessarily consciously, regard such spiritual grotesques as headache-inducing, stomach-souring, and vagina-dehydrating weaklings.

The only other bearers of psychological and social weight within the religion—economic identity and work identity—can be easily pulled out from under the structure of a man by the engineers, collapsing him essentially at their will. Like the aforementioned women, the engineers would be hard-pressed to *not* find the overly domesticated beasts of burden that are CAD's male adherents contemptible: Nature, God, and all of humankind abhor men who are suckers.

Convince enough people to follow this critical doctrine of the new faith, and the vast majority of the population suffers: The man becomes defensive, unstable, and lacking in self-direction; the wife/girlfriend grows insecure, neurotic, and resentful; and the dog gets ever more confused (because he can never figure out who is at the head of the pack). Only the cat fares well enough—a result of his leisurely indifference and willingness to eat whoever dies first. From the perspective of the engineers, this vast and growing reservoir of woe is more feature than bug.

Drugs, Bad Religion, and the Gates of Heaven

Religion, as historically defined, is no longer *the opium of the people* (to the extent it ever was). *Opium* is no longer the opium of the people. A century of better living through chemistry has given us far more powerful substances than those used metaphorically by Marx. Fentanyl, carfentanyl, lofentanyl, and whatever else underground scientists started dumping onto the global black market this week put the primitive drugs to shame. As the old drugs have been replaced, so has the old faith: Their replacements are powerful, having resulted from years of scientific research and artistic efforts.

At this point, a few may doubt that what has been described thus far truly meets the criteria for a religion. Belief in the virtues of romantic love, economic prosperity, and hard work would seem to be little more than convention or common sense. Were that the extent of it, such might be correct; however, as it now stands, the CAD requires a *leap of faith* in favor of *the* (legal, economic, and cultural) *system*(s) for one to practice it without reservation.

To establish that the CAD is a religion, one must begin with a question: *What defines a religion?* Even for an *abstraction*, religion is challenging to describe. Rather than reinventing the wheel, the simplest method to establish that CAD is a religion is to assess it using the framework of Ninian Smart, whose seven dimensions of religion include:

1. Ritual (ceremonies—things people do specifically for the sake of the religion. In Christianity, baptism would be an example of this.)

2. Narrative and mythic (stories—creation myths, for example)

3. Experiential and emotional (specific emotions associated with the religion—fear of God or a sense of awe, etc.)

4. Social and institutional (ways to spread/share beliefs—proselytizing, for example—and ways to identify group members)

5. Ethical and legal (rules for behavior)

6. Doctrinal and philosophical (systematic religious teachings)

7. Material (physical objects or places that are considered holy)

Smart's dimensions are both extensive and slightly redundant (one could see how *ritual* and *social and institutional* overlap).[15] They also have an apparent bias against less-structured belief systems. Chinese folk religion (also called *Shenism*), with its motley crew of merciful and protective Bodhisattvas; money, agricultural, and chief-bureaucrat-of-hell gods and goddess; and semi-deified military leaders, might not meet all of Smart's criteria if narrowly interpreted, particularly in regards to doctrine and philosophy, yet Shenism may be practiced with every bit as much fervor and faith as Islam, Catholicism, or Judaism, possibly more if one judges a faith by the number of incense burned or money spent on offerings. Thus, the seven dimensions may be taken as more part and parcel of an imperfect analytical framework than as a list of strict requirements. Nevertheless, it is useful.

Let us see if CAD checks all of the right boxes.

1. Ritual—YES:
    a. Romantic holidays and weddings; remarriage (because losing half of what you own once is not enough); constant praise for women's capacity for love and decency
    b. Success rituals—reading toxically sunny self-help courses and guides on self-affirmation as the key to success; participating in company retreats and programs to encourage positive, prosperity-oriented thinking
    c. Attending and graduating from college (both a consumer/status ritual and a way to establish one's bona fides for employers); proving one's virtue by putting in as much time at the office as possible

2. Narrative and mythic—YES:

    a. Myths of love, romance, and chivalry (including the soulmate myth)

    b. Myths (really, exaggerations) of self-made men

    c. Myths of hard work making a person inherently stronger and more moral

3. Experiential and emotional—YES:

    a. Adult romantic-attachment building (as opposed to the more understandable adolescent variety)

    b. Absolute pride in success; absolute shame in failure

    c. Encouraged pride in workplace identity; shame of job loss; trying to look busy, with busyness being a source of pride or identity

4. Social and institutional—YES:

    a. CAD being spread through schools, media, and even traditional religious institutions

5. Ethical and legal—YES:

    a. Enforcement of family law and complex and counterintuitive ethical obligations surrounding marriage and dating

    b. Presentation of economically successful people as being inherently good and economically failed people as being inherently bad

    c. Ethical duty to work, even when not in need of money

6. Doctrinal and philosophical—YES:

    a. Belief that romantic love is a necessity (institutionalized or semi-institutionalized in everything from psychological theory to pop motivational theory)

    b.   Ingrained theories in economics, political science, and social sciences that treat material wealth as ultimate goals and only meaningful measures of success; theories that present life in the United States as fundamentally fair (meaning that life outcomes are just)

    c.   Work being elevated to ultimate life purpose and source of fulfillment; belief in meritocratic function of society—that hard work will pay off and that the unsuccessful deserve their fate

7.   Material—YES:

    a.   Rings, romantic gifts, flowers, etc. being regarded as necessities

    b.   Signs of wealth worn as symbols of merit; home ownership being treated as a sign of virtue, not as a (potentially) rational investment

    c.   Replacement of the social space (third place) with the work environment, which serves as an ersatz community structure[16]

One of the limitations of the Smart dimensions is that they do not explicitly address the matter of locus of control. In the more fatalistic religions, the locus control (where the decisions and authority rest) is almost purely external: We are powerless. We are subject to whims and mercies of the gods. Let us try to appease them! In others, Buddhism for instance, the locus of control is almost purely internal: We control our intentionality. The world around us may change, but our religious/spiritual development is the product of our personal efforts.

The CAD is somewhat unique in this regard in that it *appears* to treat the locus of control as being purely internal: *You have no fate but what you make. All success is to your credit. All blame is to your discredit.*

In practice, this is contradicted by the requirement that one assess his spiritual success using criteria in which chance plays a great role—romantic success and economic success. Of course, how hard a man works is largely his own decision, but the effectiveness and outcome of that work are influenced by external factors. The confusion resulting from this contradiction is useful in that it makes a man's self-worth easy to manipulate.

The CAD and its locus-of-control model relates to the *Big Three* (Chapter 3) in a curious way. The CAD encourages a man to see his life as being under his control while actively taking steps to diminish that control, partially by way of the Big Three (which financially bind him) and partially by suspending his powers of individual reason.

Why Bother to Assess the CAD as a Religion?

The purpose is to demonstrate that the CAD has the same potential for social and psychological control as any other religion. That a belief system exerts influence on a society is not necessarily bad. Even countries with strict separation of church and state are likely to be somewhat socially influenced by the values of their dominant faith.

A problem is most likely to arise when a religion so permeates a society that its practices become invisible to believers, leaders, and the less-thoughtful members of the citizenry, many of whom

230

may find parts of the belief objectionable but are unable to imagine a society without them. What might be *a matter of faith* becomes *just the way things are done*.

The organic predecessors of the CAD are superficially similar to it, but are in actuality, quite different. Marriage as a functional social institution has a long history in most cultures. *Love* (in the non-romantic sense) has played a role in Christianity since its beginning. Efforts to rationalize differences in economic success and failure as being signs of a deity's favor or disfavor are as old as recorded history, and the notion that hard work is virtuous is hundreds of years old, if not older.

The CAD relies on subtle shifts in these beliefs. Pragmatic marriage, Christian love, belief in the flesh-mortifying goodness of hard work, and a vague 1970s-era mysticism were synthesized into an uxorious goddess cult, with a touch of prosperity gospel and a *fuck-you-buddy* attitude toward less fortunate men (both of which fit nicely within the *just-world hypothesis* on which the CAD depends, albeit selectively) added to the mix. Wealth becomes the default way to establish status and status is conflated with virtue. And *work ethic* turns from an emphasis on self-sufficiency to the belief that martyring oneself for his employer is a sign of holiness, with increased *productivity* serving in lieu of a heavenly reward. None of these beliefs hold up well under close scrutiny, but as is the case for many religious beliefs, close scrutiny is something they rarely receive.

And this leads to a warning: Because the CAD is both *derived* from traditional beliefs and is a deeply held (if poorly understood) faith in its own right, its adherents can demonstrate a fair amount of zealotry. Arguing with zealots is singularly pointless. Arguing with zealots who are profoundly ignorant as to the nature of their beliefs is worse. Suggest that not every job matters, that life can be more than the accumulation of money and toys, and that the hole between a woman's legs is not the gate to heaven, and some will argue, many will ignore you, and a few will agree, at least in theory. Almost none will change their behavior accordingly: There is a chasm between *having knowledge* and *applying knowledge* that few can cross.

The Merciless Homophobic Homo-mania of Our Lords and Masters

We are a homo-obsessed society, meaning that there is a tendency to identify *any* close friendships between men as evidence of homosexuality or homosexual tendencies.[17] Consider this and discover an interesting trend—while the range of socially acceptable behavior for women (homosexual, heterosexual, or indeterminate) has grown, as has the range of socially acceptable behavior for homosexual men, the range of behavior deemed acceptable and appropriate for heterosexual men has narrowed by the year.

At this point, it seems almost impossible to be *not* gay, unless you simply growl at every other man you meet while extolling the virtues of/fixating upon/sexually pursuing women from dawn to dusk. Despite protestations to the contrary by both women and men (left- and right-wing), the *idealized* man—the man who is unquestionably masculine—is part brawler, part pickup artist, and part useful idiot. Those who deviate too far from this risk being looked at with the queerest of eyes.

This is not a universal social norm, nor was it the standard within American culture until relatively recently.[18] The conflation of sexual attraction and friendship is peculiar. For most of us (straight men—I cannot speak as to the minds of gays), the relationship between being attracted to someone and valuing that person as a human being is imperfect. Most of us can think of at least one woman to whom we were attracted physically but disliked as a person. The distinction of obvious, yet there seems to be some engineered confusion on the matter.

A minor contributor to this befuddlement may be our overly broad use of the term *friend*—a word we have watered down to the point to mean *someone who clicked a button connected to my social media profile* or *a person with whom I have occasionally had sex* rather than *someone who has some (if limited) concern for my survival*. One's *girlfriend* need not be a *friend* in the substantial sense of the word. One's *internet* friends need not even be human: One can *friend* a corporation. Remembering this is easy, but language can influence perception. Use a word to describe enough different things and some of those things may blend together in your mind. This confusion keeps us more isolated still.

Heretics, History, and the Company of Men

Although they may be ostensibly at odds, corporatists, bureaucrats, and ideologues all have a shared interest in promotion of the CAD. Blind adherence to the doctrines of the Cult does much to enervate and destroy the organic and rational compacts men have built with each other over the eons and to replace them with subservience, dependence, and bondage to merciless external powers.

The rejection of a religion should not necessarily lead to the adoption of an anti-religion. Those who abandon Christianity need not become Satanists. Those who abandon tree hugging need not cut down a forest. The impulse to jump from one extreme to the other is understandable: It is the reason that some of the most rambunctious, hard-partying, and criminally inclined youths of the small town in which I was raised were the children of preachers. However, *understandable* is not synonymous with advisable.

We should not simply *react* to the CAD. A *Cult of American Nightmares* (CAN)—the mirror image of the CAD—would have problems of its own, namely that it would lead its adherents to be as manipulated as the CAD followers, although by way of different techniques. The best ablutions to cleanse us of the CAD's anointing oils of stupidity are creative and independent thought and carefully constructed free associations of men. Building these takes work, particularly in a society in which men have had their capacity for group-building suppressed. The structures of influential social groups in the United States are essentially neuter or feminine (even if men participate in these groups), and given that such groups are all a significant percentage of younger men have seen, it would be entirely unexpected for them to assume that such soft, status-quo-maintaining, hierarchically flat structures are the only sort that *can exist* outside of history books or fantasy novels.[19]

Yet throughout most of human history (and prehistory, in all likelihood), the greater part of human achievement has been the result of groups of men working together. *Community* as defined in the meaningful and practical sense of *a group of people with shared values, norms, rules, language, and culture* has also been built and maintained largely by men. This is not to say that women were *irrelevant* to the community or that they were unable to contribute in complex and important ways, only that every technologically advanced civilization and every complex social structure within them was built largely *by men*.

Thus, the unique nature of social groups of men (when compared to the feminized modern social structures) is worth considering. My analysis of different, effective groups of men suggests that they share more traits than not, including:

1. Common goals, values, and beliefs—Members of the group share certain common goals, values, and beliefs; however, most groups do not require absolute ideological conformity.

2. Trials by fire or endurance—Members gain admission to the group by demonstrating toughness, ability, and utility to the group. The more demanding the trial by fire, the more exclusive the group (with very few exceptions).

3. Hierarchy—Members have clearly delineated roles within the group, with a hierarchy that determines authority. Those groups with poorly defined chains of command either resolve power ambiguities or disintegrate. Many groups rely on a mixture of fraternal-(brother/brother) and paternal/filial-(father/son) type relationships, with those that place greater emphasis on paternal relationships generally being more stable and with less in the way of internal conflict than their fraternal counterparts.

4. Symbols—Members of the group share an understanding of a complex group-specific symbolic system that provides a visual representation of both the organization itself, its mission, and the members' roles and ranks within the organization.

5. Exclusive knowledge—Members are expected to learn certain codes, practices, and information that are not known to the general public and to not disclose this exclusive knowledge to those outside of the group.

6. Respect—Members are expected to treat both other group members and the group's symbols with a certain amount of respect. Usually, a code of etiquette governs how the members interact with each other, with violations of the code resulting in either discipline (frequently of a physical nature) or expulsion from the group.

7. Mutual aid—Members are expected to help their peers. Practical and meaningful help is considered more valuable than commiseration or feigned emotionalism.

8. Regulated interaction with women—Members are expected to interact with certain (if not all) women in a specific way. At a minimum, the group's code of conduct will dictate how members interact with other members' wives, girlfriends, daughters, and mothers. Some codes will be far broader and will address anything from mandatorily circumscribed interactions with women (as is the case for monastic orders), to regulations on wife swapping and girlfriend sharing, to how captured women are to be divvied up, to anything in between. Regardless of the specifics of any given code, it will serve to prevent or reduce in-group conflict over women.

Groups of women may share some of these traits: Women are not *entirely* egalitarian—some women will be more equal than others—and some hierarchy will eventually emerge in most groups of any size or complexity. The differences are those of degree. Women's groups generally have less in the way of mission emphasis—the idea of shared goals—and they appear to rely less on clear trials by fire and other measures of worth for individuals to gain group acceptance. This is not to say that all women automatically accept all other women into their social circles

236

(despite their pronounced homophily); however, women's groups generally place more emphasis on compliance with the collective will than on active demonstrations of ability.[20] This closely relates to the dynamics of women's in-group bias. Women *generally* favor each other over men, but they make less of a distinction between one woman and another.[21]

On the other hand, men appear to be more likely to favor *specific individuals*. This distinction—that of being *one of our guys*—is earned. The more variable an input (in this case, candidates for group membership), the more robust testing and sorting mechanisms need be deployed to distinguish the *suitable* from the *unsuitable*. This makes the sorting of men into in-group and out-group status more critical than it is for women.

Instead of considering these points in the abstract, it would be worth analyzing two radically different organizations: One-Percenter Motorcycle Clubs (1%er MCs) and monastic orders (Buddhist and Trappist).

One Percenters

The term *one percenter* (*1%er*) comes from an apocryphal statement by a representative of the American Motorcycle Association (AMA) that *99% of motorcyclists were law-abiding citizens*, suggesting that one percent were *not* law-abiding citizens.[22] Despite the limited documentation of who coined the moniker, it remains in common usage, meaning *a member of a biker gang or motorcycle club (MC)*, which is distinct from a *riding club*—a generally aboveboard club for motorcycle enthusiasts. Obtaining detailed information as to *what* exactly one-percenter MCs require of their members is difficult—this being the sort of information that *if you have to ask (about it), you wouldn't understand (the answer)*—but there is enough material available to sketch out basic group operational codes and requirements. All available evidence suggests that one-percenter club membership is almost exclusively male. Beyond that, let us see to what extent these groups have the anticipated characteristics.

1. Common goals, values, and beliefs—Taking pleasure (largely of the hedonistic sort) in life and in riding motorcycles; nonconformity with the expectations of conventional society; and a belief in the virtues of physical toughness and aggression are the one-percenter goals, values, and beliefs.

2. Trials by fire or endurance—Steps to becoming a one-percenter club member include starting as a *hang-around* (the easiest part—it entails just getting to know a bit about the club); serving as an associate (several more years); becoming a prospect (additional years of being allowed to attend events, but not vote); and becoming a fully patched member (requires a unanimous vote by all chapter members). The process of becoming a full member of a one-percenter club is time-consuming, and many potential members do not complete all of the required stages.

3. Hierarchy—Club chapters have members, officers, and presidents, and the national organization of a club has a president as well. One must slowly work his way up the ranks to be a one percenter. Clawing ones way higher up the organization would take even longer.

4. Symbols—Patches, with each part of the design having a specific meaning, are critical parts of the one-percenter uniform. Unauthorized use or possession of patches is strongly discouraged, with violence as a potential punishment.

5. Exclusive knowledge—Precise and accurate information on the exact customs and rules of club conduct is difficult for outsiders to obtain. This is very much by design.

6. Respect—Respect for other members, their motorcycles, their property, and the symbols of the club are all serious matters for the MC.

7. Mutual aid—In the case of many clubs, members are generally obligated to stand together in a fight. This may be incorporated directly into the bylaws.

8. Codes dictating interaction with women—These rules can be incorporated directly into the bylaws. They usually prevent the men from stealing/pursuing any woman to which a member has already laid claim. Supposedly, some groups require that all wives of members be shared by the entire group; however, there is little in the way of readily available evidence of this, and it may well be a myth.[23]

Monastic Orders

Distinct from one-percenter clubs, religious orders have allowed women membership for years; however, sex segregation is the norm.[24] This equal opportunity of access would seem to invalidate an examination of these groups as worthy of study as to how groups of men operate; however, it does not, as the women's groups were established after those of the men and were patterned closely on them. Additionally, most women's religious orders are *led* by a man, if only at the highest levels (be it by a bishop, an abbot, or by someone else). If anything, monastic orders should meet all of the criteria laid out for male hierarchy and operation *at least* as well do one-percenter clubs do, as a result of their significant separation from communities in which women have economic or cultural influence. Now, let us test this hypothesis by examining the extent to which religious orders have the relevant traits:

1. Common goals, values, and beliefs—Both Buddhist and Trappist (Catholic) monastic orders require acceptance of a core set of beliefs and values. Buddhists monks are required to live by a list of more than 200 rules that are designed to guarantee that they behave as models of virtue for the entire community. They are also required to accept the underlying ethical tenets of Buddhism. Trappist monks must have a professed faith in Christ and a willingness to serve the Lord. They are also subject to a large number of rules of conduct.[25]

2. Trials by fire or endurance—Becoming a Buddhist monk is a laborious process. First, one must undergo novice ordination, which involves having one's head shorn, the undertaking of ten precepts (rules), and the formal taking of robes. Only after one has lived as a novice for some time may he be fully ordained. The process of becoming a fully recognized Buddhist monk is slow, and the average amount of time one must live as a novice before becoming a fully ordained Trappist monk is similar—at least several years.[26]

3. Hierarchy—Both Buddhist and Trappist monastic orders have ranks and recognized degrees of seniority. Some Buddhist monastic orders have a relatively flat hierarchy. Others (in the Tibetan tradition for one) have quite elaborate power structures. The Trappist tradition also has has a moderate degree of organizational complexity.[27]

4. Symbols—Both Buddhist and Trappist monks have distinct dress, with colors chosen for their specific

240

symbolic value, and both wear simple, unadorned clothing that is quite distinct from that worn by the laity. Additionally, Buddhist monks carry alms bowls, which both serve the traditional purpose of enabling them to collect food donations and also serve as a symbol of their poverty.

5. Exclusive knowledge—Depending upon the monastic order, one may need to spend years demonstrating worthiness before receiving training in esoteric customs and practices.[28]

6. Respect—Elaborate codes of etiquette and behavior are incorporated into Buddhist and Trappist traditions. Higher-ranking officials in the monasteries/temples (usually abbots) are afforded specific deference.[29]

7. Mutual aid—Although mutual aid may not be written into monastic codes, the organization in which monks live (temple/monastery) is a collective. Monastic orders may be somewhat weaker in this regard than are one-percenter clubs, but given their more restricted lifestyles, they may be in need of such aid less often: The odds of a monk getting into a bar fight are relatively rare. However, some monastic or quasi-monastic orders—think Knights Templar or the Shaolin Temple—have trained members to fight. Presumably, they would demonstrate loyalty to their comrades-in-arms.

8. Codes dictating interaction with women—Both Buddhist and Trappist monks are expected to live as celibates and to maintain a certain appropriate distance from women. Buddhist monks are not even supposed to be in a closed room with a woman without a witness present.[30]

Group Building, the Rules, and Equilibrium

Building a useful social group or network outside the existing structures of work and religion is bound to be challenging, yet such may be necessary for men who do not desire to remain isolated. Work relationships are fragile, and a great many religious groups are either so lacking in rigor that they are little more than feel-good social clubs or are so focused on marriage, family, and the placating of women that they provide little in the way opportunity for men to get to know each other except in the most rigid and constrained ways.

Nevertheless, several opportunities to get to know other men willing to help each other exist. The key is to find or create a group that is structurally hostile to being commoditized (meaning *rendered interchangeable with every other group of a similar type*) and effeminized.

A few outlier religious groups, such as some Eastern Orthodox churches, may meet these criteria, but such groups may well be closed to (or at least *understandably suspicious of*) outsiders. And for those of either a non-Christian faith or of no faith in particular, the existence of Christian churches that have not been stripped of their pre-consumerist customs and practices is interesting, but tangentially relevant at best.

Much of what makes a group useful and durable and allows it to become something more than a temporary collection of transient individuals is *difficulty*. That which can be had too easily is simply not valued all that much.[31] In the same way, groups for which there are no physical, intellectual, or moral barriers to entry provide membership that amounts to little more than a card in one's wallet. For those men interested in forming useful groups and associations, the first question should be *around what?*

Around what interest, skill, or shared set of goals should a group form?

Whatever is chosen should be at least somewhat demanding. High standards of both the physical and intellectual variety do much to encourage stronger group cohesion and prevent group membership from being diluted.

Beyond these, there is the matter of considering social isolation and group formation in the context of the Rules. Balancing the imperatives within the Rules, which demand rational self-interest, with mutual aid, is not impossible, so long as the members of a group are capable of operating logically and dedicated to doing so. This is another reason that any social group of worth has meaningful cognitive and behavioral entrance standards—to weed out those too stupid or sluggish to engage in disciplined thought. If the members of any given group more or less follow the Rules and *they have roughly equal levels of power (or have power aligned with commensurate responsibility) or utility within the group*, equilibrium should be reached. Functionally, any group of men bound to endure for a length of time should have the eight relevant traits described on the previous pages.

The group should also be structured in such a way that it does not become too large for effective networks within it to be built. At largest, a group (or chapter of a larger group) should not exceed about 45 members, with functional subunits of between 5 and 15 members. If these numbers are exceeded, the group or chapter should be restructured accordingly.[32] Slowing group growth to manageable levels is a *third* benefit to high entrance standards.

Women, as a result of their ability to persuade men to act contrary to the Rules (meaning contrary to rational self-interest),

243

have an advantage of influence that will allow them undermine the functionality of any given group (from the perspective of male members). Either the group is bound to become more oriented towards women's social expectations of talk without sacrifice (a coffee klatch or gossip club) or become a group that demands tremendous sacrifice *but only by its male members for the benefit of its female members.*

This leads to our next point.

Women and the Amorphous Mass

When complex social groups allow women to enter them in significant numbers, as full members without restriction or segregation, the dynamics of these groups change: They go from competitive, hierarchical, and largely fractal structures to flatter, amorphous social masses with little in the way of cohesion. Although some individual women can contribute a great deal, once a tipping point in the sex ratio is reached, the integrity of the group will be compromised.

Physical and intellectual standards will drop, and efficiency will decline as ever more elaborate bureaucratic procedures are put in place to address the inherent complexity of having the males and females of a sexually reproducing species work together for prolonged periods of time in a theoretically (if not practically) neuter environment.[33] Even in the unlikely event an entirely desexualized culture is put into place, allowances for women's inferior strength, physical resilience, and limited ability to exert themselves without interruption for prolonged periods of time must be enforced with the heavy hand of close management and constant oversight.[34]

In order to sustain a mixed-gender group, the men within the group must constantly accommodate the women therein—

effectively lightening the women's loads—while pretending that they are doing nothing of the sort, lest the women realize their limited utility.[35] The doublespeak and doublethink required to maintain this illusion are corrosive to intragroup honesty and camaraderie as well as to group members' sanity.

High and Low: Having Friends and Allies at Every Level of Society

One should have friends at different levels and stations of society—high and low alike. Sometimes, it is useful to have friends in high places, and sometimes friends in low places can be every bit as helpful (if not more). Every social class has a unique body of knowledge that enables its members to survive at a certain level.[36] Knowing how to make money is a skill, just as is knowing how to survive without any of it, and you will find geniuses and idiots; saints and demons; those with initiative and those without; and potentially loyal friends and guaranteed backstabbing bastards in mansions as often as shanties, and country clubs as often as dive bars.

You should learn how to assess people beyond first impressions. Be no respecter of persons. This is not a *kumbaya-and-hands-across-the-globe*, *give-peace-a-chance*, *we-are-all-equals* lot of communist nonsense. Yes, everyone has their faults, and yes, most people have at least some decency in them. But that is largely without consequence. The point is to learn to look past the superficial markers of status and class and to recognize the ability (or lack thereof), decency (or lack thereof), and intelligence (or lack thereof) of the individual.

Realize how deceptive packaging can be. Marketers know this —they know that a crappy product with bad design can be made to appear (at least at first glance) to be something more than it really is. Titles, wealth, and mannerisms are all packaging. While I would urge you to avoid discounting the less prosperous, I would also urge you to avoid developing a sense of *anti-elitism*. Do not allow yourself to develop resentment or envy for someone simply because he has more than you do. Even if his success is *purely* a matter of luck, blaming him for that is unreasonable. One is no more at fault for having good luck than he is for having bad luck.

Plenty of people with money and power are tremendous fools, just as are many people without money. Competence has little, if any relationship, with abstractions and symbols, and money is an abstraction and a symbol, albeit it a useful one.

Learning to evaluate other men without regard for their status is tricky. After all, we are a status-oriented species. You probably have at least one or two superficial biases. Most of us do. If you can learn to take note of your reactions as they arise, you will soon become more adept at recognizing their effects on you.

If you see a man driving a Ferrari down the street, what is your first reaction? *Envy? Approval? Indifference?* Whatever your reaction is, be it good, bad, or indifferent, it is likely to color your assessment of him. If you see a man driving a badly rusted 1985 Ford F150, what is your first reaction to *him*? If you can learn to recognize reactions as they occur, you will be able to account for the way they shape your thinking. This will make you a more objective, more rational, and less oblivious person.[37]

You should also diversify your interests. Consider what you do for fun and profit. We are all ignorant about far more things than we are knowledgeable. However, if you have only *one* interest, you really are restricting yourself. Obviously, the more diverse skills and interests you have, the more you can do for yourself. Less obviously, the more diverse skills and interests you have, the more readily you can relate to and understand others, and the broader your skill set, the more you can trade your knowledge with others.

They Want You in Solitary

The social isolation of men in America is not, by and large, accidental, and that which is not the product of happenstances of geography or tradition is the work of government, international concerns, feminists, and social manipulators and engineers of every form. Very generally speaking, their reasons are all the same —to create men who are easy to control. The isolated man is easier to manipulate. He is easier to enslave. He is easier to erase from the collective memory.

Remember, the world will take all it can get from you and leave you without a damn thing. There will be no remorse. There will be no guilt, only mocking and derision—that is all you will get in exchange for your efforts and labors to serve others while demanding nothing in return. *All things live through the process of destruction.* This is neither good nor bad. It is natural.

The key is to be the *eater* (not the *eaten*) as long as possible while remembering that someday *you will be lunch for something*, if only bacteria. The latter thought gives one perspective.

You can delay this inevitable failure with the help of friends and allies far better than you can alone. Those who argue against this rational position are predators or the (possibly ignorant) agents of predators. Beware of them.

Learn to build alliances. Learn to build friendships on common and diverse interests. And learn to turn your competitive nature into a tool to be *used by* you, rather than allowing it to dominate your thoughts and action. Learn to derive happiness from your friends' successes.

247

This is how you keep from being singled out, isolated, and destroyed. This is how you keep the predators and the slavers away.

The Thinking Man

(Ten Questions for Review and Consideration)

1. Think about the old customs (of the 1950s) and the new customs (of today). Do you mix and match in such a way that you put yourself at a disadvantage? If so, how?

   _____

   _____

   _____

2. Consider the myth of the totally independent man. To what, if any, extent does it influence you?

   _____

   _____

   _____

3. Do you enjoy solitude? How is solitude different from loneliness? Do you behave differently during a period of solitude than when lonely?

   _____

   _____

   _____

4. Can you think of any way in which dark forest theory relates to your day-to-day thinking? Does it explain any of your biases for or against anyone or anything? Does explain any of your behaviors? If so, what?

    _____

    _____

    _____

5. Think back on the *Commonwealth of Nowhere*. Are some people more a part of the Commonwealth than others? If so, why? What distinguishes those who are fully immersed in it from those who are less so?

    _____

    _____

    _____

6. How does having your girlfriend/wife as your only/best friend make you more vulnerable?

    _____

    _____

    _____

7. Do you subscribe to the *Cult of the American Dream* (CAD)? If not now, did you ever? What part(s) of it appealed to you? What about the *Cult of the American Nightmares*(CAN)? To what extent do you (or have you) subscribed to it?

_____

_____

_____

8. Aside from the two groups mentioned (*1%er MCs* and *monastic orders*), can you think of any groups that meet the seven criteria of effective groups of men? If so, what are these groups, and what do they do?

_____

_____

_____

9. Are all of your friends and associates of a single class and group? If so, how might it benefit you to diversify your social network, and how would you go about doing so?

_____

_____

_____

10. If you are isolated, what would be the ideal first step to remedy this problem?

_____

_____

_____

12) On the Living, the Sick, and the Dead

Here is the lie that you have been told, at least indirectly: Act like a big enough pussy, and you can postpone death indefinitely.[1]

This is, of course, impossible. Birth, life, and death are brutal at best. At least they don't take all that long. (*Being* dead, however, seems to be a rather drawn-out experience, unless one manages to get himself *undeaded*, which has the potential to lead to any number of complications.)

There is no getting around the inevitability of your own demise. Denial of this somber truth is at the root of some of the greatest cons in America. Down equally far in the dirt is an apparent contradiction. Let us descend to the *zone of rhizomes* and inspect each of these with due care.

First, the seeming contradiction: You should simultaneously be suicidally heroic and health-obsessed. In truth, there is no contradiction. Think back to the last chapter. *The shovel should keep itself clean and in good working order until it is no longer needed.* It should be equally willing to put itself away in the shed or jump on the scrap heap, possibly at the same time, if such is what the shovelers wish.

But you are not a shovel. You are not merely a tool for others. You need not pogo about the farm when others will it. Autonomy is the essence of the Rules. *Can you dig it?*

Next, oblivion!

Healed to Death

We are a people being medicated to agony and ruination.[2]

Not all medicine is bad, but it is limited in its utility. The problem with both medic and medicine is not their imperfection, but that we cannot accept that they are imperfect.

Some medicines work most of the time. Reasonably effective preventive medicine, such as getting a tetanus shot, is not terribly expensive and does more good than harm for the vast majority of the vaccinated. Antibiotics, properly used, can be lifesaving as well. Unfortunately, the more a medical treatment costs, the less positive effect it is likely to have. As prices go up, benefits go down, eventually reaching the nadir of investment return—obscenely expensive end-of-life care (EoLC).[3] This correlation is as one would expect. As a technology matures, its reliability increases while its price decreases. Conversely, in their first few iterations, a great many marvels of science and engineering spend more time in the shop than they do running.

And the more people involved in a non-routine process (meaning one where not everyone can work on autopilot), the greater the risk of mistakes and cascading failures. By some estimates, 210,000 people in the United States die each year as a result of preventable medical harm (screwups).[4] For comparison, there were approximately 39,773 firearms-related *early terminations* in the United States in 2017 (23,854 of which were suicides).[5] One is about five times more likely to die from medical treatment than from *acute lead poisoning*—something to think about before running to the doctor for every sniffle. The safest shot in the arm many of us are likely to receive may well be manufactured by Hornady. To state these facts is not to attack the members of the medical community; however, such does provide evidence of the limitations of the complex and still-developing systems upon which much of modern medicine depends.

254

Thirty-six years ago, the IBM PC sold for the equivalent of more than $4,000 (inflation adjusted for 2018), whereas the computer on which I am writing this manuscript weighs less than 20% of the original, is several thousand times faster, and consumes a small fraction of the electricity used by the original PC.[6] With tax, I paid about $190 for it. Internal combustion engines, while not having seen the same price drop as computers, have improved considerably over the last 40 years, requiring less maintenance and functioning longer than their predecessors, and costing no more.[7] No one should be surprised that cutting-edge medicine works terribly (when it works at all). If *it*—whatever technology *it* happens to be—had truly been perfected, it would be cheap, ubiquitous, and of such awesome reliability that only its rare non-performance is noticed. This is the nature of engineering—it is bad enough to be noticed until it is good enough to be ignored.

In any fair and reasonable society, people who reach such a condition of profound hopelessness that they require the care of a team of doctors and technicians to survive the day, that they must rely upon technology barely in the alpha phase, would be made comfortable to the extent doing so is possible and gently encouraged to shuffle over the deadline and into the great beyond, before they bankrupt the rest of us.

Yet such rarely happens soon enough. Instead, we throw fortunes after lost causes. *Why?* Some reasons are almost certainly personal: While family members may realize that the family member/patient/victim of medicine would be better off dead, they may have a difficult time bringing themselves to save on the household electric bill by hitting the big red button on grandma's ventilator. Family politics can come into play as well: All of the children of an ill person may genuinely wish that he or she would die, but none may want to suggest that treatments stop, lest they actually do what the others *want to do*. This can turn into a costly (and sadistic) game of chicken—who will hold out longer, who can authorize the infliction of more pointless suffering upon the practically dead in the name of *love?*

Other reasons are those of business. Milking the well-insured unfortunate can yield great profits, but I suggest that money is not the primary motivator for many of these tragic and futile efforts.

And let us first acknowledge this: Many of these efforts *are* genuinely tragic. Witnesses to the death-extension process, even those parsimonious with their sympathy, would be hard-pressed to ignore the sheer terribleness of these last-ditch efforts to *do something*. Multiple rounds of chemotherapy are sickening. Surgeries may result in monstrously painful injuries. Tubes, pumps, constant injections, *nosocomial* (hospital-acquired) infections—these, combined with almost non-stop humiliation of being poked, prodded, and tested are what await a great many of us in our final days.[8]

Aside from profit, family dynamics, and (sometimes) religious concerns, and *intervention bias* (the tendency to believe it is better to *act* than to *not act*), a great deal of this pointless suffering is the result of a largely unwarranted techno-optimism. This optimism, particularly in older Americans who lived through an era of great advancements, is somewhat understandable. The fiction and predictions of the 1960s and 1970s were wildly unrealistic, and according to their timelines, flying cars, Martian colonies, and sentient computers should have come into being more than fifteen years ago.

We may not have all that, thinks the man raised on *Mystery Science Theater, Starship Troopers,* and the writings of Isaac

Asimov, *but we should at least be able to cure a little cancer!* Yet we cannot, and adjusting to such disappointment must not be easy. Even quite a few members of the post-Boomer generations—who were promised far less in technological marvels than were their parents—have confused relatively slight *visible* improvements in entertainment and communications systems for signs of radical innovation that simply has not occurred.[9]

Faced with death, the effects of techno-optimism and intervention bias are magnified. Technology becomes a quasi-god —a savior to which one prays and pleads, rather than a limited toolkit born of fallible, violent primates' sporadic efforts—and intervention bias festers ever more acutely. *We must act!*

Let us not forget that a great many doctors do not relish defeat. If they had given up easily, they would not have been able to complete their medical degrees and residencies. And some simply hate to tell their patients that there is no better treatment to be offered than learning to quiet one's soul and stare long into the abyss.

Ironically, the kindest thing the physician may be able to do to guide his patients through these dire straits is to *be a bastard* and admit the hopelessness of the situation without too much concern for feelings or niceties. But being a proper bastard can be difficult, even for those who follow all of the helpful instructions in the unambiguously named "On Being a Bastard" (Chapter 14).

As a society, we may be uniquely afraid of dying. Any explanation for this is bound to be speculative. We likely suffer from an excess of good luck. The Europeans saw their countries torn apart twice in the last century. Japan was very nearly burned to the ground in the Second World War. Russia survived Lenin, Stalin, Nazi invaders, and the economic upheavals of the 1990s.

China, a place where corpses were long as common as tea leaves, experienced more than thirty years of domination by warlords, a bone-crushing invasion by the Japanese, a civil war, a multi-year famine, and the Cultural Revolution. Even England saw more trauma than did the United States, with German bombing raids flattening civilian and soldier alike. Relative to the nonstop suffering that was most of the 20th century for billions of people, the American experience was a cakewalk on a pleasant Sunday afternoon.[10] Our modern, post-WWII culture developed in a time of plenty, which leads to my next point:

Sick Children Make for Sensible Adults

If you ever meet anyone who seems almost totally unable to comprehend his own mortality—the kind of guy who seems shocked (*shocked!*) to learn that he could ever get sick, that he could ever get injured, that he might eventually suffer the incredibly minor inconvenience of needing to wear glasses in his 50s—ask about his childhood health. Chance are, it was good, *too good!* This is a man (or woman) who has never had to face the awful truth that his body is a poorly constructed, difficult to repair, and incredibly slipshod assembly of kludges that may well self-destruct at any moment. And for that reason, this person is inclined to become a horribly irritating pain at the first signs of a head cold.

On the other hand, a childhood of sickness, assuming that the sufferer eventually outgrows it, gives a certain strength. The victim of middling biology comes to understand that he is but one missed heartbeat away from ceasing to exist. Yet as is the case for salt, sugar, tea, or tobacco, too much of that which is positive becomes a negative in its own right.

258

An overabundance of sickness and death can cause one to give up altogether. The sweet spot for a character-building (if not necessarily enjoyable) youth is that at which a child is sick, weak, and vulnerable enough to recognize that his time in the land of the fallen may be cut short, but strong enough to know that he has at least a fair chance of having more days than he can count on stubs of fingers and toes gnawed away during a bout of leprosy.

This is the point of *optimal unwellness*.

Those who were *optimally unwell* during their youths have the advantages of knowing that their existences are limited and precious, of understanding that medicine can only do so much, and of appreciating the importance of humor in the face of uncertainty. The idiot boy who fancies himself ten-feet tall and bulletproof at the age of 17 may well become a hypochondriac and coward by the age of 57, when he finally notices that no combination of pills, sprays, and powders can return to him the missing hair on his hair or the spring in his penis, both stolen by Chronos in the night. The optimally unwell are not so afflicted.

Perspective, Risk, and Motivation

Immortals need not make haste. To them, time is truly unlimited, which makes any amount of it valueless. Immortals need not pay any mind to risk either. Punishment and suffering are both irrelevant to the immortal. The death penalty would certainly be off the table for them, and even a sentence of a thousand years of being sexually violated by rabid bears would not amount to much. The experience might be unpleasant, but an immortal would have *forever* to recover from it.

Immortality would be liberating, as immortals can live without fear, but given that everything in the universe would eventually change around them—that they would come to see all things

259

crumble away—even those with overwound personalities of the worst sort would settle into equanimity.

But we are not immortals, and despite the veneer of hyper-optimism, despite our can-do attitude even as the icy hand reaches up from the depths for us, we know, deep down, that we will soon pass. The optimally unwell may be more *aware* of their impending expiration, but none of us are truly ignorant of the nearness of the grave. Our cognitive dissonance has left us in a state of perpetual befuddlement, and the befuddled are easily manipulated. They are perfect suckers, primed to buy one nostrum after the next, convinced that this potion or that miracle diet will extend their days long enough for them to be extended further still. They are perfect daredevils as well, sold on the notion that any amount of recklessness can be undone, that *the Great They*—the white-coated workers of miracles—can put anyone or anything (Humpty Dumpty included) back together again.

In order for this little psychological charade—that which allows men to entertain the notion that they have unlimited time remaining—to continue for any length of time, they must learn to ignore a *huge* number of day-to-day risks and injuries, lest the game is disrupted by that most charmless of killjoys, *reality*.

When reality does finally stop the merrymaking, some players do not respond with much in the way of rationalism or maturity.

Such is a major reason that terrorists can so easily send us into a tizzy. The danger *Osama al Bomba* and his minions pose the average person, while statistically small, *appears* outsized due to a conditioned ignorance of probability. One is more than twenty times likely to be killed while driving to the store to buy a terrorist-hacking machete (with blood grooves and a lard coating) than he is to be killed by the *Brothers Terrisamazov* or anyone else from those far-off countries where apostasy is a serious crime.[11]

The other great problem caused by the American death-is-optional mindset is that it encourages a peculiar form of time mismanagement. Sometimes, this takes the form of simple procrastination. Remember, *immortals have no motivation.*

It can also manifest as an odd, eternal hopefulness that, somewhat paradoxically, makes digging one's own grave that much easier. Older generations of men, particularly those born in the 1950s and 1960s, seem afflicted with this to the point of absurdity.

Consider the fellow who has been married more than once and has insisted on having at least one child with each of his wives (to *make the marriage real* or some other such nonsense). Chances are that this schlub's exes did not have the good grace to die while he was out of town with an airtight alibi. Instead, it's dollars to doughnuts that each took her fair share (meaning *everything*) of his assets before departing. Yet being probed and penetrated once by the cruel hand of the family courts is not enough for the masochist: He repeats his mistakes, thinking probability will someday grant him mercy. And while being frogmarched down the aisle for the umpteenth time, the words *I reckon this one sure does love me!* ricochet through his empty head like a BB hitting a steel backstop at a shooting gallery.[12]

Stupid is as stupid does.

If he just keeps trying *long enough*, romantic love will eventually find the schlub. Unfortunately, *eventually* has a countdown timer attached, and so a great many *penis-guided putzes* end up dying with one hand clutching their chests and the other clutching the divorce papers (and accompanying protective order) they have just been served on behalf of *Wife No. 7.*

Hope beyond sense and reason is all but guaranteed to spoil whatever peace of mind a man might achieve. One so cursed is forever stuck discounting the present for a potentially happier and better future, and a man can focus too much on the future, especially if he forgets that in the future we will all be dead. The myth that can *you do/get whatever you want if just put your heart into it* is a terrible thing. It is a lie. Any of us *could* do anything if given unlimited time, but unlimited time is something we do not have.

Poisons and Medicines

The optimists and the if-you-can-dream-it-you-can-do-it types have dumped poison on our heads. Most worthwhile goals are incredibly difficult to achieve, and many of them are downright unachievable. The medicine to soothe one's misery is the wisdom to prioritize actions. None of us have the time to do otherwise.

If you can focus your efforts on select goals that you really want, be they large goals (writing your novel, making your first HALO jump, or patenting your fantastic invention) or smaller ones (avoiding too much heavy work and making time to watch more movies), and learn to drop almost everything else, you will be all the happier. You will probably not live long enough to build a perfect business, buy a mansion, follow whatever creative interests you have, pursue sex to the fullest of your interests, *and* make all the money you would like to make. If you lose sight of the sheer amount of time all of this would take—centuries for most of us—you are that much more likely to be crushed under the weight of your fantasies.

Think Like a Frail Boy

You can learn the wisdom of the frail boy, even if you are fit as a fiddle. Do this: Imagine you are a boy who is optimally unwell—

the diseases you have *may* not kill you anytime soon, but they just might, and they most certainly keep you from bouncing off the walls—trying to decide how to spend his days. This boy knows his time may be quite limited. He knows his energy is limited as well. Unlike his irritatingly healthy peers, he takes careful stock of his health for the day, weighing out how much he cares to exert himself for any given thing. The boy is thrifty. Minutes, calories, and movements count, so the boy is deliberate.

Now, consider the Rules.

Give as little as possible.

This applies not only to money but also to matters of exertion. Strain yourself too much for one thing, and you will be left unable to do another.

Take as much as possible.

Maximize the most you get from each movement and calorie spent on doing anything that you absolutely do not *enjoy* doing. The optimally unwell boy may not wake up tomorrow: If he is going to put forth the effort to do something, he is going to try to get the most out of it he possibly can.

Always have an exit.

The boy who is optimally unwell is too weak to have much energy to waste, but he is strong enough to get up and leave before he tires too badly. This contradicts some popular advice. Sunzi wrote that the best approach to making soldiers fight harder is to give them no opportunity to flee.[13] In military strategy, this makes sense, particularly if you do not care how many of your soldiers are killed in battle. But for the optimally unwell boy, this is exactly the *wrong* strategy to take. The frail boy is not fighting so much to achieve a single, fixed goal, as he is fighting against time. Apply the

263

Third Rule to everything from work (and always having a viable alternative source of income) to relationships (always be ready to find someone else or do without) to home ownership to everything in between. The unwell boy knows life is too short to waste on lost causes or that which bores him. He recognizes that it okay to **not care** about anything and that losing interest in something can be a perfectly good reason to walk away from it. The frail boy does not cling to any one thing, save the preciousness of his time, and he locates the exits before he has taken his seat.

Enjoy your life to the fullest.

The boy knows that one breath does not guarantee another, so he tries to enjoy the day. At the same time, he does not overstrain his body, lest he bring about his death faster than it need occur, or he worsen his illness. He balances his search for enjoyment against conservation of energy.

The truth is that we are all unwell. We are all rotting from the inside out. This should not drive you to despair. It should drive you to pragmatic efficiency, to making the most of your life—and by that I mean trying to live as *you* wish to live, not as others wish you would—and to setting goals that align with the time you have remaining and that can fit through the windows still open to you.

Think like the frail boy and live the better for it: This is how you balance your mind—by accepting the uncertainty of each day and the limits of your powers and energies and by rationally making the most of them.

And here's a paradox to remember: The boy with the sickly pallor and the weak body may have the healthiest mind and strongest spirit of us all.

The Thinking Man
(Eight Questions for Review and Consideration)

1. Were you ever really sick as a child? If so, what did you think about during that time? Did you think that you might not survive?

    _____

    _____

    _____

2. How is the thinking of the frail (*optimally unwell*) boy different from that of the always-well child?

    _____

    _____

    _____

3. When considering the limited amount of time and energy you have remaining, are there any goals that you are less interested in pursuing than you were before? Are there any goals you are more interested in pursuing?

    _____

    _____

    _____

265

4. Are there any life goals that others have tried to impose on you that you now think are a waste of time? If so, what are these goals and who tried to impose them on you?

_____

_____

_____

5. Can you think of any ways to increase the number of non-suicidal *exits* in your life, aside from building additional income streams? These could relate to anything, from possible exits from meetings that you find boring to ways to terminate relationships that prove more trouble than they are worth.

_____

_____

_____

6. Is there anything you could do today to spend less time (*Give as little*) on that which you do not enjoy while getting more (*Take as much*) out of your time?

_____

_____

_____

7. Have you known anyone to waste his life because he simply did not take into account its brevity? If so, who was this person and what wasteful things did he do? Did he express his regrets to you? What do you think he should have done differently?

_____

_____

_____

8. Are any of the Rules violated by obsessing over health? If so, *which* Rules are violated and *how* are they violated?

_____

_____

_____

13) On Addiction

The Disease

America is a nation of addicts.

Despite having only 5% of the world's population, we use about 80% of the global opioid supply, and as of 2017, more than 47,000 Americans died from opioid overdoses.[1] Given that the American economy is largely post-industrial (meaning that there are relatively few jobs in which people are seriously injured), these rates of drug use and death are almost bizarrely high.

And our culture of addiction is not purely limited to that which can be swallowed, shot up, or snorted. Our fixation on romantic love—on marriage and remarriage, a never-ending cycle of sexual and emotional hits—leads to an addiction of one sort. The equally pernicious emphasis on excessive consumption—on having and accumulating—leads to a different form of addiction. The third form is the addiction of aspiration—the notion that life is bound to *get better*, not because of particular luck or initiative, but because *improvement is a natural (and inevitable) process*—this may well lead to more suffering than do the previous two combined.[2]

Why? Why do we suffer so?

Let us begin with this: *You are not made to be happy most of the time.* Your death fast approaches. Every womb is a tomb. How happy can you truly be? Satisfaction is impossible. Our appetites are not made to be sated, but they can be brought to heel, as can our misery. The uncontrolled urge to binge and purge and binge again is the lifeblood of addiction.

These observations do not contradict the Rules. A great deal of *enjoying your life to the fullest* is finding a sustainable middle and interests to keep you there. It is not being hungover half of the time.

Many of the experts claim addiction is a *disease*.[3] With a limited number of exceptions, I disagree. I would also suggest that this theory is not taken all that serious by the very government agencies that promulgate it. If addiction really were regarded as a disease, the vast majority of our public policies for addressing it would be cruel to the point of unconstitutionality—no better or worse than sentencing someone to prison for having cancer. At worst, even the most unstable (and potentially disruptive) of the afflicted would be sent to sanatoriums, not prisons.

Rather than seeing addiction as a disease (as it is regarded in theory) or as a crime (as it is treated in practice), addiction is largely *a symptom* of the soul-destroying ailment of *psychosis-inducing expectations disorder* (PIED). Those suffering from PIED are afflicted by hopes and dreams so fantastically high that God himself would struggle to reach them were he flying a nuclear rocket strapped to a warp drive being dragged through the sky by a cast of peregrine falcons on steroids.

Here is the good news: PIED does not require a conventional cure—it is a *societal disease* more than a personal one, which is to say that it is an *illness of proximity*. One simply needs to distance himself from the sources of PIED and the symptoms will dissipate in short order. If this seems confusing, read on. All will be clear soon enough.

Welcome to the Jungle

The jungle may have fun and games, but it is also a good place to die. The jungle itself does not make you sick. Rather, that it is a warm, humid environment, friendly to pathogens, is the problem. Our jungle is metaphorical—a place the germ of PIED finds quite hospitable. In the jungle—*our jungle*—there are two great threats. One is PIED. The other is the plenitude of surfaces on which the PIED microbes multiply.

Too Much is Never Enough

Almost everyone has a hedonistic streak—that desire to feel more and feel better. This is a part of what enables us to survive as a species. Without the desire to eat, we would starve. Without the desire to procreate, the species would not continue. In the natural environment, these instincts cannot easily run amok. Those who doubt this should search for photographs of *any* technologically primitive tribe. Where the tribe is located does not matter—Asia, South America, Africa, or Australia. Some of these peoples have nose rings, some wear unusual or colorful dress, some are nearly naked, some are of a darker complexion, and some are of a lighter complexion. Some are famously violent, and others are comparatively peaceful. Despite these tremendous differences of geography, culture, and genetics, they almost all share a common trait: *They are very rarely fat.*

It is unlikely that many (if any) of these groups have much in the way of a scientific understanding of nutrition. They have no dietitians, no counselors, no weight-loss gurus. Yet they do not seem to need them, at least to stay trim. *Nature* keeps them thin. There is no *opportunity* in the natural environment to get fat. Food is relatively scarce in hunter-gatherer societies. In these societies, there is no need for *intentional moderation*. The nature of the environment makes anything but moderation impossible, which, in turn, makes developing a profound addiction difficult.

None of this is to say that life in technologically primitive cultures is easy or wonderful. Many of these societies are barbaric in a way that exceeds what is described in all but the most gruesome of post-apocalyptic fantasies, and the lives of their members of are often nasty, brutish, and short; however, *addicted* they are not.[4] This relates to the matter of *abundance*.

For better or worse, ours is a land of plenty, where even the poorest suffer from diseases of excess. The solution to this is to put distance between the person and the problem. You can avoid places where addictive substances are in ready supply. Bars, liquor stores, and drug dens are obvious examples. For some people, the list of places and things to avoid may also include restaurants, houses of ill repute, certain smartphone apps (*Tinder* comes to mind, but there are probably others), and whatever else proves difficult to resist consuming to excess. And more than just avoiding these things, you must absorb (rather than just understand intellectually) the limits of potential pleasure and the sheer fleetingness of it. This deeply incorporated knowledge makes avoiding temptation less difficult, which is not to say that avoiding addiction will necessarily be easy. By design, we are not animals of well-moderated impulses. And the primitive mind, left unattended, can adeptly manipulate the higher levels of consciousness.

Hope, Dope, and Hungry Snakes (Oh My!)

Disciplining one's mind is difficult, not only because we are not naturally suited to the task, but because doing so requires one learn to operate in a manner radically different than that encouraged by our consumerist, toxically optimistic society. PIED is not an entirely man-made illness, but it is close. It might best be thought of as an *enhanced disease*—an ancient affliction made more virulent by science.

271

Keeping you doped—dependent on one high after the next—is an excellent means of economic, cultural, and political control. First and foremost, it is a way to sell you that which you do not want, do not need, and cannot afford. The never-ending chorus of *More! More! More!* is really a call for *More sadness (for you)! More debt (for you)! More pain (for you)!* and *More money (for your enemies)! More power (for your enemies)! More slaves (of which you are one)!*

Yet one can never have all of these *wants* (not *needs*) met: *More!* is a goal that retreats two steps for every one step you take towards it. And with each inevitable disappointment, the need to self-medicate grows. Addiction leads to addiction, which leads to more addiction still. The snake eats its own tail, but you are not so doomed to have your head and ass bound together.

Truth!

Here is the truth that will set you free and make you healthy again:

Everything you have been told about **desire** is a lie: Human desire is never extinguished by excess, but by discipline. This is quite distinct from *martyrdom*, which leads to our next point:

Everything you have been told by **sacrifice** is a lie. You will rarely be respected for your sacrifices for others, especially if those *others* are women, who are likely to regard you as a sucker. This is not to say that you should never *make* sacrifices, only that you should expect no one to care or appreciate these sacrifices, that you should do them expecting nothing more than the satisfaction of knowing that you are living according to your values. Sacrifice is different from *mutual aid*, which occurs in certain very specific groups.

Everything you have been told about **bastards** is a lie. Bastards get ahead. Bastards do well in life. Granted, they must be able to *control* their bastard natures—all things in moderation. But you if ever need to decide between being a bastard and being a *nice guy*, be a bastard. It is a better that the world hate you than that it sneer at you.

Everything you have been told about **concern** is a lie. Despite frequent statements to the contrary, you are never obligated to care, about anyone or anything. Likewise, no one is ever obligated to care about you.

Everything you have been told about **debt** is a lie. Debt is a con. It allows the makers *of abstractions* to dominate the makers of *things*. Money is an abstraction, and the unrestricted production of it enables the crooks to impoverish honest men. Unless you are a bank or a national government, you cannot *legally* print money, so flooding the markets with cheap money—be they markets for housing, consumer goods, food, or medicine—is all but guaranteed to screw you, the man without the printing press. The only good debt is the debt that no one can force you to repay.

Everything you have been told about **duty** is a lie. You have no non-reciprocal duties. You must *assume* a duty. One cannot be forced upon you. *Give something; get something.* And if you get nothing, if there is no consideration, you are not fulfilling a duty— you are making a sacrifice.

If you are *made* to sacrifice yourself for a cause, a people, a nation, or another person and receive nothing in return, your time, your money, and possibly your life are being stolen from you. This is robbery, nothing more. Feel free to use any tool at your disposal to fight those who would steal from you. Whatever you do, without bounds or restrictions, to resist such deprivations is ethical. Just try to win.

Everything you have been told about **education** is a lie. To be educated is great, but this has little to do with school. You can learn just as much on your own about *almost* any subject, and for less money. School and education are frequently miles apart.

Everything you have been told about **fairness** is a lie. Almost no one even *wants* fairness. They want what is in the best interest of them or their preferred group. The only people who seem to care much about the nonsense of fairness in the abstract, impartial sense are a select group of Western men. This is a strength, but it may well also become a suicidal weakness. If one group tries to conduct itself fairly and the others do not, one group is bound to lose. Can you guess which one?

Everything you have been told about **family** is a lie. Family gives you no stability. Have a family and become a resource to be exploited. You will sacrifice much and receive little good in return. Certain people and organizations may *want* you to have a family so that you will borrow and spend more, work more, and be more thoroughly enslaved, but they will not reward you for it. This behavior is largely a sign of their arrogance. These people believe that they know everything about you. They believe that you can be manipulated with relatively crude psychological tools. They believe you are too stupid and helpless to survive without a woman shrieking at you, a child bleeding you dry, and the approval of *everyone and no one in particular*.

Everything you have been told about **happiness** is a lie. You can make no one else happy. You may be able to alleviate another person's suffering. You may be able to give them the tools to make themselves happy, but you can make no one happy. Happiness is the responsibility of each individual if he (or she) chooses to pursue it. Those who would demand others make them happy are either dullards or tyrants. And even the happiness you provide yourself will be in limited measure. The fastest route to agony is the pursuit of never-ending happiness of the most ecstatic sort— the fast-burning happiness that consumes as it is consumed.

Everything you have been told about **harmlessness** is a lie. Harmlessness is not a virtue. It is not an aspect of compassion or kindness. Be merciful as it suits you, but harmless, never. The harmless man is a tool, a fool, and an abomination. This point will be considered more in the following chapter.

Everything you have been told about *home ownership* is a lie. Houses are not great investments (if they are investments at all). They give you no real security, and if the mortgage market ever collapses, a great many of them may end up being sold for pennies on the dollar. Easy credit almost inevitably leads to inflation, and the housing market has been flooded with easy credit for more than three decades.

Everything you have been told about *love* is a lie. This is not to say that love does not exist, only that it has less value than we are encouraged to believe. Recognize love for what it is: a series of neurochemical and neuroelectric chain reactions. Love, at least worldly love, is weak. (A man of faith might argue that God's love is stronger, but that is a topic of its own.) Love is a fragile thing because the system in which the processes of love occur—the brain—is a fragile machine.

All emotions are fragile as a result of the system in which they occur, but love is a uniquely fickle one. It spreads far more slowly through groups than does *rage*, and it has far less motivating effect.[5] Consider this: We are at least mildly surprised when

275

someone sacrifices himself for love, yet for someone to sacrifice himself for rage is not shocking at all. Rage motivates us to fight, to kill, and work against almost impossible odds. Whole nations can be brought together by rage. Peoples can be wiped from the map by those empowered by rage. Yet how many wars were set aside for love?

Love fades, but rage can endure for a lifetime.

Take note of how little love is worth relative to almost *anything* else. Glass is tougher. And romance is little more than dangerous frivolity.

Everything you have been told about **opportunity** is a lie. Some people may well get rich through hard work, but luck will always play a huge role in success. There is no reason to resent the lucky, just as there is no reason to despise the unlucky. Our fortunes are not entirely our own to make. This is not to say that you should not *try*, it is not to say that you should disregard the Rules, only that you should not ignore that importance of God, the Fates, Ganesha, the Flying Spaghetti Monster, chaos, or whatever you think is responsible for events beyond your control.

Everything you have been told about **shame** is a lie. Those who would shame you are rarely motivated by a desire for a greater good. With few exceptions, *shamers* are either charlatans who would manipulate anyone and anything for the own benefit or the benefit of their favored group, or they are hollow men and women who have a desire to dominate and feel superior to someone, *anyone*, lest their own worthlessness overwhelm them.

Everything you have been told about **submission** is a lie. Submission earns you contempt—from women, from authorities, from anyone and everyone before whom you bow, scrape, and grovel. Sometimes you may have no choice but to submit, at least temporarily, but you should not be inactive during this time. You should look for an exit—a way to break free from whatever compels you to bend to the wills of others—or a way to sabotage those who demand your submission.

And for whatever it is worth, there is no faster way to earn the admiration of tyrants than to take all that they have and violate their every right and every orifice. Dominance is all they understand. They *will* love you for your severity—they will regard you with awe—for whatever little love and awe are worth.

Everything you have been told about **symbols** is a lie. The only value they have is in the value we assign them. Sometimes a symbol is a useful currency, but like all currency (itself a symbol) a symbol must not be too easily had, lest the value drops to nothing. *Scarcity* constitutes a large part of the value of any symbol. You have been taught to define *yourself* by the symbols you possess or that are attached to you: This provides the symbol givers power. Beware of surrendering your power to abstractions and their makers. Do so only with the greatest care and hesitancy.

These are the truths you must remember.

Slaughtered Sacred Cows and Shot White Elephants

Have a seat and take a moment to consider the content of the previous section. We are switching from one overworked metaphor to the next, and such is easier to do after having caught your breath.

The blood of sacred cows has made the floors slippery. Standing is not advised. The bolt gun was fired for the last time, and the bovine lowing has ceased. Blessed silence makes thinking less laborious.

Now, if you *do* drink, drug, shop, screw, or do anything else to the point of self-destruction, *why*? Almost everyone I have known who appears an addict is actually attempting *self-medication*. That people would self-medicate is not unexpected. Given the sheer craziness of what men in America are told to believe, it is remarkable how *few* of them need something to fortify themselves against the insanity.

Rather than treating the symptoms through self-medication, it is better to cure oneself outright, which can be done easily enough. Ignore everything everyone else has ever told you about what you need, what you *should* want, or what you *should* attempt to achieve. Now, there are two things left to ask yourself:

1. What do *I* want *for myself*?

2. What can I realistically hope to get?

Have you ever heard or read the story of the white elephant? Believe it or not, real *white elephants* exist. They are extremely rare, and they can only be found in certain parts of Asia, particularly Thailand, where the legend (and the metaphor) of the white elephant came into existence.

According to the legend, the kings of Thailand would give those who annoyed them a white elephant as a form of punishment. White elephants were revered animals with great symbolic worth, so it would seem that being given one from the leader of the country would be a unique privilege—a symbol of the king's high regard. In theory, it was. In practice, it was a great burden.[6]

Elephants eat quite a bit—sometimes more than 200 pounds of food a day—making keeping one of them in good health an expensive proposition, and they can live for decades, further

278

adding to the cost.[7] A white elephant from the king, wondrous gift that it was, simply could not be chained to a tree or allowed to wander the village as it pleased—such would be both unseemly and dangerous. The elephant's *much-honored* owner had to find somewhere respectable to keep it. Unless he had an unusually well-floored domicile, the recipient of royal largesse was bound to find even the most pleasant and placid of pachyderms a house pet of the troublesome type (although it is unlikely to get underfoot, which counts for something). Thus, the owner would be stuck with the cost of building a dedicated elephant barn, preferably of an attractive design. This leads to a question:

Why not sell the elephant to someone who wanted it?

Some Nobel laureates have sold their medals.[8] Unfortunately for the owner of a white elephant, such was not an option. To hawk a gift from the king would have been seen as a great insult to the honor of the king himself—more than a *faux pas* in a country where people are still jailed for *lèse-majesté*—defaming or insulting the members of the royal household (or even the royal pets).[9]

So the owner of the white elephant was stuck with something he most certainly did not need, very likely did not want, and almost certainly could not afford. A white elephant was a gift that would keep on giving (grief).

Much of what you have been *told to want* amounts to a white elephant of some form or another. A home may well become a white elephant. Family *is* a white elephant. Status is oftentimes a white elephant. If you are not careful, you will end up with a dozen white elephants trailing you everywhere you go, knocking down buildings, demanding food, and insisting that you scratch their trunks for them. Fortunately, you have some options that the poor/revered owner of a real white elephant did not.

279

Here is the best one: **Do not accept white elephants.**

Here is the second best one: **If you have a white elephant, shoot him, sell him, or send him off to the circus.**

The first option is easier and *better*. You may be *pressured* to take a white elephant under your roof, but you are rarely forced to do so. It is in your best interest to give the big fellow a bag of peanuts, a few gallons of water, and send him on his way.

Reject the white elephant. Return him to the king. Certain people will belittle you for this action. Others will attack. Most will be indifferent. If you pay any attention at all to those in the first two groups, you will drive yourself to drink, drugs, suicide, or some combination of them. Such people do not matter. Their opinions do not matter.

The next best option is a bit trickier. Shooting the white elephant can be as easy as abandoning your concern with status or as difficult as trying to free yourself from a bad contract. There is no one right way—no single magic bullet—to drop the beast in its tracks. The first step is always the same: *Stop being bullied into caring. Do not care unless you choose to care.* Beyond that, there are so many elephants, so many rifle calibers, so many brands of bullets, and so many external variables (windage, et cetera) that meaningful advice is almost impossible to give.

Setting Goals and Freedom from Addiction

Unless you have a truly all-consuming goal—curing a major disease, for instance—you are better off aiming for those things that will give you some realistic chance of non-misery and that will not require too much in the way of cooperation from others. These sensible things are not white elephants. Do not allow yourself to become isolated, but do not assume that even your most loyal friends will have unlimited free time to help you with one interest or the next.

Want little, and there will be little you want that you cannot have. Want much, and you will always find yourself coming up short. This is not to say that you should *want nothing*, only that you should bear in mind that ownership is never free.

Once you have set your sights on things that you want and can realistically achieve, bearing in mind their costs, you should find your addictions fade away. In a few cases, addictions may persist. Occasionally, the experts are right, and a person does have a unique neurological condition that makes avoiding addiction all but impossible. This is an essentially incurable disease for which even the most expensive treatments offer few benefits.[10] The best advice for this who suffer so: Absolutely *do not* have children.[11] Willfully passing down this curse to another is not *being a bastard* (which is fine). It is being a psychopath.

Your Life is Your Own

Addiction takes control of every part of your being. For the duration that you are in its clutches, it owns you, which is not to say that you can never be free of it. *Most* can recover. Once the underlying problem—that of *psychosis-inducing expectations disorder* (PIED) and of believing that you must accumulate one encumbrance after the next—is resolved, your mind can clear itself. Send the elephant back to the one who sent it to you. Or shoot it. Cure yourself of PIED.

Free yourself from addiction. Get the elephant off your back: It is heavy. You will walk all the better for it.

The Thinking Man

(Eight Questions for Review and Consideration)

1. Do you drink, drug, spend, or do anything else to the level of addiction? If so, do think your addiction is an *addiction resulting from circumstance* or an *addiction resulting from neurology*? Why do you give the answer you do?

   _____

   _____

   _____

2. Do you think that *addictions resulting from circumstance* have a relationship to suicide? If so, what is that relationship?

   _____

   _____

   _____

3. What are places or institutions where one might feed an addiction? Bars, liquor stores, or drug houses are obvious. Try to think of some less conventional answers.

   _____

   _____

   _____

4. Think back on what you have read about lies and truth. Have we missed anything? Is there anything else about which everything you have been told is a lie? If so, what was this thing (or *were these things*)? What were the lies you were told?

_____

_____

_____

5. Has anyone tried to push you into accepting a white elephant? If so, *who* pushed you? *What* was the white elephant in question? *Why* do you think they pushed you into accepting a white elephant?

_____

_____

_____

6. Think about the things you own and the costs of owning them. Consider the time, energy, and even emotional investments involved in keeping them. Are any of them white elephants? If so, can you rid yourself of this thing (or things)? How would you go about doing so?

_____

_____

_____

283

7. Does self-destruction through self-medication violate the Rules? If so, which of the Rules are violated? How are they violated?

_____

_____

_____

8. Does accumulating white elephants violate the Rules? If so, which of the Rules are violated? How are they violated?

_____

_____

_____

14) On Being a Bastard

You have a right to be a bastard.

You have a right to be *not nice.*

This is good. Being nice is a terrible life strategy. You have an absolute right to like, love, dislike, hate, or be indifferent to anything or anyone for *any* reason (or no reason at all), without explanation or rationalization. It is great to understand your motivations and preferences, but you never need make excuses for them. Stop apologizing for them. Your inner bastard will show you the way.

You *need* to get in touch with your inner bastard: He is a great guy to have on your side. He cares more about you than anybody else ever has (or will), and he is the person who will keep you from being turned into a doormat; from being abused or bullied; from being hung upside down, beaten with a stick, and screwed over 50 ways to Sunday. Getting to know this charmless prick is a critical survival skill.

For most of us, our inner bastards are not all that hard to reach. Clear away all the trash saccharine pleasantries and shibboleths of political correctness that fill your mind. Turn down the voices of others—people claiming *you owe them*—even though you receive nothing from them in return. Look and listen. Your inner bastard is there, patiently waiting to help you say *screw those losers!* He always has been, and he has always been looking out *for you.*

You should not ignore your friends, certainly not one as loyal as is the bastard within.

Even if you were born without much of an inner bastard—a potentially fatal and (fortunately) rare birth defect—keep reading. Even if you are one of those rare men who is naturally pleasant and is in a good mood most of the time, follow along. The advice herein applies only slightly less to you than it does to irritable bastards such as me. Everyone should know how to be a bastard from time to time.

What is a Bastard?

Before we going any further, the term *bastard* need be defined. It does not mean an explosively violent person, nor a psychotic one, nor a sadist.

Rather, it means *someone who understands that the opinions of the vast majority of the world's population* **do not matter***, because* **most people do not matter***; someone who is as severe as necessary to achieve his goals; someone who is not confused, conflicted, or upset by his own irritability, who knows that life is too short and resources too scarce to waste on placating idiots*.

The bastard knows that all actions are selfish. Even empathy is selfish. He knows that there is no such thing as a selfless act, only chicanery and delusion masquerading as such. The bastard is not an egomaniac. He does not discount *everyone's* value, but he is parsimonious in his concern. *That* is a proper bastard—a bastard of the best kind.

As the proper bastard matures, he becomes more honest by the day, simply because such is easier than trying to remember which lie has been told to whom. And as death draws nigh, the proper bastard grows ever more adept at focusing on *his goals, his passions, and his welfare*. He does not apologize for looking out for Number One. He does not play the part of spaniel, for he knows that *he* would despise those who bowed and scraped before him—

this is a fundamentally human response—and he expects others to be no more generous in their regard for weaklings. A proper bastard has no problem absolutely and permanently cutting off anyone, man or woman, who mistreats or annoys him. A proper bastard is one of the sanest men you are likely to meet, and he is far less dangerous than those who fight against their true selves and struggle to be *nice* every moment of every day. A proper bastard makes his intolerance for nonsense known—with his frankness filling the air like steam from a rolling boil—but he is not a pressure cooker. He rarely explodes, nor does he *vent*. He simply does not care to pity fools, and even the most harebrained of them ascertain as much in short order.

Mother Nature is a Vicious Whore, and That is Not Your Problem

One of the most moronic beliefs to have ever been perpetuated is that it is the duty of every *real man* to protect the weak, even if doing so involves sacrificing himself for those who have no connection to him aside from being members of the same species. Like any number of statements regarding *real men* (a decidedly ill-defined notion), *altruism as masculinity* is better in theory than in practice. In an earlier era, where communities were extensions of family and where only so many resources could be expended to enable to unfit and vulnerable, altruistic masculinity had a place and a purpose.[1] The conservation of altruism across generations is superficially paradoxical: *Why should an animal sacrifice its resources and (quite possibly) the ongoing opportunity to pass down its genetic material?* After all, suicidal behavior is not beneficial to the individual engaging in it in most circumstances.

Yet masculine altruism persists. A major evolutionary benefit of masculine altruism in ancient times was that it worked to perpetuate the man's germline, either directly (by way of him protecting his offspring) or indirectly, by way of him protecting more distant relatives. The drawbacks to altruism were also relatively limited at the level of the collective. Nature, vicious whore that she was and remains, still had sufficient force to thin the herd quite effectively and keep the number of undesirables at an acceptably low level.

In its current form, masculine altruism has become horrifically maladaptive. It is overly broad in its current application—leading to the rendering of aid to genetically disconnected groups—and worse yet, *overly effective*. Sacrifice too many of the strong for too many of the weak, and only the weak remain.

Finally, there is the matter of men's natural sympathy for women's vulnerabilities and discontentment. When life was genuinely difficult for a great many women—childbirth was dangerous and physical threats were forever present—women's complaints had rational bases. Now, much of the real misery has stopped, but women's expectations have been raised to the point that anything other than a life of unadulterated, orgiastic bliss is considered reason to grouse.

Even were an existence of bottomless strawberry daiquiris; glass-ceiling-shattering promotions; free abortions, contraceptives, childcare, and shipping (of anything, children included); and nonstop dates with young Dwayne-Johnson lookalikes made available to every woman, the complaints would not cease. The *ideal* would just move forward, slightly over the horizon, where it shall always be. Dissatisfaction is integral to the *human* condition. The Gordian knot is tied by the modern man's toxically altruistic and female-friendly desire to *fix* this—to make women happy— rather than simply telling the ladies to *suck it up*, which is what

288

adults should be expected to do when grumbling about nothing in particular.

Too much altruism, and the weak terrorize the strong, civilization declines to levels so low that even a nitwit among nits does not find his intelligence threatened, the species devolves to primordial ooze, and Death and Abomination rule as co-sovereigns over a hellscape of flaming sulfur. Bastards can solve this. Bastards —people who are cold-hearted enough to stop throwing money, labor, and lives at lost causes—can lead the way. Bastards do not mind that Mother Nature is a sadistic slattern, whose only passion is for the highest bidder and the biggest penis—that she only wants to bang the winners. They do not begrudge her for this. They do not idolize the natural world, but neither do they ignore the necessity and organic origins of competition. Rather, bastards grab the old gal between the knees and give her a grope hard enough to make her jump out of her fishnet stockings and acrylic platform heels. This is the bastard's way. This is the way of victors.

Of course, proper bastards need not care about saving the world. Nor should you.

Being a bastard is its own reward.

Nicegeist: Not Really German, Not Really Nice, and Not Really Sane

We, Western men, are too damned nice. And it is killing us. Given time, it will kill everything. Here are two questions to ponder:

1. Why do so many men detonate—act out in bizarrely violent ways—seemingly without warning?

2. Why do they seem to do this more often than they did in the past?

Most of the obvious answers do not hold water. Crimes rates have dropped over the past 40 years, so we do not appear to be turning into a generally more violent civilization, and the availability of weapons has not changed all that much in the United States either.[2] So what is it?

The genesis of the problem can be found (at least in part) in the *nicegeist*—the deeply held and culturally specific belief that we (men) should always be charming, helpful, mild, and agreeable, except when we *should not*, meaning when aggressing in service of those who have little loyalty to us. Our society has come to expect men to be almost bizarrely nice, in a way that even the most proper lady of a century ago would have found difficult to maintain. This is horribly unhealthy. It is every bit as unnatural as was foot binding, and probably less humane.

For a few people, a pleasant disposition is natural. That is fine as well. I know of at least one man who seems to feel great nine days out of ten, and as one would expect, he is usually a cheerful, pleasant, and upbeat person. Good for him! I write that without sarcasm. Generally, he should be (and is) true to himself, as we all should be true to ourselves. Yet even he will find it advantageous to at least *play the part* of a bastard from time to time, which is not to suggest that he need glower at all and sundry as a matter of habit.

This is not me, however, and I suspect it is not all that many of you. If you are a naturally irritable person, believe it or not, you are ultimately doing those around a great favor by exposing them to your ill humor. You may even be saving their lives. Here is why:

The Wages of Nice

The wages of sin may be death, but the wages of nice are far worse. At least the former cuts its checks reliably. *Nice* doles out its horrors irregularly. You can only take so much, and once you have reached your sugar-and-spice quota, there is bound to be a problem. The *wages of nice* are failure, surrender, and despair—at best. At worst, the trail of bodies left behind those men who played nice until unable to continue the charade shows that sin and nice dispense their compensation in the same currency of oblivion more often than one might think.

What you have been taught, largely by women and effeminate men, is to feign harmlessness. You are *not* harmless. Be glad for that. A truly harmless thing is extraordinarily vulnerable—it has no way to defend itself. Even plants develop defense strategies. Nicotine—the alkaloid of the gods—is a powerful pesticide tobacco plants and other members of the nightshade family have developed to protect themselves.[3] If you were truly harmless, you would be even more vulnerable than the favorite vegetable of the late Frank Zappa.

Nothing lives without the destruction of something else. That includes you. Being truly harmless is an impossibility. Feigning harmlessness, pretending that you have no bastard capacity, is more than to deny all understanding of yourself, it is to deny all understanding of life, the universe, and everything.

This strategy of simulating harmlessness may make women and weak men feel more comfortable in your presence, but it will lead to consistently lousy outcomes—for you, for those around, and for all of humanity. If anything, the odds of you prospering will increase if people overestimate your capacity to harm them.

Consider who is treated better: the 120-pound, Prius-driving, lisping weakling or the 250-pound, semi-retired boxer with a Harley and a Slavic accent? Regardless of what anyone may *claim* to prefer, they will almost certainly treat the boxer with more respect.

291

The more harmless you are perceived as being, the more others will expect of you and the less they will give you in return. You will be put upon to no end. Eventually, your *non-harmlessness* will get the best of you. Remember, you *do* have an innate capacity for destruction. Teaching someone to conceal this capacity can be done through years of training and social manipulation—castration by conditioning—but this is a matter of *concealment*, the actual potential remains: Eliminating it is almost impossible.

Given enough abuse and suppression, your destructive tendencies will manifest in one of three ways—outward-directed destruction, inward-directed destruction, or some combination of the two. Suicide is but the most obvious inward-directed destruction. Self-injury by small measures (heavy drinking or profoundly reckless behavior) has about the same effect, but it takes longer. Outward-directed destruction also has the potential to be fairly obvious (killing sprees, for one), but it can just as easily take the form of the subtle sabotage of others. Frequently, it flares up on the pretext of moral outrage. This at least partially explains the sheer number of people who have *nice* public personas but demented online ones—the bloodthirsty netizens who advocate that six-month-long gang-rape sessions be administered as punishment for unpaid library fines, but would hesitate to say *boo* if someone broke into their homes.

Dual inward-outward destruction can be anything from a murder-suicide to adopting blindly Pyrrhic life and business strategies—being willing to go to any lengths to get even, regardless of how much harm your actions cause you.

Little of this destruction is will prove useful to you: Seeking revenge against the world is a poor use of time and energy. Fortunately, there is a better way.

Black Hearts and Happy Songs: The Mantra

Inoffensiveness is impossible.

No matter what you say, it will offend someone, somewhere.

Do not start down the dark path of unmitigated consideration for the feelings of others. The more effort you put into this, the more you will paint yourself into a corner. The more solicitous you are perceived as being (beyond a very reasonable point), the higher the bar for your behavior will rise. Eventually, the bar will be so high that *no one* could possibly reach it. However, if you develop a reputation for a thoroughly Germanic directness, the standards of accommodation and *niceness* to which others hold you will be quite low. Low standards are easy to maintain.

This is the same reason it is generally better to play the bad guy: The good guy makes one *small* mistake and his reputation is ruined. He needs to be perfectly good *all the time*, which is impossible. The bad guy, however, does not need to be infallibly bad all of the time in order to maintain his reputation. He can *occasionally* be pleasant or kind, just so long as he does not make a habit of it.[4]

The best strategy—meaning that which is most effective and consumes the least effort—is to let your words land flat and where they may. This is different from being *intentionally* offensive, which can take quite a bit of work. Insult comics get paid for their labors of belittlement. Anyone who does likewise should be commensurately compensated.

This strategy is all the more easily implemented by those who recall the Mantra, which is:

I do not care.

I will not care unless I choose to care.

Soon I will be dead. I do not have the time to care about bullshit.

Mantras can be sung, this one as well as any. Day and night, the bastard carries the Mantra in his heart. Its melody swells, and given time, it drowns out the cacophony of *nicegeist* pleasantries, the hymns of the Church of the Sacred Vagina (CoSV), and the clamor of the furies within the bastard. The Mantra gives the bastard peace, and its steady rhythm matches that of his deliberate and rational actions.

Gramps Was an Ornery Son of a Bitch (Not That There's Anything Wrong With That)

What of the fruits of bastardry?

From 1870 to 1970, mankind developed powered flight and supersonic aircraft; programmable digital computing; modern physics and the atomic bomb; spaceflight and satellites; almost all modern vaccines; and movies and radio.[5] This was an era of out-and-proud bastard behavior. The *70-to-70 Century* was governed by *not-nice* men of the highest order, with the predominant leadership style of the day having bordered on the psychotic. Yet without all of these terrible people and the terrible things they did, we might well be stuck riding horses and pushing plows—living the slow and terrible existences of our forebears.

And since we have become a more genteel species, what have we achieved?

Better computers and video games, (slightly) better commercial aircraft and medicine, higher quality and more readily accessible pornography—these are the great innovations of the last five decades. Of course, comparing a period of about 50 years (1970 to present) to one of 100 years is stacking the deck. Still, if we only compare the last 50 years of progress to that made from 1920 to 1970, the pattern holds: The nicer we get, the less we achieve.

Assuming current trends continue for even another generation, we may stop achieving anything at all, aside from standing up for those with hurt feelings and bruised egos. Of course, the bastard/progress relationship could be entirely the result of correlation, but it would seem a near-total unwillingness to even *bruise* any eggs would slow down omelet production, if but ever so slightly.

There is no reason to set out to impress the world unless that is what *you want to do*. However, the lesson remains the same, and it is that:

Bastards Get Things Done!

Unless your only goal in life is to be a martyr, you will need to learn to be a bastard to get much of anything done. Let us consider some top-notch bastards, *what* they achieved, and *how* they behaved like bastards (their particular *bastardry style*).

1. Jeff Bezos—founder of Amazon.com—built a brutally competitive workplace where weak, sick, or lazy employees are terminated without apology, expects employees to work 80 hours a week (or more)[6]

2. Henry Ford—founder of Ford Motor Company—employed criminals, boxers, and ex-cops to intimidate workers using techniques that would almost certainly be illegal today[7]

3. Ray Kroc—founder of McDonald's Corporation—screwed the McDonald's brothers (the men who built the first McDonald's) out of their name and millions of dollars[8]

4. Steve Jobs—founder of Apple—tremendously critical of his employees, fired people without notice, hurled insults pretty much whenever he felt so inclined[9]

Obviously, not all bastards are productive. Some of them achieve relatively little. It is also safe to assume that you are probably better off *not* working for a *pure* bastard. People who get on board with bastards at the right time may make considerable fortunes—stock options can be a great thing—but you should remember just how difficult meeting the demands of a bastard can be.

The Deepest Well: Tapping Into Your Bastard Nature

Almost everything you have been taught about how to interact with others is designed to give them the impression that you are harmless, weak, and essentially a willing victim. Fortunately, our instincts are not so easily destroyed. Returning to the natural state *is* possible. Here is how you can do so:

Practice Being Less Empathetic

One need not become a drowner of kittens to succeed, but the ability to ration empathy is a critical survival tool.

You have been taught to be far too empathetic and sympathetic when dealing with women. This makes interacting with them needlessly challenging. Most of their emotional displays mean relatively little, so you can safely ignore them.

There are few legitimate reasons for a woman to cry. One of the most obvious instances would be if her child has recently died or been diagnosed with a serious illness. Being sympathetic to this is entirely fine. A woman might also have a legitimate reason to cry if her immediate relative, close *female* friend (or infrequently, a *male* friend she has had since childhood), or dog has died. Being

296

diagnosed with a terminal illness would also warrant tears. If a woman cries in front of you for pretty much any other reason, such as *stress* or the loss of her male partner, she is very likely either weak or manipulative. You should avoid weak or manipulative people—men and women—to the greatest extent possible. They can be trouble.

As for men, give them the *dead-kid/dead-dog pass* as well. Men are vastly more likely to be attached to the women in their lives than the other way around, so extending some sympathy to a man whose wife was hit by a bus a few hours prior is reasonable. That does not mean his alleged grief should be accepted as an excuse for behavior that is out of bounds.

You also might give men a certain emotional allowance if they lose their jobs. Ideally, men would not invest so much of their identity into their jobs that they are deeply traumatized by the loss of them. Any other displays of extreme emotionalism on the part of men should be regarded as signs of psychological instability. Avoid such men just as you would unstable and manipulative women.

Practice Displaying Indifference

One of the great weaknesses of American culture is that we are taught to care (or *pretend to care*) about almost everything. To counteract this, you will need to practice displaying indifference. This is different from *rudeness*. You can still maintain the appearance of etiquette without suggesting that you care. This is largely about *tone*. Develop a certain consistency of speech that suggests that your emotions are not affected much one way or the other by what happens to most of the people around you. Bear the Mantra in mind wherever you go, and sensible behavior will follow naturally.

297

Even when you *do* have an empathetic response, try to avoid displaying it openly. In an ideal world, displays of concern for others would not be punished, but we do not live in an ideal world. The more empathetic you seem, the more others will be disposed to assume you are a sucker.

If you give anything to charity, do it anonymously. Otherwise, you will risk ending up on one of *those lists*—the lists that charities sell to each other of whom they can hit up for money time and again.

Practice Dropping People

Is there anyone in your life who is more trouble than he (or she) is worth? A problematic girlfriend? A relative who is always begging for (or demanding) money? For many of us, getting rid of these tenacious ticks and fierce fleas is difficult. They know how to manipulate—usually with guilt, flattery, fear, calls upon the better angels of your nature, or some combination of the aforementioned. These people will wear you down and bleed you dry.

Drop them. Drop them now.

Dropping people requires a certain bastardry, particularly if the people you are trying to drop appeal to your generosity to extract resources from you. But dropping them is worth doing. You may be able to run these people out of your life by simply ceasing to help them. Some will be too persistent for this to work. You may need to move out of state or country. Some will argue that the last is impossible for them—that they cannot move. This sentiment is understandable, but unless you have a truly unusual job or have tenure, chances are that you can find some other way to pay your bills in a far-off community. This may take great effort, but freeing yourself from tons of dead weight is one of the most liberating things you can. Bastards know this.

And if you move, be willing to drop *everyone*. Failing to do this is what gets criminals caught after they have otherwise made perfectly clean getaways. They simply cannot resist the urge to check in on someone from *the neighborhood*. This is how the FBI finds them. And this is how your personal parasites will find you if you lack the resolve to remain true to your bastard nature.

Practice Extreme Bluntness

Practice being blunt at least once a day. Even if it is only over a small matter—*This deal is terrible* or *No, son, I am not impressed. Any moron can get a participation trophy*—cultivating bluntness is worth doing. This may not even qualify as being a *bastard*. It may just qualify as practice in being *anything other than an American*. The Chinese have no great problem with bluntness. The French are, well, French. The Israelis have all the subtlety of a sledgehammer wielded by a drunkard with a bath-salts habit.

What we may perceive as *being a bastard*, anyone anywhere else on earth might well perceive as just *being normal*. Nevertheless, the notion that *bluntness = bastard* is an integral part of American thought, so for the purposes of a largely American readership, bluntness has a place in this chapter.

The Balanced Bastard: Pragmatism and Bastardry

Friends and allies are great, but they are only useful if you remember the principle of *consideration—give something; get something*. And there is no reason that a bastard cannot have a certain number of friends. And a (reasonably) honest bastard, might well be one of the best friends a man can have, if only because he will be refreshingly, efficiently direct. But just as the bastard is bold whenever feasible, he is cautious whenever necessary, particularly when at risk of attracting parasites and hangers-on.

299

Whatever your goals are, you need to keep them first and foremost in your mind, and you need to pursue them aggressively. Remember that most people are quite indifferent to you, and generally, they are not obligated to be otherwise. The goals that are pushed upon you—the things you are told to want—are rarely for your benefit. Either they are the odd vestiges of an earlier era— they continue to be done simply because they *have been done* for a long time—or they are designed to turn you into a sucker. Many habits and activities are promoted by different segments of society so that you may better serve *their ends*, not your own. And a fair number of the promoters are already bigger, better bastards than most of us could ever hope to be.

Rather than focusing on the desires of others, keep *your goals* in mind. If you do not, who will? Apply the Rules, and friendship, business, and life should all balance out.

The Thinking Man

(Ten Questions for Review and Consideration)

1. How would you define *a bastard* in your own words?

   _____

   _____

   _____

2. What are some advantages to being a bastard?

   _____

   _____

   _____

3. How can being nice hurt *you* and those around you?

   _____

   _____

   _____

4. Is anyone harmless? Why might supposedly harmless people become dangerous?

   _____

   _____

   _____

301

5. How much tolerance do you have for dealing with the public?

_____

_____

_____

6. What is one part of your life that could be improved by your being a bastard?

_____

_____

_____

7. Is there anyone whom you would like to drop from your life? If yes, *why*, and *how* can you go about doing so?

_____

_____

_____

8. Would being painfully blunt make any part of your daily life better? If so, what part?

_____

_____

_____

9. Who is your favorite bastard, real or fictional?

_____

_____

_____

10. How does being a bastard make following the Rules easier? (Try to tie being a bastard to each of the Rules. Doing so should not be terribly difficult.)

_____

_____

_____

15) On Liberation

The smartest wardens are tricksters. The prison with bars, walls, and guard towers has a weakness: The men confined therein *know* that there is a world beyond their circumscribed existences, they *know* that world is forbidden to them, and as is the case with all things forbidden, a life outside the gates becomes all the more tempting.

But those with a certain carceral aptitude can decorate the bars with ivy and trumpet vine, can camouflage walls—paint them so that they look to be something else entirely—and can hide the guards in ghillie suits. Those with a true genius need not do even these things. Rather, they can, through pure force of persuasion, convince the inmates that all these things are for their protection. The walls become *security barriers*; the guards, *dutiful sentries*; and the bars, *the last line of defense from a cruel and destructive world*. The inmates are not inmates anymore. They are *guests*, and they should pay for the privilege of their protection.

And then there are the chains—*jewelry*, so claims the warden/ host. See them for what they are, and only then can you tear them away.

1. The chain of addiction—that binds you to the notion that you cannot achieve peace of mind without a fix, be it gambling, drugs, alcohol, or sex, that keeps you dependent on those who provide these things

2. The chain of compulsory concern—that binds you to the notion that you must care

3. The chain of consumption—that binds you to the notion that you are what you consume, even though almost

everything you consume is obsolete from the moment you purchase it and you will keep none of your prizes for any length of time

4. The chain of false hope—that binds you to the notion you that someday, if you just buy enough, waste enough, or work enough, somehow everything will be okay, even though nothing is ever truly okay—things simply are—and *someday* is a fiction that will never arrive

5. The chain of ownership—that binds you to the notion that you own anything or have more than the temporary use of anything, even though anything you own can be taken without a moment's notice

6. The chain of possible longevity—that binds you to the notion that, if you just take enough pills, run to the doctor frequently enough, and hunker down in a corner, avoiding all risks, you will be able to postpone death indefinitely

7. The chain of romantic love—that binds you to the notion that *someday* some woman will regard you as the center of her universe, she will become the center of yours, and this mutual fixation is somehow *good*

8. The chain of sex—that binds you to the notion, not just that you can have sex (which anyone can do for the right price), but that the sex should be fantastic, frequent, and free of obligations and that without sex you are less of a man

9. The chains of shame and status—that bind you to the notion that what other people think of you is more than a short-lived combination of electrical and chemical signals in the brains of those around you

10. The chain of utility—that binds you to the notions that your only value is your ability to serve others and that your career and your role as a provider are all that you are

Ten chains, each one of them heavy, each one of them made of links stronger than steel, heavier than gold, and harder to melt than tungsten—these are what bind you to the people and systems that will gladly take what that you have and leave you for dead, all while heaping scorn and ridicule upon you. These are what keep you bound to the prison walls. *How can you snap the chains?* What should you do, and just as importantly, what you should you avoid doing so that you may achieve the closest any man may get to freedom?

Do not: Flaunt your resources or abilities/
Do: Keep a low profile

Conspicuous consumption hurts you in three ways. First, it causes you to burn through your resources faster than you otherwise would. Second, it acclimates you to dedicating effort to making an impression on others, which leads to a greater psychological investment in *status*. Third, it may well attract the wrong sort of attention. Flash your money around long enough and people of the worst sort *will* notice you. These people want only to exploit you, and whatever it is that you flaunted will be taken away in short order. Flaunting your abilities is not much smarter.

Would you walk around the most dangerous neighborhood imaginable wearing gold and diamond rings and a sign that says *I am a totally helpless idiot. I do not know how to defend myself or call the police. Please do not rob me*, or would you rather not? If your answer is *rather not*, you obviously have enough sense to know that making a show of your assets is not a good idea. If you actually *would* do as much, there is no hope for you.

306

Never try to make people jealous, not with what you own, not with what you can do, not with the strength of your mind or body, and not with your social or professional connections. There is little upside to cultivating envy in the hearts of others. Doing so may give you a very short-lived sense of smug glee, but you pay a high price for this—by making yourself a target.

Do not: Buy more house than you need/
Do: Consider buying an RV

The average American home is simply too large—an absolute albatross for the average man.[1] Remember, homes are not really investments, and due to current market distortions resulting from an overabundance of credit, a great many of them are overpriced, oversized, and shoddily built.[2] If you *do* want to buy a home, waiting a few years—until the bulk of the Baby Boomers have lurched off to the great classic rock concert in the sky—will serve you well. There should be a veritable glut of extra-large houses, extra-padded furniture, and extra-collectible Allman Brothers memorabilia for the lowest of low prices.

Here is another one: Buy a recreational vehicle (RV).

Consider a few points. First, you need somewhere to live. Second, you need transportation. Third, you may need to move at any time, and the less mobility you have, the more beholden you are to others.

An RV addresses each of these problems perfectly. An RV gives you a place to live. An RV *is* a form of transportation, and an RV gives you the ability to relocate at the drop of a hat.

Consider how many men have been made slaves to their employers because *they (the men) thought could not afford move.* This makes a man vulnerable, and any employer with the slightest

307

bit of sense knows as much. The more vulnerable others think you are, the more likely they are to mistreat you. Having a massive debt around your neck (and nowhere else to go) is no less disabling than having your legs broken. With an RV, however, the highway is your home, and you can easily migrate to wherever your interests and opportunities take you.

Owning an RV is not free. Gas, taxes, and insurance can all add up, but if you follow the conventional approach to life, you will need to pay for all of these for your car *and* pay taxes, insurance, and utilities on your house. Remember you *do not* own a home. No one does. No one owns *anything* in the immutable, permanent sense of the word. We only have the use of things. Learn to regard your residence, be it on stilts, a brick foundation, or wheels, pragmatically, rather than as a sign of who or what you are.

Do not: Care unless you choose to care/
Do: Learn to be direct

Some good points are worth repeating, the Mantra most of all:

YOU ARE NEVER OBLIGATED TO CARE.

There are no exceptions to this. You may sometimes be compelled to *provide* care (money or labor), but you are never obligated to care.

Here is another point worth remembering: An honest man is hard to con.

How do these two fit together?

Your capacity to care is limited. You must prioritize. The problem arises when you get in the habit of pretending to care. Here are some issues about which I do not care at all:

1. The rain forests

308

2. The availability of shellfish in Argentinian coastal regions

3. The quality of bait available at any convenience stores in Hell, Michigan (which proved to be a surprisingly pleasant small town the last time I visited it)

4. The women (or *womyn*, if you prefer)

5. The children (particularly when preceded by *won't somebody please think of . . .*)

6. The opinions of more than 99.999999% of the 7.7 billion people on the planet[3]

7. Whatever peculiar ideology or faddish claptrap is floating around academia today

8. Demographic, racial, and ethnic shifts *anywhere*

Of course, this is a partial list. The complete list of matters about which I am indifferent would be a book in and of itself. You may care about some of these things. If so, fine. You may not care about any of them. That is fine as well. Care about whatever suits you. *Do not* care as it suits you. Make no apologies for it. I know all of the irritating counterarguments, and I suspect you do as well. *If you do not care, who will? Who will make our world a better place?*

Whoever is asking the question, I suppose. Let them deal with it. Or not.

The point is that we—American men—have been beaten down and shamed by those who insist that we must care about this, that, or the other. We cannot and should not care about *everything and everyone*. As for the *woke folk* (and their cousins on the right, whoever they are), one would be wise to regard them with suspicion. Feigned compassion is the bastion of scoundrels.

The truth is that I *do care* about some select things and people. I *would* be willing to help them, and sometimes I have, occasionally quite a bit. I do have some interests and concerns, and I tend to those with effort and diligence. At best, one's passions may be a mile wide and a foot deep or a foot wide and a mile deep. Often, they are a foot wide and equally shallow. But deep and wide they cannot be. Diversity of interests is a wonderful thing, but only to a point. No man is island. No man is an ocean either. Only so much water can be drawn from the pools of love, time, energy, and life.

But if you care about nothing, that is fine as well.

YOU ARE NEVER OBLIGATED TO CARE.

To switch to a drier metaphor: Break this chain of compulsory concern. It is a heavy one, and strongly made, so breaking it will not be easy, but such is the case for most worthwhile endeavors.

Do not: Marry your job/
Do: Learn marketable skills and build revenue streams

We all know men married to their jobs. Some of them really are bound by economics—either they work or they starve—but their prospects are rarely as limited as they may think them to be. If a man has no wife or children (or has grown children and no wife), he should have a quite a bit flexibility as to what he does for a living. From a practical standpoint, most of us can regard our work as a way to pay our bills, nothing more and nothing less, and paying our bills should not be at all that difficult if we plan carefully.

Even if your job does matter, you are better off not becoming a *company* man. Work on developing multiple sources of income and aggressively strive to reduce your expenses. If you spend less, you can make less and still be okay.

Whatever it is that you do, there must be *something* else you can do to make a living. If you build things, start a side business taking on small projects. If you push a pencil for a living, look into ghostwriting or editing. If you really cannot do anything, consider learning something, be it house painting or more highly skilled labor. The point is this:

ALWAYS HAVE A PLAN B.

ALWAYS HAVE SEVERAL REVENUE STREAMS.

The greater the number of revenue streams you have, the less vulnerable you are. Diversifying your earnings sources is probably the single best thing you can do to put yourself in a stronger financial and psychological position.

Do not: Entertain false hope/
Do: Look for convenient ways to improve your life

Sometimes, hope is not warranted.

Things *may not* get better. You may never get that promotion. No one may ever love you. Even your dog may think you are an irredeemable ass. Additional education may do you no good. And death may be the only cure for what ails you.

Fantasy keeps men weak. It prevents them from moving forward, from effectively cutting their losses, from focusing on what is in front of them *now*. It makes them supremely stupid. Have you ever known a man to cling to a job he hates? Have you ever known a man to refuse to sell a house he obviously cannot afford? Have you ever known a man to get married four times? Have you ever known a man to try to reclaim youth lost decades ago?

311

If so, you have seen misery and suffering sprung of damnable hope.

Long is the list of people and industries with an incentive or two to keep you deluded—of betting on odds that make playing the state lottery a viable retirement program by comparison. Self-deception is the bedrock on which marketing is built. *Buy this magical pill, and look and feel young again, be rid of all your maladies, improve your sex life, and gain 60 IQ points (per day)!* Such an example may seem a bit extreme, but not by much. Stop wasting time trying to improve that which is unimprovable and you may actually be able to make your life better.

Here is a simple, easy-to-understand question that you should ask yourself every 24 hours or so: *What can I do before the end of this day to make it less miserable and more comfortable than the one before?*

And then answer it. And follow your own good advice.

Do not: Base your sense of self-worth on the opinions of others, especially women/
Do: Develop a proven sense of self

Boys in the West are taught to seek the approval and validation of women for much of what they do. This is odd. That adult men continue to do this is a testament to the power of acclimation and (quite possibly) the power of Stockholm syndrome.

A boy would do better to form his identity on the opinions of men than on those of women, but he would be wiser still to build an identity based on actual accomplishment—on finding out what he can do and what he is, rather than what others *think* he can do or what he is. It is great for a boy (and then a man) to have friends to whom he may turn in his times of trouble, but *no one* should be

312

able to dictate to a man what he should think of himself. He who has tried, failed, tried again, and eventually succeeded—even if his failures vastly outnumber his successes—has a huge psychological and informational advantage over the emotionally dependent and codependent.

The accomplished man knows what he is capable of doing and not doing *based on experience*. Actual experiential knowledge is far more valuable than speculation. Thus, the accomplished man's sense of self is also considerably more stable than that of the man who has done little. A man may appreciate having his friends and colleagues tell him that they think he would be a good mountain climber, but whatever happiness kind words give him is likely to pale in comparison to the far more substantial happiness and sense of accomplishment he stands to gain from looking down from the majesty of the summit.

Opinions change as easily as the wind, but for a man to know that he has overcome and triumphed gives him a pride that cannot be easily taken away. Finally, he who has built his sense of self upon experiential knowledge, not the criticism, condemnation, or speculation of others, has *learned how to fail*, which is one of the most valuable skills a person can acquire.[4]

Anything significant, anything in which a person can take pride for a lifetime, comes with a significant risk of failure. If it (whatever *it* is) is easy, there is no pride to be had from it. Trying that which is worthwhile will almost certainly lead to failure. You may *not* be able to climb that mountain. You may *not* be able to learn Korean. You may *not* become a good guitarist or write a great book. Even if you do succeed, there is almost certainly going to be a tremendous amount of frustration along the way. Let us say that you write a potentially bestselling book, the kind that will be read by millions over the course of decades. *Zen and the Art of Motorcycle Maintenance*, a national bestseller in the 1970s, was rejected more than 100 times before a publisher finally accepted it, and *Carrie*, a bestseller by the extraordinarily successful Stephen King, was rejected 30 times.[5] The resilience that comes from efforts of this sort cannot be gained by way of mere talk.

Worrying about what men think you can do will make you miserable. Worrying about what women think you can do will make you psychotic. Worrying about what *no one* thinks you can do, because you know *from experience* what you can do (and what you are), will make you strong, stable, and realistic.

Do not: Obsess over your health/
Do: Avoid becoming medically dependent

Here is a point I have made more than once: YOU ARE GOING TO DIE!

Medicine *may* be able to delay this process somewhat, but it is just as likely to speed it up. Medicine is somewhat of a crapshoot.

Your best strategy is to try to stay out of the hospital and the doctor's office as long as possible. Doing this does not require any unreasonable efforts on your part. Other than a sensible diet, moderate amounts of exercise, and avoiding the never-ending and soul-raping hell that a great many long-term romantic relationship is likely to be, there is not that much you need to do. Do not put your hand into a wood chipper. Do not grab live high-voltage power lines. Do not drink or drug yourself into oblivion. Do not drive it like you stole it (unless you really did steal it, in which case, you might want to drive especially cautiously, lest you draw the attention of the police). Beyond that, there is really is not much for you to do.

314

Do not: Medicate yourself to oblivion (unless all hope is lost)/
Do: Get to the root of the problem

Drinking and drugging recreationally is quite a bit different from drinking and drugging to ease the pain of existence. While the decision to drink or drug is a personal one, alcohol and drug use is not a good *first-line* strategy to address problems readily (and more effectively) addressed through other means.

Before you decide to undertake a one-man reenactment of *Leaving Las Vegas* (which is even less joyful than the film—no golden-hearted hooker), ask yourself a question: *What makes me miserable, and can I free myself from it?* More often than not, there *is* a solution. Sometimes, the solution is *more or better*— more money, a better place to live, better transportation, et cetera. Just as often, the answer is *less*—less interaction with other people, less self-deception, less time spent trying to accommodate others, or less in the way of unneeded possessions to maintain.

If you can free yourself from the other chains that bind you— those of consumption, ownership, shame, or status—you will likely find that chain of addiction falls away on its own.

Do not: Take pride or shame in your sex drive/
Do: Figure out how much you are willing to pay to get laid

Straight men pay for sex.

Regardless of whatever feminist or counter-scientific nonsense you have read about women wanting sex, you should never lose sight of the fact that sex with a woman, regardless of her looks, age, desirability, or lack thereof, will cost you *something*. There is no way around this. Anyone who claims otherwise is either a fool or is out to screw you (and not in an enjoyable way). The decision to pursue sex (or not) is entirely up to you. Just bear in mind that

315

every time you have sex with a woman, a transaction is occurring. This transaction probably will not be *sex in exchange for love*. It will only in the most extraordinary of circumstances be *sex in exchange for sex* (unless you have a remarkably high HSP score). That simply is not the way the world works. You may pay in time. You may pay in money. You *will* pay in liability. You may pay in all of these ways or in some way that may not be immediately apparent.

Some deals are fair. Some deals are not. *Fair* is largely in the eye of the beholder. The critical point is that you understand the nature of the deal. You should carefully consider the price. Sex is a luxury service. There is nothing wrong with luxury services or products. Flying first class can be great if you have the money. Eating at a fine restaurant run by a celebrity chef might be wonderful as well.

What *is* a bad idea is buying luxury products or services with money you cannot afford to spend simply so that you *may* impress other people. *This* behavior is the mark of a sucker. Only suckers try to impress with conspicuous consumption, because only suckers believe anyone cares about what they buy or consume. You are not your purchases. You are not what you consume. All conspicuous consumption proves is that you are desperate for approval. The same goes for sex. Having it because you enjoy it is fine (assuming you have considered the price). Having it to wow others with your prowess is merely a form of conspicuous consumption.

Remember all of these things when asking yourself the critical question: *Exactly how much am I willing to pay to have sex with a particular woman?*

Set an upper limit in your mind *before* you start negotiations, not after. And beware of purported freebies. In reality, free lunches are more common by orders of magnitude than are free sexual encounters.

Do not: Believe the myth of romantic love/
Do: Make friends

Romantic love is so antithetical to reason that it would be taken as a sign of mental illness were it to emerge today, rather than having been grandfathered into our culture from an earlier time. This idea that someone should love or be loved deeply simply because *that is the way the world should work* is, at best, incoherent. Even worse is the notion that you are exciting/moral/fantastic enough to be someone's be-all and end-all. Most people, even the best, are not interesting. Chaining your happiness to that of another person is bound to make both of you miserable. One could attack the idea in the abstract, but a better approach is to simply ask *why?*

Why should anyone else consider you the center of her world?

Why should you consider anyone else the center of your world?

This leads to another question:

What makes either you or a given woman think that you (or she) is so overwhelmingly special that *anyone* should be all that concerned with the happiness of either of you?

The questions differ, but one word answers them all:

Arrogance!

Why do you think someone should consider you the center of her world?

317

Arrogance! For you to believe that anyone should consider you great (or even highly interesting) is arrogant. For the purposes of any sexual relationship, you can be easily enough replaced.

Why should you consider anyone else the center of your world?

Arrogance! For a woman to believe that you should consider her great (or even highly interesting) is arrogant. For the purposes of any sexual relationship, she can be easily enough replaced.

What makes either you or a given woman think that you (or she) is so overwhelmingly special that *anyone* should consider either of you highly interesting or be all that concerned with the happiness of either of you?

Arrogance!

The reason that the notion of romantic love has survived as long as it has is that it plays to our egos. This belief that each and every one of us *deserves* great concern from another person is baffling in that it suggests that *you* are great and *your lover is* great. According to the assumptions underlying romantic love, we *all* are great. Greatness, much like tallness, is relative. If everyone is great, greatness has no meaning.

This is miles apart from the belief in a god of boundless love, whose concern for humanity is not a testament to the greatness of people, but to the greatness of the deity. A god of this sort loves people *despite* their flaws, not because of them. This is far less absurd than the idea that everyone *deserves* to be loved by someone else.

Someone *should* care about you. Someone *should* be dedicated to improving your life. Someone *should* think that *you matter.* That person is *you. The world does not owe you a damned thing.*

That includes love. The only person who owes *you* real concern *is you*.

The other appeal to romance is that it puts each of us in our own little dramas. Not everyone likes drama, but enough people do so that this is a major draw. Life can be boring, particularly for those who lack the initiative to test themselves or cultivate any interests, so the petty intrigues, the hurt feelings, and the occasional blowup add at least *the possibility* of a break from the tedium of life. Eventually, many tire of such high-school nonsense, but some do not, and even those who do, may take quite a few years to abandon the last traces of their adolescent mindsets.

Ideally, you can and will make friends who are concerned with your welfare, but friendship is about as similar to romance as sugar is to gasoline. They share a common trait—high caloric density in the case of sugar/gasoline and emotional involvement in the case of friendship/romance—but they are not interchangeable. Good friendships are built and earned over time. Like most things of value, they are very rarely given.

I offer no more in the way of *do/do not* statements. Instead, I urge you to consider a fundamental truth:

Everything is a Transaction

You may have friends, and you may have allies, but let us be honest on this point: All interaction is transaction. And that is fine. *Give something; get something.* The question is if you are getting a deal that is fair to you.

Let us think back to what I wrote some pages before. The Rules are a rational strategy to getting what you want. You *give as little as possible*: That is the way you conserve your time and effort, both of which you recognize are valuable. You *take as much*

319

as possible: That is essential to getting the best deal. You *always have an exit*: The man without an exit is vulnerable. He is backed into a corner. He becomes desperate, and the desperate cannot negotiate well. And you *enjoy your life to the fullest*: Doing otherwise is a waste of life.

But to make effective use of the Rules, you *must* know what you want. You must know yourself, and you must remember the sheer indifference of the world. The petty symbols others offer you in exchange for your life and time are rarely worth much. Break free of this connection to symbols. Do so as soon as possible.

So now that you have learned how to follow the Rules—how to take the clay of your life and shape it according to your will, as much as it can be shaped by human hands—what do you do?

How will you make use of your newfound freedom?

What will you do for yourself *today*?

The Thinking Man

(Ten Questions for Review and Consideration)

1. What are some disadvantages of letting others know about your resources or abilities? Do these outweigh the advantages (if there are any)?

    _____

    _____

    _____

2. Aside from buying a conventional house, renting an apartment or house, or buying an RV, can you think of any ways to provide yourself with an adequate place to stay for a reasonable price?

    _____

    _____

    _____

3. What is one popular cause or issue about which many people *claim* to care but about which you do not? Do you believe that many of the people who claim to care about this issue actually do?

    _____

    _____

    _____

4. Other than your current job, what is way you could make money (an alternate revenue stream)? If you cannot think of anything at the moment, what would be something you could *learn* to do in a reasonable period of time that would allow you to make money?

_____

_____

_____

5. What is one thing you can do to make today and tomorrow less miserable and more comfortable than yesterday?

_____

_____

_____

6. What do you *do* (or have you done) that gives you a sense of pride and self-worth independent of the opinions of others? If you cannot think of anything, what is something you *could* do (or learn to do) that would give you a sense of pride or self-worth?

_____

_____

_____

7. What is a reasonable length of time for a man to live? What would you consider to be a sensible lifespan target *for you*? Try to think of this in terms of years, rather than providing an open-ended answer.

_____

_____

_____

8. If you do drink or use drugs, why? If you do so mainly to medicate your way out of a problem, are there any steps you could take to solve this underlying issue?

_____

_____

_____

9. Imagine you meet a woman whom you consider to be a solid 8 /10 aesthetically, you find her to have a tolerable personality, and she seems at least somewhat willing to have sex with you. How much would you be willing to pay (in terms of time, money, and risk) to have sex with this woman *today*? Assume for the sake of this hypothetical that you are not currently involved with another woman.

_____

_____

_____

10. Other than those already mentioned in this chapter, does anything else bind you to a life of misery? If so, what are these chains and how can you break free of them?

_____

_____

_____

Conclusion

This is a book of hope—hope of the *realistic* sort.

The world of our fathers' has passed into darkness. You cannot *uncook* the burger. Community has collapsed. Long-term and stable employment is but a distant memory for those old enough to remember it. For the rest of us, it is myth. The family, at least as historically defined, fares not much better. This is fine. Life is what it is. Death, the same. Let the dead bury the dead.

There is hope.

We may well be dominated by abusive, intrusive, overbearing, and soul-crushing bureaucracies, ideologues, and corporate interests, yet they cannot know all. They cannot see all. Their powers are limited. Their powers are less than they would have us believe.

The marketers, the Marxists, the utopianists, and the feminists won—they won *half* the war. They annihilated one civilization so that they could build another on the ashen ruins. They have built things. They have built a great many of them, and some of that which they have built *looks* quite impressive.

But all they have constructed stands on an assumption—that you may *react*, that you may *fight*, but that you will eventually comply.

They never thought you would adapt. They never considered the possibility that you could. For this, they have no plan. Here is the problem with deluded dreamers and their fantastical castles: In their wild imaginings, no one but the dreamer has agency. No matter how psychedelic the view behind their eyelids, one fact

325

remains—dreamers think that only they have souls. Everyone else is but an automaton or a piece to be moved around a board.

In the long run, the strongest—the best suited to a given environment or task—lose out to the most adaptable. Remember that when you hear some fool brag of momentary success. You can adapt. You can prosper, but it will not be easy. So long as the world is not engulfed in flames, all is not lost. So long as you keep breathing, you probably need not despair.

Your adversaries and oppressors are well-funded, well-trained, and well-equipped—*good for them, bad for you!* They are also rigid, singularly unacclimated to hardship, and lacking in creativity —*bad for them, good for you!* They can excel when they make all the rules, so long as they can change the rules whenever doing so suits them.

But you have rules of your own. You have the Rules.

So how do you win?

First, stop deceiving yourself and stop believing the lies of others. The standards and expectations to which you are told to hold yourself are as contradictory as they are insane. Efforts to shame and manipulate you into compliance can be identified as such, dissected, and rendered harmless.

Second, learn to distinguish between that which you *have been told you* want and that which you *really* want. After that, setting priorities for yourself is easy.

Third, starve the beast. Work every day to *take more from* and *give less to* the people and systems that would destroy you.

Fourth, take the path of liberation. It has been opened for you, ironically enough, by those who wish you to remain in bondage. You have been given an entire corridor filled with exits. *Know where they are and how to open them, always.* With few exceptions, men surrender their freedom before it is taken from them. Do not be one of those men.

Life has been hard for the vast majority of people (men and women) in every country, in every culture, and in every era. Aside from the inherent brutality of nature, much of what made life hard for men was the effort they needed to expend to support and aid others. The technologists, inventors, and scientists did much to free humanity from labor and drudgery. The ideologues did also, but quite without intent or understanding. That the efforts of the former have improved our lives is obvious, that the efforts of the latter did is less so.

Marriage, family, religious traditions, employer/employee loyalty, established social obligations and connections—soon nuclear shadows and history books will be the last extant testaments to their existences. Even the books will mold and decay in time.

Here is the thing about winning half a war: The supposedly triumphant also lost half of it. If he (or it) really *won* at all is debatable. That matter is not settled.

So now you stand with eyes clear and open. Your enemies may see you, but they cannot see what you have become—a free man, capable of thinking for himself. Their ignorance is your advantage.

Do not waste this opportunity to enjoy your short and precious existence. Follow the Rules. Apply them to all that you do. Beware of tyrants. You owe this to yourself. To others, you owe respect for their rights. And unless you have *chosen* to obligate yourself to another, you owe no one else anything at all.

You are free. This is your life. Fight for it. Win.

Notes
0) Introduction

(1) Knowing what occurs in the mind of another is a challenge no one—neither scientist, sage, nor charlatan—has met with much success. But outcomes *can* be measured. It is worth noting, however, that complaints of misogyny in higher education continue, despite women outnumbering men in the student population.

Apparently, women's higher college graduation rates are the fault of the patriarchy—a sexist power structure constructed expressly for the oppression of women that, paradoxically, benefits women. An interesting notion indeed:

Guo, J. (2014, December 11) **Women are dominating men at college. Blame sexism.** *Washington Post*. Retrieved from https://www.washingtonpost.com/

Next is an article written by a (somewhat) respected academic. It is not indicative of the views of all women in higher education, but the fact that it was published in one of America's largest newspapers, apparently without overriding editorial objection, says much about the mindset of those in education and journalism. (*Why don't you tell us how you really feel, sweetheart?*):

Walter, S.D. (2018, June 8). **Why can't we hate men?** *Washington Post*. Retrieved from https://www.washingtonpost.com/

Just as importantly, the article serves as a cautionary note on the wages of being an overly accommodating husband.

Meanwhile, a considerably milder argument that certain academic institutions and practices may be biased in favor of women leads to a leading (male) professor being suspended:

Erickson, A. (2018, October 2). An Italian professor set out to prove 'physics was built by men.' He ended up suspended. *Washington Post*. Retrieved from https://www.washingtonpost.com/

As for biases in academia (and elsewhere) against men and the origin of these, an entire book has been written on the matter:

Sommers, C.H. (2000). *The war against boys: How misguided feminism is hurting our young men*. New York, NY: Touchstone.

(2) Women, oppressed creatures that they are, make most (85%) consumer purchasing decisions. Also note the products for men marketed to women (as they are the ones doing the buying):

Ekaterina W. (2012, March, 19). Marketing to women: How to get it right. *Fast Company*. Retrieved from https://www.fastcompany.com/

(3) The decision to use "owe you a *damn* thing" rather than "owe you a *damned* thing" was not made lightly. I opted for *damn thing* after checking usage trends throughout the 20th century. Prior to the 1930s (1933, according to the Google Books Ngram Viewer), *damned thing* seemed to have a slight edge over *damn*). After that, *damn* took the lead. By 1980, *damn thing* was the clear winner. *Ambrose Bierce* wrote the "The Damned Thing" (1893) whereas Johnny Cash said, "Success is having to worry about every damn thing in the world, except money." Choose whichever one you prefer. *Language is just the damnedest thing, is it not?*

Cash, J. (n.d.). "Success is having to worry about every damn thing in the world, except money." *AZ Quotes*. Retrieved from https://www.azquotes.com/

(4)

Consideration. (2015, September 12). *Legal Dictionary*. Retrieved from https://legaldictionary.net/

(5)

Alter, C. (2016, April 22). U.S. suicide rate rising precipitously, especially among women. *Time*. Retrieved from https://time.com/

(6)

Smith, H. (2013). *Men on strike: Why men are boycotting marriage, fatherhood, and the American dream—and why it matters*. New York, NY: Encounter Books.

1) The Rules

(1) *Maximax*, *Maximin*, and *Minimax* game theories are fairly easy to understand. Stanford University provides pleasantly accessible explanations:

Chen, J., Lu, S., & Vekhter, D. (n.d.). Strategies of play. Retrieved from https://cs.stanford.edu/people/eroberts/courses/ soco/projects/1998-99/game-theory/Minimax.html

(2) Social mobility and earnings have declined considerably over the last generation, and a growing number of Americans (and citizens of other developed countries) will end up poorer than their parents:

Dobbs, R., Madgavkar, A., Manyika, J., Woetzel, J., Bughin, J., Labaye, E., . . . Kashyap, P. (2016, July). Poorer than their parents? Flat or falling incomes in advanced economies. *McKinsey Global Institute*. Retrieved from https://www.mckinsey.com/

Davis, J., & Mazumder, B. (2017, July). The decline in intergenerational mobility after 1980 (WP 2017-05). *Federal Reserve Bank of Chicago*. Retrieved from https://www.chicagofed.org/

(3) Keeping up with one's neighbors increasingly means keeping up with their debt accumulation, buying on credit what previous generations might well have bought with cash:

Andriotis, A., Brown, K., & Shifflett, S. (2019, August 1). Families
go deep in debt to stay in the middle class. *The Wall Street
Journal*. Retrieved from https://www.wsj.com/

(4) Work as religion—*workism*—appears to be more a part of American culture than that of some others. It can affect women, but it is more integral to the lives of wealthy men than anyone else. Perhaps this—constant work—is why they are wealthy. Either way, treating work as religion stands to make a man vulnerable:

Thompson, D. (2019, February 24). Workism is making Americans
miserable. *The Atlantic*. Retrieved from
https://www.theatlantic.com/

To the surprise of no one even vaguely familiar with modern American culture, these hard-working men are resented. After all, they make women look bad:

Thompson, D. (2016, April 27). Too many elite American men are
obsessed with work and wealth. *The Atlantic*. Retrieved from
https://www.theatlantic.com/

2) The Lists

(1) A few decades before watchmaker and inventor Pierre Jaquet-Droz built his first automatons, Jacques de Vaucanson constructed his mechanical duck. The creation, much like those of Jaquet-Droz, was surprisingly lifelike:

Andrews, E. (2018, August 30). 7 early robots and automatons.
History.com. Retrieved from https://www.history.com/

(2) Everything from pointless social customs to elaborate religious practices was categorized as *conspicuous consumption* by Thorstein Veblen, the developer of the concept. One of the most curious points of American culture is that Veblen's *leisure class* now readily engages in conspicuous consumption, just as described, but without much in the way of leisure. The leisure class just so happens to be not very leisurely at all. Nevertheless, the Veblen's

book makes for a better (and more amusing) read than one might expect:

Veblen, T. (1899). *The theory of the leisure class*. London, England: Macmillan & Co. Ltd. Retrieved from http://www.gutenberg.org/

(3) Since *Kelo v. City of New London*, 545 U.S. 469 (2005), the government (local, state, or federal) can seize private land for essentially *any* reason. Despite the Fifth Amendment specifically stating that "nor shall private property be taken for public use, without just compensation," private property can be condemned through eminent domain and immediately transferred from one private owner to another.

For example, it would be entirely constitutional for a city government to seize your home, pay you whatever it deems it to be worth, and immediately convey title to a car dealership so that it can expand its sales lot.

Although lawful use of civil asset forfeiture was somewhat restricted by *Timbs v. Indiana*, 586 U.S. ___ (2019), government agencies still have relatively broad powers of seizure. For those curious as to *how* broad it was until 2019, I would refer them to a few articles on the matter, both of which demonstrate the naked greed of a great deal of drug-related law enforcement:

Brown, P. (2014, September 8). Parents' house seized after son's drug bust. *CNN*. Retrieved from https://www.cnn.com/

Anderson, A. (2015, June 9). After the government takes his life savings, this 22-year-old fights for justice. *The Daily Signal*. Retrieved from https://www.dailysignal.com/

Even now, civil asset forfeiture powers are still stronger than those with a concern for property rights might hope:

Andersson, E. (2019, March 15). The Supreme Court didn't put the nail in civil asset forfeiture's coffin. *ACLU*. Retrieved from https://www.aclu.org/blog/

As for the other matters—loss of property during divorce, et cetera—they should be familiar to anyone who has ever even known a divorced man.

(4) I explore the concepts of self-imprisonment and voluntary bondage more in Chapter 15 ("On Liberation").

(5) Although the evidence is not conclusive, there is some research to support the notion that men (at least in the West) pay more in taxes than do women, and generally receive less in return:

Aziz, O., Gemmell, N., & Laws, A. (2013, June). The distribution of income and fiscal incidence by age and gender: Some evidence from New Zealand. *Victoria University of Wellington*. Retrieved from https://papers.ssrn.com/

(6) I have based the length of this list on research by Robin Dunbar, the originator of the *Dunbar's Number*, which is really a series of numbers. Dunbar theorized that one can have a maximum of about 150 social relationships of the vaguely significant sort, 50 friendships of any consequence, 15 close friendships, and 5 strong family/bosom-buddy relationships. These are approximations, and some people can have slightly larger (or significantly smaller) social circles. People can move from one circle to another or be dropped altogether, but maximums do not change:

Konnikova, M. (2014, October 7). The limits of friendship. *The New Yorker*. Retrieved from https://www.newyorker.com/

Dunbar, R.I. (1993). Coevolution of neocortical size, group size and language in humans. *Behavioral and Brain Sciences, 16*, 681-735.

(7)

Britt, R.R. (2006, June 23). Americans lose touch, report fewer close friends. *Live Science*. Retrieved from https://www.livescience.com/

3) On Shaming and the Big Three

(1) Relevant information about women and friendship: A recent survey found that at least 57% of women are closer to their best friends than their husbands. This certainly suggests that women like other women more than they like men. Women's *in-group bias*, which is largely responsible for this, has been well-documented, and it will be examined in depth later in this text:

Reid, R. (2018, April 6). Over half of women prefer their best friend to their husband. *Metro*. Retrieved from https://metro.co.uk/

Insight into the nature of women's friendships can be had easily enough:

Angel, H. (2010, July 8). Are you closer to your best friend than your husband? Hannah was—and here she evokes a magical bond every woman will recognise. *Daily Mail*. Retrieved from https://www.dailymail.co.uk/

In regards to women's in-group biases, see Note 3 for Chapter 5 ("On Education").

(2) Sperm counts appear to be dropping so quickly throughout the Western world that parthenogenesis may be the only viable route for reproduction by 2100:

Stone, L. (2018, September 6). Study: If trends continue, all men may be infertile by end of century. *The Federalist*. Retrieved from https://thefederalist.com/

(3) The notion that all pornography somehow relates to or encourages rape was heavily promoted by radical feminist (and generally peculiar woman) Andrea Dworkin. In fairness, not all feminists agreed with her assertion, and some even produce pornography, arguing that it is liberating:

Gracen, J. (2000, September 20) Andrea Dworkin in agony. *Salon*. Retrieved from https://www.salon.com/

Agnew, R. (2015, June 18) Feminist porn: Putting female desire in the picture? *The Irish Times*. Retrieved from https://www.irishtimes.com

(4)

Amnesty International publishes policy and research on protection of sex workers' rights. (2016, May 26). Retrieved from https://www.amnesty.org/

(5)

Crouch, D. (2015, March 14). Swedish prostitution law targets buyers, but some say it hurts sellers. *The New York Times*. Retrieved from https://www.nytimes.com/

(6)

Intelligent machines: Call for a ban on robots designed as sex toys. (2015, September 15). *BBC News*. Retrieved from https://www.bbc.com/

(7) At the risk of being cruel, I would suggest that one simply search for photographs of two of the most popular sex-negative feminists, Andrea Dworkin and Valerie Solanas. Of course, both were failed artists—Dworkin, a middling author of fiction and Solanas, an unproduced playwright—and that might have had every bit as much to do with their vitriol as their abominable forms. What is more, Solanas did not take rejection of her creative endeavors well—a fact Andy Warhol learned the hard way:

Maeder, J. (2017, August 14). When 'flower child' feminist and failed playwright Valerie Solanas shot Andy Warhol. *New York Daily News*. Retrieved from https://www.nydailynews.com/

(8)

Arum, R., & Roksa, J. (2011, January 18,). Are undergraduates actually learning anything? *The Chronicle of Higher Education*. Retrieved from https://www.chronicle.com/

(9)

Frailich, R. (2018, November 29). Your home is not an investment. *Forbes*. Retrieved from https://www.forbes.com/

Morrell, A. (2016, October 28). A Wharton professor explains why you shouldn't consider buying a home an investment. *Business Insider*. Retrieved from https://www.businessinsider.com/

Homes sizes have nearly doubled since 1973, despite the average family getting smaller:

Vinopal, L. (2016, June 16). Guess how big the average American house has gotten since 1973. *Fatherly*. Retrieved from https://www.fatherly.com/

(10) Hanlon's Razor: *Never attribute to malice that which is adequately explained by stupidity.*

(11) This is essentially an argument for the concept of *organic morality*—morality that has developed within a society, without orders from on high. Even below the level of human social consensus, there is some limited evidence of *natural morality*—moral codes so basic that they need not be taught at all. A crude sense of moral or behavioral acceptability rightness appears to exist in non-human primates, such as chimps:

Choi, C. (2012, March 7). Primate police: Why some chimps play the cop. *Live Science*. Retrieved from https://www.livescience.com/

And at least one philosopher has suggested that a great many other animals may have limited moral capacities:

Rowlands, M. (2012). *Can animals be moral?* New York, NY: Oxford University Press.

(12) Definitions of *investment* vary from one text to the next, but a fairly standard one states:

An investment is an asset or item acquired with the goal of generating income or appreciation. In an economic sense, an investment is the purchase of goods that are not consumed today but are used in the future to create wealth. In finance, an investment is a monetary asset purchased with the idea that the asset will provide income in the future or will later be sold at a higher price for a profit.

Taken from:

Chen, J. (2019, Jun 30). Investment. *Investopedia*. Retrieved from https://www.investopedia.com/

By this definition, a college degree is either *not an investment* or a highly speculative one—an investment that *may* improve one's earnings potential but cannot be properly sold (meaning the debt and title transferred) and that is likely to come with nondischargeable debt.

(13) For more insight into the Christian view of happiness, I would invite you to read "We Have No Right to Happiness" by C.S. Lewis. Lewis focused on sexual happiness (and divorce—not such a common thing during Lewis's life), but his thoughts can be more broadly applied.

Arguing that one has a right to *pursue happiness* is quite different from arguing that one has a right to catch it. A fishing license provides one with the *right* to fish in public waters. It is not a lawful order compelling the fish to bite:

Lewis, C.S. (1963, 21 December) We have no right to happiness. *The Saturday Evening Post*, 236, 10-12

(14) The rise of *romantic love* and the increasing emphasis on *keeping mamma happy* cannot be disentangled. Romantic love is not Christian in any real sense:

Lewis, C.S. (2013). *The allegory of love*. New York: Cambridge University Press. (Original work published 1936).

As for the bizarre emphasis within modern church practice of keeping women placated, I refer the reader to an article on *Lazy*

*Mother Mus*ings. The writer (a woman it seems, for whatever it is worth) provides quite a bit of insight into what is expected in the modern marriage. Sensibly, she is against such nonsense:

Counseling, feelings, and the roles of husband and wife. (2018, October 29). *Lazy Mother Musings*. Retrieved from https://lazymothermusings.wordpress.com/

Finally, the *submissive husband* perspective is in almost total opposition to the actual biblical teachings, such as can be found in 1 Peter 3:1-4.

Given all of the aforementioned evidence, one can reasonably conclude that a great many people in the church (pastors included) spend relatively little time reading their Bibles, or if they do, they are ignoring a goodly portion of the contents.

(15)All biblical quotes are from the King James Version.

(16)For a reasonably good overview of the life of the Buddha, I recommend *Introduction to Buddhism* by Geshe Kelsang Gyatso. As for the relationship between Buddhism—an essentially monastic religion—and family, "Buddhism and the Family" by Reiko Ohnuma (Oxford Bibliographies) provides quite a few references on a decidedly complex matter:

Gyatso, G. K. (2008). *Introduction to Buddhism*. Glen Spay, NY: Tharpa Publications. (Original work published 1992).

Ohnuma, R. (2014, June 30). Buddhism and the family. *Oxford Bibliographies in Buddhism*. Retrieved from https://dx.doi.org/10.1093/obo/9780195393521-0201

(17)As is the case with so many Chinese names and texts, there is more than one way to write the words in the roman alphabet (romanize). *Laozi* has also been written as *Lao Tsu* and *Lao Tse*. *Daoism* is also written as *Taoism*, and the *Dao De Qing* is also written as *Tao Te Ching*. I use the Pinyin romanization system throughout this book, but to each his own.

As for Laozi, if he was a man who became legend or was never a man at all—a composite—may never be known. If he *was* a real person, he supposedly left civilization on a water buffalo. This may or may not be true, but it is certainly consistent with the tradition of mystics and wise men retiring from civilization:

Lin, S. (2019, April 23). The story of Laozi's servant. *The Epoch Times*. https://www.theepochtimes.com/

(18)After the Bible, only a few books have been translated more than the *Dao De Qing*. Many good translations are commercially available and many others are in the public domain. Unfortunately, there is sadly little overlap between these categories. Thus, I have attempted a translation of the relevant passages on my own.

I offer my apologies to Laozi's ghost in advance.

(19)Like many abstract concepts, there are about as many ways to interpret *wu wei* (无为) as there are people who have studied it. Mine *seems* to make about as much sense as any, but I invite any Chinese language or culture scholars or philosophers (professional or amateur) to provide me with a better explanation of the concept.

(20)Given that men have higher reproductive elasticity than do women, *male disposability* makes a fair amount of sense when considered from an evolutionary perspective. There is no reason to rail against this: Human nature is what it is, but you had better be aware of reality if you are to avoid being crushed by it.

(21)*Golden handcuffs*, like most slang, has several meanings. One of the most popular is *a pay or benefits package that is large enough (or that is structured in such a way) to make quitting a job difficult, if not impossible, to justify*. This definition is popular, but it is incomplete. Economic need is determined by expenses. Said another way, it is easier for a man to quit a well-paying job if he has low expenses and has managed to save a large amount of his income than if he spends all that he makes. *This* is where the expenses of family come into play.

(22)The abandoning of wasted efforts is *almost* inevitable. This is fundamentally similar to *extinction*, as defined in psychology—the termination of behavior that is not reinforced.

4) On the Evil Five

(1) Depending upon the sources and hypotheses cited, competition for access to vaginas/sexual access may well be *the greatest* source of male-to-male violence:

McDonald, M.M., Navarrete, C.D., & Vugt, M.V. (2012). Evolution and the psychology of intergroup conflict: The male warrior hypothesis. *Philosophical Transactions of the Royal Society B, 367*, 670-679.

(2) It is easy to underestimate quite how difficult it would be to assemble a small crowd of even ten Americans with minds uncorrupted by drugs, even if only taking into account the legal ones:

Miller, S.G. (2016, December 13). 1 in 6 Americans takes a psychiatric drug. *Scientific American*. Retrieved from https://www.scientificamerican.com/

(3) An example of the significance of chirality: A left-landed thalidomide molecule is relatively innocuous and is effective in controlling nausea, whereas the right-handed molecule is toxic and can cause severe birth defects:

Newcastle University. (2016, February 8). Nature's mirror: The code for chirality. *Science Daily*. Retrieved from https://www.sciencedaily.com/

(4) The notion of a *love* based courtship is fairly recent, with families playing a major role in spouse selection throughout the 17th and early 18th centuries. At least in regards to marital relations, our ancestors were a more practical lot than are we:

Mintz, S., & McNeil, S. (2019). Courtship in early America. *Digital History*. Retrieved from http://www.digitalhistory.uh.edu/

(5) In 1915, the United States divorce rate was 1 per 1,000, whereas the childbirth mortality rate (for the mother, not necessarily the child) was about 6 per 1,000. These numbers cannot be directly compared as a result of women oftentimes having more than one child, but they do suggest that *till death do us part* was more likely to be the case than *till I can find an even bigger sucker to screw over in divorce court*—the vow for the modern era:

Plateris, A.A. (1973 December). 100 years of divorce statistics: 1867-1967 (HRA 74-1902). *National Center for Health Statistics*. Retrieved from https://www.cdc.gov/

Singh, G.K. (2010). Maternal mortality in the United States, 1935-2007: Substantial racial/ethnic, socioeconomic, and geographic disparities persist. *U.S. Department of Health and Human Services*. Retrieved from http://www.mchb.hrsa.gov/

(6) California introduced the no-fault divorce in 1969. Other states followed shortly thereafter:

Coontz, S. (2010, June 16). Divorce, no-fault style. *The New York Times*. Retrieved from https://www.nytimes.com

This can be seen as the beginning of the end of marriage as historically defined in the West. The disintegration of marriage in Russia occurred earlier, not long after the Bolshevik rise to power. If the intent of the Russian law was to destroy marriage and family, it appeared to have worked fairly well, just as did similar laws in the West:

A Woman Resident in Russia. (1926, July). The Russian effort to abolish marriage. *The Atlantic*. Retrieved from https://www.theatlantic.com

(7) See Chapter 9 ("On Women") to determine your sexual desirability, which will influence how easily you can obtain sex.

(8) Fentanyl was invented in the 1960s and not commonly used until years later. Deaths from overdose increased greatly from 2014 to 2015, and the problem does not appear to be going away soon:

Porter, T. (2017, April 28). **What is fentanyl, the drug linked to thousands of deaths in North America?** *Newsweek*. Retrieved from https://www.newsweek.com/

As for divorce and break ups, I refer one to accusations that have emerged *decades* after an alleged act and their ability to harm these men's reputations. Some of these may be true, and some of them false. Proving or disproving them is impossible.

5) On Education

(1) I have yet to find a formal declaration against men going to college by an organization with power in academia—the American Association of University Women, et cetera—but there is research supporting the notion of an overall anti-male bias in higher education. (See *The War Against Boys* as referenced in Note 1 for the Introduction). Additionally, there is anecdotal evidence of the academy's hostility towards men:

Sacks, G. (2002, November 19). **Why males don't go to college.** *ifeminists.com*. Retrieved from http://www.ifeminists.com/

As for scholarships, far more of them have been made available to women than men, at least in Canada:

Abraham, C. (2018, April 28). **Designated scholarships overwhelmingly favour women.** *The Globe and Mail*. Retrieved from https://www.theglobeandmail.com/

The pattern in the United States appears to be similar:

Ny, R. (2013, February 27). **4x as many scholarships for women — a disadvantage for men?** *NerdWallet*. Retrieved from https://www.nerdwallet.com/

(2) "Hell is filled with musical amateurs," said George Bernard Shaw. As much as I like *Man and Superman*, I am going to disagree with the *Überschreiber* on this point. *Hell is filled with judicial amateurs*. And that is exactly what one is likely to face if he is a man attending a college or university within the United States. God help the man who is accused of violating any school codes or policies developed under Title IX or who fails to get affirmative consent.

Occasionally, a woman gets trapped in the demon claws of Title IX administrators. Laura Kipnis (admittedly one of the more sensible feminists) did not seem to much care for the experience:

Gersen, J.G. (207, September 20). Laura Kipnis's endless trial by Title IX. *The New Yorker*. Retrieved from https://www.newyorker.com/

Regarding coitus, I invite any man thinking of attending college and dating while there to read the Duke University sexual misconduct policy's section on consent:

Duke University Student Affairs. (2019). Student sexual misconduct policy and procedures: Duke's commitment to Title IX. Retrieved from https://studentaffairs.duke.edu/

(3) Women favor women *far* more than men favor men:

Rudman, L.A., & Goodwin, S.A. (2004). Gender differences in automatic in-group bias: Why do women like women more than men like men? *Journal of Personality and Social Psychology, 87*(4), 494-509.

As for grading bias, female teachers favor girls, but male teachers do not favor boys.

Ouazad, A., & Page, L. (2013, July 3). Students' perceptions of teacher biases: Experimental economics in schools (INSEAD Working Paper No. 2013/66/EPS). Retrieved from https://ssrn.com/

(4) The majority of lower-grades teachers are middle-aged White women. Although this changes somewhat by high school, students learning habits and self-perception may largely be formed by that time:

Loewus, L. (2017, August 15). The nation's teaching force is still mostly white and female. *Education Week*. Retrieved from https://www.edweek.org/

(5) *Passivity* may be hard to quantify, but the ability to sit still for long periods of time can be more objectively measured. One small example of schools favoring the passive and physically inactive is the elimination of recess. This may not have been engineered by feminists, but it does seem to harm boys and their ability to learn (which is not to say that it is *ideal* for girls):

Pappas, S. (2011, August 14). As schools cut recess, kids' learning will suffer, experts say. *Live Science*. Retrieved from https://www.livescience.com/

Passivity might also be said to relate to agreeableness and lack of aggression. Generally, women are *more agreeable* and *less aggressive*. See Note 6 for this chapter.

(6) Observations about personality are tricky. Obviously, that which is generally correct may not apply to any given individual; however, clear sex-specific personality differences have been identified. Women have been found to be more agreeable, warmer, and open to feelings, whereas men have been found to be more assertive and open to ideas. In a highly cooperative (and conformist) environment, such as school, women and girls are likely to have an advantage:

Costa, P.T., Terracciano, A., & McCrae, R.R. (2001). Gender differences in personality traits across cultures: Robust and surprising findings. *Journal of Personality and Social Psychology, 81*(2), 322-331.

Chapman, B.P., Duberstein, P.R., Sörensen, S., & Lyness, J.M. (2007). *Personality and Individual Differences, 43*(06), 1594–1603.

Testosterone levels demonstrate a strong inverse correlation with risk aversion:

Apicella, C.L., Dreber, A., Campbell, B., Gray, P., Hoffman, M., & Little, A.C. (2008). Testosterone and financial risk preferences. *Evolution and Human Behavior, 29*(6), 384-390.

(7) Men generally have lower grade point averages, earn fewer credits, and are less likely to complete their degrees than are women:

Conger, D., & Long, M.C. (2010). Why are men falling behind? Gender gaps in college performance and persistence. *The Annals of the American Academy of Political and Social Science, 627*(1), 184-214.

Men's college grades have been lower than those of women for quite some time; however, one could still openly argue that they demonstrate superiority in the sciences as late as the 1980s:

Goldberg, S. (1989, July 5). Numbers don't lie: Men do better than women. *The New York Times.* Retrieved from https://www.nytimes.com/

(8)

Carnevale, A. P., & Smith, N. (2018). Balancing work and learning: Implications for low-income students. *Georgetown University Center on Education and the Workforce.* Retrieved from https://cew.georgetown.edu/

As far as attractive waitresses getting better tips than their snake-haired colleagues, blame women:

Weller, C. (2015, September 11). Pretty waitresses earn bigger tips —and they have female customers to thank. *Business Insider.* Retrieved from https://www.businessinsider.com/

(9)
Morgan, J. (2013, 24 October). Women 'better at multitasking' than men, study finds. *BBC News*. https://www.bbc.com/

(10)The history of colleges and universities is surprisingly complex, and there is no universally agreed-upon antecedent to the modern college. I trace them back to the cathedral schools, which were run by various churches. Others might trace their history back to Middle Eastern institutions or find similarity between modern college and institutions in China and India.

(11)This list is based on informal interviews and discussions I have had with current and former college students in both the United States and China. I regret that I am unable to provide percentage breakdowns; however, I would note that economic concerns were most frequently mentioned by the members of my decidedly non-random sample.

(12)From time to time, some researcher will claim that a great many adults can learn languages about as easily as can children *if only the right teaching methods are used*. Much as is the case with popular diets, the supposedly magical method of language learning/ weight loss goes in and out of vogue, but the paucity of compelling evidence as to the effectiveness of the *méthode du jour* remains the same. The fact remains that *most* adults are unable to achieve fluency in a second language:

Newport, E.L. (1990). Maturational constraints on language learning. *Cognitive Science, 14*, 11-28.

Snow, C.E., & Hoefnagel-Höhle, M. (1978). The critical period for language acquisition: Evidence from second language learning. *Child Development, 49*(4), 1114-1128.

(13)

Defense Language Institute Foreign Language Center. (2018).
    General catalog 2019-2020. Retrieved from
    http://www.dliflc.edu/

(14)

Arum. R., & Roksa, J. (2011). *Academically adrift: Limited
    learning on college campuses.* Chicago, IL: The University of
    Chicago Press.

(15)There is compelling evidence that the Chinese invented movable type far before the Germans, but the technology was not well-known outside of Asia. Gutenberg almost certainly devised the idea on his own, without Chinese influence:

Palermo, E. (2014, February 25). Who invented the printing press?
    Live Science. Retrieved from https://www.livescience.com/

(16)In the age of widespread internet access, e-books, and free shipping (and fast delivery) for millions of titles, it may be easy to forget about the public library and its historical role in small-town America. For many rural communities, the opening of a public library was a big deal. Almost 2,000 libraries were started with grants from Andrew Carnegie, one of America's more generous businessmen and immigrants:

Kevane, M.J., & Sundstrom, W.A. (2016). *Public libraries and
    political participation, 1870-1940.* Santa Clara, CA: Santa
    Clara University. Retrieved from
    https://scholarcommons.scu.edu/

(17)I am not the first person to make this school/conformity observation:

Deresiewicz, W. (2014). *Excellent sheep: The miseducation of the
    American elite.* New York, NY: Free Press.

(18)There is substantial evidence to support the *greater male variability hypothesis* across multiple domains. Observations regarding the greater variability traits in men go back to Charles Darwin's *The Descent of Man, and Selection in Relation to Sex*. Research in this area includes:

Intelligence (at least during childhood):

Arden, R. & Plomin, R. (2006). Sex differences in variance of intelligence across childhood. *Personality and Individual Differences, 41*(1), 39-48.

Height:

Sauro, J. (2019). Fundamentals of statistics 2: The normal Distribution: Introducing the normal distribution. *Usable Stats*. Retrieved from https://www.usablestats.com/

Loquaciousness or laconism (both the most and least talkative people were found to be men):

Swaminathan, N. (2007, July 6). Gender jabber: Do women talk more than men? *Scientific American*. https://www.scientificamerican.com/

Suicide (women are more likely to attempt it, whereas men are more likely to be successful, even in England, where access to firearms is limited):

Schumacher, H. (2019, March 18). Why more men than women die by suicide. *BBC News*. Retrieved from http://www.bbc.com/

(19)There are two major ways in which a culture can be viewed: *etic* and *emic*.

The *etic* perspective is that of the outsider looking in at a culture alien to him. This is anthropology exactly as one typically thinks of it—a researcher disappearing into the jungle to study spear-wielding tribesmen. He remains distant from the people, not engaging with them too much. A similar type of knowledge might be derived from flying drones over a primitive people, watching how they hunt and live from above.

The *emic* perspective is that of the insider analyzing elements of the culture that cannot easily be understood by outsiders. Emic knowledge often derives from first-hand accounts of group members, but it can just as easily by produced by outsiders who embed themselves in a culture for a prolonged period of time (usually years).

I like to think I have both an emic and an etic understanding of academic culture, but I might simply be equally ignorant in both domains.

(20) I am paraphrasing Sunzi, who wrote, "He wins his battles by making no mistakes."

Taken from:

Giles, L. (1910). *Sun Tzu on the art of war.* London, England: Luzac & Co.

(21) Peter Drucker, a famous business consultant, probably said something quite similar to this; however, I have not been able to locate the exact quote. Regardless of the phrasing, *no measurement = no improvement* has become a truism.

(22) At best, the human memory is a poor tool. By some measures, most unreinforced information fades from memory within a day or two. The capacity to remember what one sees is bad, with the reliability of a memory decreasing as one's confidence in it grows. Thus, grades from years prior may indicate little about current levels of competence, particularly if the information studied has not been refreshed in years. Memory limitations are also relevant when considering the utility of eyewitness accounts:

Albright, T., & Rakoff, J. (2015, January 30). Eyewitnesses aren't as reliable as you might think. *Washington Post*. Retrieved from https://www.washingtonpost.com/

(23) The reasons for medical license suspension vary from state to state. More common ones include drug use, malpractice, and

conviction of a serious crime (felony). The reasons for losing a law license (disbarment) are somewhat more varied, but oftentimes involve mismanagement of funds.

Loss of a medical license (in Texas):

The Hart Law Firm. (2019). Major causes of physician license revocations in Texas. Retrieved from https://www.thehartlawfirm.com/blog/

Disbarment (in Minnesota):

Cole, M.A. (2009, August). 55 ways to lose your license. *Bench & Bar of Minnesota*. Retrieved from http://lprb.mncourts.gov/

(24)If you think you might have seen a certain teacher *somewhere*, but your memory is a little foggy, it may be that you met her (or him!) at a whorehouse or on a street corner, where a surprising number of them supplement their incomes. In comparison, Walter White's job at a car wash was almost dignified:

Gee, A. (2017, September 28). Facing poverty, academics turn to sex work and sleeping in cars. *The Guardian*. https://www.theguardian.com/

(25)Impostor syndrome is not limited to academics, and it is fairly common. Contrary to early speculation, it is about as common in men as in women:

Sakulku, J., & Alexander, J. (2011). The impostor phenomenon. *International Journal of Behavioral Science, 6*(1), 73-92.

(26)I have been unable to find a breakdown by academic discipline of college protesters (student or faculty); however, a general trend *seems* to be that soft disciplines (the social sciences, anything with the word *studies* in it) yield more campus rabble-rousers than do the more rigorous ones.

For contrast, I compare three academics on the two sides of campus ideological battle.

For the protesting side:

Melissa Click, famous for her University of Missouri protest actions, is an expert on popular media and culture, such as that related to the *Twilight* books series.

Her activism (and how similar activism affected her former employer):

Hartocollis, A. (2017, July 9). Long after protests, students shun the University of Missouri. *The New York Times*. Retrieved from https://www.nytimes.com/

Her dissertation (provided as evidence of her intellectual competence or lack thereof):

Click, M.A. (2009). *It's 'a good thing': The commodification of femininity, affluence, and whiteness in the Martha Stewart phenomenon.* (Doctoral dissertation). Retrieved from https://scholarworks.umass.edu/

Dwayne Dixon, a teacher at University of North Carolina at Chapel Hill, was active in antifascist protests in Durham, North Carolina. His multimedia dissertation appears to focus primarily on Japanese youth and skateboard culture—a field sufficiently hipsterish to choke even the most dedicated *maté lattes* sippers, assuming they could see well enough through their fashionably oversized horn-rimmed glasses to find their eco-friendly mugs:

Dixon, D. (2014). *Endless question: Youth becomings and the anti-crisis of kids in global Japan.* (Doctoral dissertation). Retrieved from http://scalar.usc.edu/students/endlessquestion/index

For the non-protesting side:

Bret Weinstein, who resigned from Evergreen State College after being the subject of harassment by campus protesters, represents the opposition. Hardly a Bible-thumping conservative, he is an evolutionary biologist, whose dissertation is not publicly available from the University of Michigan website. Despite this, a review of his Abstract would suggest that it is *at least* as demanding a topic as Martha Stewart or Tokyo skateboarders, possibly even more so:

Weinstein, B.S. (2009). *Evolutionary trade-offs: Emergent constraints and their adaptive consequences.* (Unpublished doctoral dissertation). University of Michigan, Ann Arbor, MI.

(27)A journal's *impact factor* is a measure of the average number of times the articles within that journal are cited by other publications. A higher factor is better than a low one. *The New England Journal of Medicine*, for instance, has an impact factor of about 70, whereas *Journal of Gender Studies* has an impact factor of 1.362. Impact factor may not always be a perfect measure of the importance of a publication, particularly if it is one that publishes useful articles that are highly specialized; however, it does give a general sense of how many people see fit to cite the articles within a given journal.

If a tree falls in a forest and no one is around to hear it, does it make a sound? If an article is printed and no one cites or reads it, was it really published?

I am as indifferent to trees as I am to most research, but the above are interesting philosophical questions, nonetheless.

Explanation of impact factor:

Garfield, E. (2019). The Clarivate Analytics impact factor. *Clarivate Analytics.* Retrieved from https://clarivate.com/

The New England Journal of Medicine impact factor:

National Institute of Environmental Health Sciences (n.d.) Details for high impact journal: Superfund research program: The New England Journal of Medicine (impact factor: 70.670). Retrieved from https://tools.niehs.nih.gov/srp/publications/

Journal of Gender Studies impact factor:

Informa UK Limited (2019). Journal of Gender Studies. Retrieved from https://tandfonline.com/toc/cjgs20/current

(28) The citation rate for papers varies hugely by subject. The vast majority of research papers in the domain of medicine are cited, whereas the vast majority of social science papers are not:

Larivière, V., & Gingras, Y. (2009). The decline in the concentration of citations, 1900–2007. *Journal of the American Society for Information Science and Technology, 60*(4), 858-862.

(29) Pol Pot was a particularly interesting case of a minor intellectual who hated intellectuals. Prior to his attempt to purge Cambodian society of all foreign cultural influence, he taught French, which would make for both an ironic and amusing story if it did not end in pyramids of skulls:

Chandler, D.P. (1999). *Brother number one: A political biography of Pol Pot*. Boulder, CO: Westview Press.

(30) About 73% of new car purchases are financed. The rate for unicycles is presumably far lower:

NewCars. (2019). Auto financing: It's all about the benjamins. Retrieved from https://www.newcars.com/how-to-buy-a-new-car/auto-financing.html

(31) And you're not getting any soup either! (Those who are not *Seinfeld* fans should ignore this note.)

(32) If survey results are to be believed, the most popular reason for going to college is to improve one's career prospects. My informal research supports this assertion (see Note 11 for this chapter). Although some non-economic reasons were listed, work and money largely explained why Americans attend college. As for *herd* instinct —going because other people are going—members of a culture that emphasizes the *illusion* of independence as much as does ours may understate (and *underestimate*) their level of passivity, even denying it to themselves. Either way:

Rampell, C. (2015, February 17). Why do Americans go to college? First and foremost, they want better jobs. *Washington Post.* https://www.washingtonpost.com/

(33) About 70%. of Americans 18 to 24 years of age are ineligible to join the military:

Feeney, N. (2014, June 29). Pentagon: 7 in 10 youths would fail to qualify for military service. *Time.* Retrieved from https://time.com/

Slightly *more* than 69% of high school graduates attend college, which is not to say that they majority of them graduate:

Bureau of Labor Statistics. (2017, May 22). 69.7 percent of 2016 high school graduates enrolled in college in October 2016. *TED: The Economics Daily.* Retrieved from https://www.bls.gov/

(34) *If* the *one-in-four* claims are to be believed, college is more dangerous than prison, at least by some measures. Assuming that the average college experience is four years, the risk of sexual assault per year would be about 6.25%. This is higher than the reported 4.5% yearly sexual assault rate in federal prisons. Of course, these estimates are vague and leave room for multiple interpretations. Certain federal prisoners (child molesters, et cetera) might be raped repeatedly, with the bulk of the prison population being left well enough alone, whereas one quarter of female college students may be raped/assaulted exactly once. This would suggest that college is more dangerous for the average female student than is prison for the average prisoner (with the prison experience being uniquely negative for a select few). Conversely, the one-in-four claim does not preclude the possibility that one fourth of women attending college are sexually assaulted *at least* once, with a subset of that group being drugged and passed around fraternity houses like cheap sex dolls. Still, prison would seem to be the safer choice.

Rather than preparing his child for college, the responsible parent would do better to teach his spawn how to rob post offices and banks, given that the U.S. Bureau of Prisons (BOP) appears to run a tighter ship than do most institutions of higher learning (and entirely at taxpayer, rather than parent, expense).

Prison sexual-assault rates (about 4.5% per year):

Human Rights Watch. (2007, December 15). US: Federal statistics show widespread prison rape. Retrieved from https://www.hrw.org/

Interestingly, not all research supports the one-in-four claim, which makes the school/school-of-hard-knocks decision somewhat more complicated.

College sexual-assault rates (about 11.7% of students reported sexual assault/harassment *during their college experience*):

Association of American Universities. (2015, September 3). AAU climate survey on sexual assault and sexual misconduct (2015). Retrieved from https://www.aau.edu/

Finally, why federal prisons are better than state prisons (from someone in the know):

Fresh Out—Life After The Penitentiary (2014, June 2). *Differences between federal and state prison systems—What are they?* Retrieved from https://www.youtube.com/

(35) The least-marketable college majors are what one would expect —photography, graphic design, et cetera. The most-marketable majors typically involve a fair amount of mathematics. *Kiplinger* has published a list of each.

Most-lucrative college majors:

Rapacon, S. (2019, February 5). 25 best college majors for a lucrative career. *Kiplinger*. Retrieved from https://www.kiplinger.com/

Least-lucrative college majors:

Rapacon, S. (2019, January 29). 15 worst college majors for a lucrative career. *Kiplinger*. Retrieved from https://www.kiplinger.com/

(36) Gender-breakdown by civilian profession (2016 data):

Matt Rocheleau (2017, March 6). Chart: The percentage of women and men in each profession. *The Boston Globe*. Retrieved from https://www.bostonglobe.com/

That most combat deaths are men is a fairly well-established fact. Even looking at post-2010 deaths in Iraq, the ratio of female-to-male deaths is about 1/45:

Simpson, R. (2011, December 15). Iraq War casualties—By gender as of end of combat missions. *The American War Library*. Retrieved from http://www.americanwarlibrary.com/

(37) The relationship between feminism and mysticism is stronger than one might think, with at least one author arguing that witches were the first women's liberationists:

Kelly, K. (2017, July 5). Are witches the ultimate feminists? *The Guardian*. Retrieved from https://www.theguardian.com/

More than a few feminists have argued that *all* women are witches. How wonderful it is to be able to agree on something!

Bois, P. (2017, December 18). No surprise here: Feminist witchcraft on the rise. *The Daily Wire*. Retrieved from https://www.dailywire.com/

(38)

Persell, C.H. (1990). Socialization. *introsocsite: Introduction to Sociology*. Retrieved from https://www.asanet.org/

(39) The California loyalty oath requirement was still in effect as of 2008, as evidenced by a Quaker graduate student having her employment terminated for refusing to sign an unmodified version of it:

Asimov, N. (2008, February 29). Quaker teacher fired for changing loyalty oath. *SFGate*. Retrieved from https://www.sfgate.com/

(40) If anything, college may actually make people *more* fragile than they would otherwise be. This is difficult to establish as fact, and rather than college encouraging weakness, weak people may simply be more likely than strong ones to attend college. The possibility also exists of a synergistic effect.

Either way, college and mental strength do not seem to go together:

Lukianoff, G. & Haidt, J. (2015, September). The coddling of the American mind. *The Atlantic*. Retrieved from https://www.theatlantic.com/

(41) As for those raised by wolves, there may be hope still. Marcos Rodriguez Pantoja spent years in the Spanish wilderness with only wolves for company, and he seems to be doing better than one might expect. Granted, he did learn to speak before being abandoned to the elements:

Plitt, L. (2013, November 27). Marcos Rodriguez Pantoja: Did this man live with wolves? *BBC News*. Retrieved from https://www.bbc.com/

(42)

Bejjanki, V.R., Zhang, R., Li, R., Pouget, A., Green, C.S., Lu, Z., & Bavelier, D. (2014). Action video game play facilitates the development of better perceptual templates. *PNAS, 111*(47), 16961-1696. Retrieved from https://www.pnas.org/

(43) In 2011, a group of gamers playing Foldit—a puzzle-based computer game—solved a complex protein-folding problem that had challenged scientists for a decade. The best supercomputers of the time could not:

Coren, M.J. (2011, September 20). Foldit gamers solve riddle of HIV enzyme within 3 weeks. *Scientific American*. Retrieved from https://www.scientificamerican.com/

(44)I have not been able to find any solid statistical data on the effectiveness of traditional martial arts (TMA) in street fights; however, anecdotal evidence suggests that TMA fighters rarely defeat those trained in practical, non-theoretical fighting. Martial arts training may have many uses (fitness, encouraging self-discipline, et cetera), but surviving combat would not appear to be one of them.

6) On Work

(1) Baby Boomer men seem unusually likely to commit suicide. That much said, reliable numbers are difficult to find in suicidology. Occurrences of suicide itself may be undercounted, particularly in cases of intentional drug overdose. Efforts to find broad and consists reasons for suicide involve even more speculation. Simply stated, *why* a given person kills himself is often never known. As for disappointment, poverty, and divorce leading to suicide, there is *some* evidence to support this hypothesis.

Suicide trends:

Tavernise, S. (2016, April 22). U.S. suicide rate surges to a 30-Year high. *The New York Times*. Retrieved from https://www.nytimes.com/

Similar data can be found in Note 4 for the Introduction, with the author of the referenced article developing a slightly different analysis.

Argument that suicide for Baby Boomers may see an increase in coming years, with emphasis on how little is known about suicidal motivations:

Bethune, B. (2019, January 15). Are Baby Boomers the suicide generation? *Maclean's*. Retrieved from https://www.macleans.ca/

Common reasons for suicide in men:

Walton, A.G. (2012, September 24). The gender inequality of suicide: Why are men at such high risk? *Forbes*. Retrieved from https://www.forbes.com/

(2) For a very lighthearted and completely unscientific view on how symbols of wealth can attract women:

VitalyzdTv. (2014, June 19). *Picking up girls in a Lamborghini without talking!* Retrieved from https://www.youtube.com/

Of course, there is no guarantee that any given YouTube video is not staged, but one would be hard-pressed to argue that luxury cars do not attract a fair number of women.

Interestingly, looking better (more attractive) seems to correlate with being wealthier *to a point*, beyond which an inversion occurs. The least attractive people (ass ugly) actually make the *most money* on average. As for what it means to *look poor*, perhaps it is not all that different from looking *very, very rich* but with cheaper clothes.

Either way, the research is interesting:

Gvozdenodic, V. (2013). *Beauty and wages: The effect of physical attractiveness on income using longitudinal data.* (Master's thesis). Retrieved from https://digitalcommons.pace.edu/

(3)

Tsosie, C., & El Issa, E. (2018, December 10). 2018 American household credit card debt study. *NerdWallet*. Retrieved from https://www.nerdwallet.com/

(4) Medical bills are sometimes a reason for bankruptcy, but loss of wages and earnings resulting from illness are likely to have as large, if not larger, an effect:

LaCapria, K. (2016, April, 22). Do 643,000 bankruptcies occur in the U.S. every year due to medical bills? *Snopes*. Retrieved from https://www.snopes.com/

(5) As of 2018, about 70% of workers in human resources (HR) departments are women. The leadership within these departments is rarely competent:

Bureau of Labor Statistics. (n.d.) Household data annual averages: Employed persons by detailed occupation, sex, race, and Hispanic or Latino ethnicity. Retrieved from https://www.bls.gov/cps/

The gatekeepers are rarely of the highest quality:

Charan, R. (2014, July–August). It's time to split HR. *Harvard Business Review*. Retrieved from https://hbr.org/

In regards to women's in-group biases, see Note 3 for Chapter 5 ("On Education").

(6) Justine Sacco's social-media debacle is a vivid example of how quickly a bad joke can damage a sensitive career. One wonders if a diesel mechanic would have suffered the same opprobrium and professional harm:

Waterlow, L. (2015, February 16). 'I lost my job, my reputation and I'm not able to date anymore': Former PR worker reveals how she destroyed her life one year after sending 'racist' tweet before trip to Africa. *Daily Mail*. Retrieved from https://www.dailymail.co.uk/

(7) I am using *bullshit jobs* in essentially the same manner as does David Graeber, an academic who popularized the phrase:

Graeber, D. (2018). *Bullshit jobs: A theory*. New York, NY: Simon & Schuster.

(8) For those lacking the financial endowments of Croesus, an excellent option for a comfortable retirement (early or otherwise) is Southeast Asia:

Peddicord, K. (2015 May 12).Enjoy a low-cost retirement in Southeast Asia. *U.S. News & World Report*. Retrieved from https://money.usnews.com/

(9)

Whyte, W.H. (2002). *The organization man*. Philadelphia, PA: University of Pennsylvania Press. (Original work published 1956).

(10)At least one Englishman has thought that he was turning Japanese. The Japanese may soon think that they are turning unemployed, at least those working in insurance:

McCurry, J. (2017, January 5). Japanese company replaces office workers with artificial intelligence. *The Guardian*. Retrieved from https://www.theguardian.com/

PricewaterhouseCoopers estimates:

PwC. (2017, March). *UK economic outlook*. Retrieved from https://www.pwc.co.uk/

It's difficult to make predictions, especially about the future. Regardless of who said the aforementioned (and there is some debate), it is undoubtedly true. Only time will tell as to what jobs are eliminated by technology, but a great deal of pencil pushing is likely to be on the chopping block. Quite a bit has been written about the end of truck drivers and cabbies, but lawyers may not fare much better:

Susskind, R., & Susskind, D. (2015). *The future of the professions: How technology will transform the work of human experts*. New York, NY: Oxford University Press.

(11)The number of Americans who pay no income tax may be even higher, with 40% non-payers being a slightly conservative estimate:

Catey, H. (2016, April 18). 45% of Americans pay no federal income tax. *MarketWatch*. Retrieved from https://www.marketwatch.com/

(12)The secret millionaire may not be quite as rare as one thinks. One such example, Ronald Read, worked a number of blue-collar jobs and accumulated a small fortune:

LaBianca, J. (2019, May 2019).These people donated millions after they died—But no one knew they were rich. *Reader's Digest*. Retrieved from https://www.yahoo.com/

(13)Given that sexual reproduction is far more demanding for women than it is for men, emphasizing achievement for men (rather than mere existence) makes quite a bit of sense.

Some of men's physical traits are relevant to their ability to provide, protect, and procreate, but deficiencies in two of these three skills can be overcome economically—one may *provide* by buying things and pay guards to *protect* his offspring—whereas a woman's fitness is fixed by biology. These differences in the mechanics of the sexual market are neither anyone's fault nor are they wrong: They are in accordance with biological differences.

(14)In parts of Europe, asking what someone does for a living may be bad form (at least during small talk); however, this is not a universal trend. During my time in China, the three questions most frequently asked me were: 1) What do you do for a living? 2) How much money do you make? 3) Are you married?

Job-related questions in France:

MacLellan, L. (2017, July 14). One of the most common questions in American small talk is considered rude in much of the world. *Quartz*. Retrieved from https://qz.com/

As for how things are done in China, I refer to my personal expertise and experiences throughout this text, which is a roundabout way of saying *trust me*. As with everything else in life, do so at your peril.

(15)Slightly more than 5% of *all* pilots are women, but slightly less than 5% of airline pilots are:

Goyer, M. (2019). Five decades of American female pilots statistics. How did we do? *Institute for Women of Aviation Worldwide*. Retrieved from https://womenofaviationweek.org/

(16) A similar, if less often paraphrased, message is found in the Old Testament (relevant parts in bold):

> Live joyfully with the wife whom thou lovest all the days of the life of thy vanity, which he [God] hath given thee under the sun, all the days of thy vanity: for that is thy portion in this life, and in thy labour which thou takest under the sun. **Whatsoever thy hand findeth to do, do it with thy might; for there is no work, nor device, nor knowledge, nor wisdom, in the grave, whither thou goest.** (Ecclesiastes 9: 9-10)

Although these words echo those of Colossians, the emphasis is different. The entire chapter addresses the fleetingness of life and the mortality of all people. This is the same book from which the oft-quoted "Vanity of vanities . . . all is vanity" is taken. If anything, the author(s) stress the importance of making the most of one's days, of appreciating life because of, rather than in spite of, its brevity. In content (if not in tone) it dovetails with Rule 4 (*Enjoy your life to the fullest*).

(17) Adjusted for inflation, American men earn less now (2010 and later) than they did in the 1970s. This trend is expected to continue, quite possibly for many more generations, if not until the heat death of the universe:

Malito, A. (2017, May 7). Why the lifetime earnings of American men are on a slow, inexorable decline. *MarketWatch*. Retrieved from https://www.marketwatch.com/

(18) The difference between a work friend and a real friend is not much less than the difference by sugar and aspartame: Both share a (somewhat) similar taste, but only the most insensitive would confuse one for the other:

Giang, V. (2012, February 13). There's a big difference between your work friends and your real friends. *Business Insider*. Retrieved from https://www.businessinsider.com/

(19)Unless, you have the chops to be a professional comedian—one of those who can be consistently funny while offending almost no one (which is challenging)—you had best leave humor at home:

Wolfe, L. (2018, December 30). Humor in the workplace and the law. *The Balance Careers*. Retrieved from https://www.thebalancecareers.com/

As for outside-of-work interaction with colleagues, simply *not* inviting a woman along may considered discriminatory. The best practice in dealing with colleagues is to avoid integrating them into your personal life. *Work at work with the people at work.* Socialize with others.

Fraternize with no colleague unless willing to socialize with all equally (or be accused of discrimination):

Kitchener, C. (2017, August 22). When it's hard for women to find male mentors. *The Atlantic*. Retrieved from https://www.theatlantic.com/

Finally, the mentoring of junior employees (and why men are hesitant to mentor women) has been the subject of much chatter as of late. As it turns out, women are not that eager to mentor women either. Perhaps the sisterhood is not as strong as the feminists would have us believe, or perhaps young women are simply too irritating for *anyone* to tolerate.

Men (not) mentoring women:

LeanIn. (2019). Men, commit to mentor women. Retrieved from https://leanin.org/mentor-her

Women (not) mentoring women:

Drexler, P. (2014, March 4). Can women succeed without a mentor? *Forbes*. Retrieved from https://www.forbes.com/

(20)Making friends in the workplace is not extremely common in the United States, which is probably just as well for the many reasons aforementioned. It is worth noting that work relationships have not filled the void left by the decline in non-work social relationships/friendships, and Americans are far more hesitant to interact socially with colleagues than are the citizens of other countries:

Kacperczyk, A., Sanchez-Burks, J., & Baker, W.E. (2011, November 17). Social isolation in the workplace: A cross-national and longitudinal analysis. Retrieved from https://papers.ssrn.com/

(21)As for the death of the nuclear family, one could cite statistics, but just as effective (if not more so) is to refer you to the words of *two* high-ranking judges who have pointed out that the traditional family is dying. Both judges are British, but there is no reason to believe that British culture differs enough from that of America to invalidate their arguments:

Slack, J. (2014, February 19). It's the end of the nuclear family . . . and that's no bad thing, insists Supreme Court judge who says he fears watching couples take their wedding vows. *Daily Mail.* Retrieved from https://www.dailymail.co.uk/

Edkins, G. (2018, June 1). Collapse of the nuclear family should be applauded due to the 'new reality' of single and same-sex parents, says top family court judge. *Daily Mail.* Retrieved from https://www.dailymail.co.uk/

For those who *do* want statistics on the decline of the nuclear family, ask and you shall receive:

Livingston, G. (2014, December 22). Fewer than half of U.S. kids today live in a 'traditional' family. *Pew Research Center.* Retrieved from https://www.pewresearch.org/

7) The Mantra

(1) The veil of ignorance is not difficult to understand. That said, a fuller explanation of it than I have offered is worth reading:

Ethics Unwrapped. (2019). Veil of ignorance. *McCombs School of Business*. Retrieved from https://ethicsunwrapped.utexas.edu/ glossary

(2) A movie quote worth remembering (from *The Departed*, 2006): "Nobody gives it to you. You have to take it." The speaker was referring to power, but fairness is no different. *Theoretical* fairness is dictated by impartial assessment. *Practical* fairness is whatever the those with power declare it to be.

8) On Debt and Taxes

(1) As of 2018, Baby Boomers (those from 55 to 73 years of age) had an average total debt of 95,095 USD. That is less than the members of Generation X had (more than 100,000 USD), but still quite a bit for a group of people who should have paid off their student and housing debts long ago:

Stolba, S.L. (2019, April 12). Baby Boomers prove high debt doesn't equal bad credit. *Experian*. Retrieved from https://www.experian.com/blogs/ask-experian/

Of course, many figures related to household income and the like are estimates, and the U.S. has no formal household debt registry. These numbers differ slightly from those referenced in Note 3 for Chapter 6 ("On Work").

(2) One study established that "50 percent of households with children living at home used their credit cards to pay for basic living expenses like rent or a mortgage, utilities, groceries, and insurance because they did not have enough money in the bank." This research was conducted in 2012, so it may reflect circumstances that were exacerbated by the 2008 financial crisis, but given the four-year time gap, this information is still disheartening:

Traub, A., & Ruetschlin, C. (2012, May 22). The plastic safety net. *Demos*. Retrieved from http://www.demos.org/

(3) The relationship between lending and inflation is fairly well documented. Given that banks *make money*—a topic explored later in this chapter—the effects of excessive lending have the potential to be profound. Simply stated, the more money is borrowed, the greater the supply of money, which eventually leads to inflation:

Folger, J. (2019, February 6). What is the relationship between inflation and interest rates? *Investopedia*. Retrieved from https://www.investopedia.com/

(4) Ideally, outsourcing leads to lower labor costs, and the savings of such are passed on to the consumer. If a given company actually does this—offers products of developed-world quality at developing-world prices—is never certain:

Patel, D. (2017, July 17). The pros and cons of outsourcing. *Forbes*. Retrieved from https://www.forbes.com/

(5) An example of the easy credit/inflation relationship is in the housing market. As mortgage rates drop, house prices rise. The more money people can access, the more they are willing to pay for the same thing:

Olick, D. (2019, June 20). Falling mortgage rates are heating home prices this summer. *CNBC*. Retrieved from https://www.cnbc.com/

Microfinance research in South Africa supports the credit/inflation relationship, but suggests that factors other than interest rates (length of loan, et cetera) also affect consumers" willingness to borrow:

Karlan, D., & Zinman, J. (2005, October). Elasticities of demand for consumer credit. (Paper 926). *Yale University Economic Growth Center*. Retrieved from https://www.semanticscholar.org/

(6) An asset-backed security (ABS) is a financial instrument (usually a bond) backed by debt connected to specific property/ properties.

A popular type of ABS is backed by consumer automotive loans. In this case, a lender provides financing to car purchasers, many of whom have bad credit. The lender then packages all of this debt as bonds, which are sold. The bond buyers get money from the borrowers' repayments (minus administrative costs). In theory, this can be a great deal for bondholders, but only if a large number of debtors do not default. If defaults become widespread, investors receive a far poorer return on investment than anticipated:

DiMartino-Booth, D. (2017, April 12). Bonds backed by auto loans look toxic. *Bloomberg Opinion*. Retrieved from https://www.bloomberg.com/opinion

(7) The process of money creation within the modern, heavily leveraged economies is somewhat different than one might believe. Private banks play a surprisingly significant role:

McLeay, M., Radia, A., & Thomas, R. (2014, March 14). Money creation in the modern economy. *Bank of England*. Retrieved from https://www.bankofengland.co.uk/

(8) There is fairly good evidence that student loans have increased the cost of education at a rate far above that of overall inflation:

Cooper, P. (2017, February 22). How unlimited student loans drive up tuition. *Forbes*. https://www.forbes.com/

(9) There is more than one definition of *rape*. One more or less fits metaphorically. Another fits literally. A third definition (of *Brassica*

napus, a Eurasian plant) fits awkwardly, if at all. Pick the meaning you deem most suitable:

Rape. (2019). *Dictionary.com*. Retrieved from
   https://www.dictionary.com/

(10) See Note 3 for Chapter 2 ("The Lists").

(11) See Note 5 for Chapter 2 ("The Lists").

(12) Excluding the few programs that generate revenue (University of Kentucky's men's basketball program, for one), sports programs are expensive, and colleges can only support a certain number of them. A school can meet the Title IX requirements for equality by either offering more opportunities for women or (more economically) offering fewer opportunities for men. Both achieve the desired result:

Thomas, K. (2011, May 1). Colleges cut men's programs to satisfy
   Title IX. *The New York Times*. Retrieved from
   https://www.nytimes.com/

There is much ongoing debate as to exactly how many money-losing men's programs have been cut as a result of Title IX. But even *trying* to establish equal representation of men and women in competitive sports appears absurd. Men are simply more likely to be interested in sports (as both viewers and participants), largely due to evolutionary reasons:

Deaner, R.O., Balish, S.M.., & Lombardo, M.P. (2016). Sex
   differences in sports interest and motivation: An evolutionary
   perspective. *Evolutionary Behavioral Sciences, 10*(2), 73-97.

(13) Rather than belabor a point beyond all measure, I offer a few example programs listed by the Small Business Administration (SBA). I would challenge anyone to find a list of similar programs offered to men. The closest thing in existence is a select number of programs designed to help veterans, most of whom are men:

U.S. Small Business Administration. (n.d.). Grow your business: Women-owned businesses. Retrieved from https://www.sba.gov/business-guide/grow-your-business/women-owned-businesses

(14)This may change, given a recent ruling by a federal judge in Texas; however, one should not count on it:

Korte, G. (2019, February 25). Q&A: A judge has ruled the male-only military draft unconstitutional. What happens now? *USA Today*. Retrieved from https://www.usatoday.com/

(15)The *Washington Post* provides two exemplary works of academic misandry. The first is by Suzanna Danuta Walters, a Northeastern University professor who has managed to write about one book *every eight years*—a shamefully slow tempo of authorship for a practicing academic. Her article is already cited in Note 1 for The Introduction.

Were the meager accomplishments of Professor Walters not underwhelming enough, she has been bested (*worsted?*) by Victoria Bissell Brown, a retired professor at Grinnell College, who has written exactly *one* book of consequence in her life—a biography of Jane Addams—and who has co-authored a few history readers.

To get some idea of the sort of feeble-minded piglets that suck from the great tits of academe, read at least one of these articles. Consider the mindset of these supposed scholars before donating to the institutions that saw fit to grant them tenure:

Brown, V.B. (2018, October 12). Thanks for not raping us, all you 'good men.' But it's not enough. *Washington Post*. Retrieved from https://www.washingtonpost.com/

(16)As it stands now, a great many Baby Boomers are already uncertain if when (or *if*) they will be able to sell their elephantine homes—the purchases of which were largely subsidized with low-interest mortgages. Some of these properties can cost almost

20,000 USD a year to maintain, making them so expensive that *giving them away* would be challenge:

Kulp, K. (2017, October 14). Boomers worry they can't sell those big suburban homes when the time comes. *CNBC*. Retrieved from https://www.cnbc.com/

(17) At least one prominent academic has suggested that 50% of United States colleges and universities will go bankrupt by 2032. I find this prediction to be rather aggressive, but not impossible. I have gone on record in predicting a significant drop in college attendance (which is almost certainly bound to have severe economic effects for the higher education system) by 2040.

The Harvard professor's prediction:

Hess, A. (2017, November 15). Harvard Business School professor: Half of American colleges will be bankrupt in 10 to 15 years. *CNBC*. Retrieved from https://www.cnbc.com/

My prediction:

Goble, B.V. (2014). A long bet: By 2040, the percentage of U.S. citizens of traditional college age who are attending postsecondary educational institutions in the United States will drop at least 50% from the level reported for the 2011/2012 academic year. *Long Bets*. Retrieved from http://longbets.org/676/

(18) Only a few countries (such as Morocco) lack extradition treaties with the United States. In even fewer of these countries is English spoken. Assuming that you are not on the lamb, an interesting choice for citizenship might well be Panama. Like most things in life, getting Panamanian citizenship requires money.

Additionally, those with at least one Irish grandparent or great-grandparent *may* be eligible for Irish citizenship, which can provide the holder with certain tax advantages.

Panamanian citizenship:

Kraemer & Kraemer. (2019). Panamanian citizenship. Retrieved from https://kraemerlaw.com/en/immigration/panamanian-citizenship/
Irish citizenship by descent:
Department of Justice and Equality. (2016, December 20). Check if you are an Irish citizen by birth or descent. Retrieved from http://www.inis.gov.ie/en/INIS/Pages/citizenship-by-birth-descent

9) On Women

(1) I am aware that a *few* small cultures, such as the Mosuo of China, are dominated by women, but these cultures are technologically unsophisticated and are almost always eclipsed by neighboring patriarchal cultures, which prove more adept in warfare, technology, and the arts.

For whatever it is worth, traditional Mosuo and modern American reproductive practices seem to be converging. The Mosuo *tiesese* (walking marriage) custom shares some similarity to the booty call/hookup culture of today: Men and women live apart, and the men visit the women at night for copulation:

Qin, A. (2015, October 25). 'Kingdom of daughters' in China draws Tourists to its matrilineal society. *New York Times*. https://www.nytimes.com/

(2) See Note 6 for Chapter 5 ("On Education").

(3) I doubt that the majority of men would take issue with a woman loving her children more than she loves her husband. As for friends and pets, the best available information should surprise no one who knows any women.

According to one (imperfect) study, the majority of women prefer their friends to their husbands, and a great many women seem to think that their pets are *better listeners* than their husbands. In the case of German Shepherds, I have no doubt that the dog is a better *hearer* than most men, but as a *listener*, who knows? They may well just be willing to tolerate anything for a Milk-Bone:

Associated Press. (2010, April 28). One-third of married women say their pet is a better listener than their spouse, poll finds. *Los Angeles Times*. Retrieved from https://www.latimes.com/

Finally, there is the matter of women allowing themselves to be inconvenienced for men. I am not one to advocate that women *should* allow themselves to be put in a bad way for the benefit of their husbands/boyfriends. Any man who expects this is a fool.

Remember that the majority of divorces are filed by women. There is no reason to think that a woman will not immediately cut her losses if her husband falls on hard times, just as there is no reason to suspect that a woman will regard her significant other (assuming said *other* is a man) as much of a friend. One need not be bothered by any of this, but he should be aware of as much. See Note 1 for Chapter 3 ("On Shaming and the Big Three") as it relates to female friendship.

(4) This is almost certainly one of the reasons women face shorter prison sentences than men for the same crime, a pattern that has been well documented (at least one the federal level):

Starr, S. (2012). Estimating gender disparities in federal criminal cases. *University of Michigan Law School*. Retrieved from https://repository.law.umich.edu/

Occasionally, a woman will honestly admit that weakness (or *softness*, if you prefer) is a more effective tool for women to achieve their ends than is imitating men:

Barnett, E. (2014, October 1). Stella McCartney's right: Women can use their 'weakness' as a form of strength. *The Telegraph*. https://www.telegraph.co.uk/

(5) See Note 3 for Chapter 5 ("On Education").

(6) A weak man is a liability to the entire community, men and women alike. We can tolerate both physical weakness in women (which is very real) and psychological weakness in women (which is oftentimes exaggerated) because they bear children. Men with these traits are pure burdens. Would you trust a weak man? Think of how you respond to an overly emotional man. Instability in a woman in annoying. In a man, it is frightening or repulsive.

As for women being *less* controlling than men (and less likely to torment weak partners), such is not the case:

Merz, T. (2014, June 26). Women are 'more controlling and aggressive than men' in relationships. *The Telegraph*. Retrieved https://www.telegraph.co.uk/

(7) Men are about ten times more likely to be killed on the job than are women:

DeVore, C. (2018, December 19). Fatal employment: Men 10 times more likely than women to be killed at work. *Forbes*. Retrieved https://www.forbes.com/

(8) The less economic pressure women face in a country, the less likely they are to study the sciences:

Khazan, O. (2018, February 18). The more gender equality, the fewer women in STEM. *The Atlantic*. Retrieved from https://www.theatlantic.com/

(9) Any creative endeavor entails certain risks, and for the most part, the risks result in little prosperity:

Most artists make little money:

Kinsella, E. (2017, November 29). A new study shows that most artists make very little money, with women faring the worst. *Artnet News*. Retrieved from https://news.artnet.com/

Most artists (at least the *great* ones—a less-than-entirely objective categorization, no doubt) are men:

Cochrane, K. (2013, May 24). Women in art: why are all the 'great' artists men? *The Guardian*. Retrieved from https://www.theguardian.com/

Most patents are not profitable:

Key, S. (2017, November 13). In today's market, do patents even matter? *Forbes*. Retrieved from https://www.forbes.com/

Most patents are granted to men:

Zarya, V. (2016, July 21). There's a huge gender gap among inventors. *Fortune*. https://fortune.com/

Even most patents granted to universities make little money. Of course, one might argue that universities engage in research more to advance the state of the art than to turn a profit:

Love, B.J. (2014). Do university patents pay off? Evidence from a survey of university inventors in computer science and electrical engineering. *Yale Journal of Law and Technology, 16*(2), 285-343.

(10) See Note 6 for Chapter 5 ("On Education").

(11)

Tierney, J. (2007, August 20). Is there anything good about men? And other tricky questions *The New York Times*. Retrieved from https://www.nytimes.com/

(12)

Diep, F. (2017, June 14). 8,000 years ago, 17 women reproduced for every one man. *Pacific Standard*. Retrieved from https://psmag.com/environment/

(13) About 92% of serial killers are men (but not as likely to be White as one might think):

Sterbenz, C. (2015, May 16). Here's a surprising look at the average serial killer. *Business Insider*. Retrieved from https://www.businessinsider.com/

As far as I have been able to ascertain, there is no national registry of heroes. The profession that would seem to be most closely aligned with that of hero—one that involves taking great risk to save others in exchange for middling compensation—is firefighter. The vast majority of firefighters (93%) are men:

Evarts, B. & Stein, G. (2019, March). US fire department profile – 2017. *National Fire Protection Association*. Retrieved from https://www.nfpa.org/

Regarding great successes and failures, I would point out that 18 of 20 of the world's richest people are men (at least according to *Forbes*). The only two women on the list—Francoise Bettencourt Meyers and Alive Walton—inherited their money:

Kroll. L. & Dolan, K.A. (2019, March 5). Billionaires: The richest people in the world. *Forbes*. https://www.forbes.com/

On the other end of the spectrum, most homeless people— 71% or so—are men:

Poole, G. (2015, August 6). Homelessness is a gendered issue, and it mostly impacts men. *The Telegraph*. Retrieved from https://www.telegraph.co.uk/

(14) These concepts were borrowed from the ancient Greeks, with some taken from John Alan Lee's book:

Lee, J.A. (1973). *Colours of love: An exploration of the ways of loving*. Toronto, Canada: New Press.

My explanations are rather simplified compared to those of Lee and the Greeks.

(15) My answers: (1) *Potaters:* Yes. (2) Mustard and biscuits: Nope.

(16) See Note 3 for this chapter.

Of course, there is *some* speculation when considering what another person is feeling, but actions mean more than feelings in the abstract. Love without sacrifice is inconsequential. And whatever love a woman may *claim* to feel for her husband or boyfriend, it is almost certain to have no bearing on her actions.

(17)*Eros* also relates to the concept of *limerence*. Although there are some exceptions, limerence typically fades in somewhat less than four years:

Silver, M. (2015, February 16). Sexual desire often fades in relationships. *The Sydney Morning Herald*. Retrieved from https://www.smh.com.au/

(18)This risk was real; however, one should not overstate it. Around the time of America's founding—1750 to 1800—the maternal mortality rate in England was 7.5 per 1,000 births (rates for the United States—an English colony for some of this time, are not readily available). Assuming that a woman had four pregnancies that did not premature terminate (not an unreasonable number during that time), she would have had a less than 5% chance of dying during childbirth. This is not terribly high, but it is high enough so that almost every woman would have at least *known of* a community member who died while giving birth. Mortality rates dropped considerably by the 1900:

Chamberlain, G. (2006). British maternal mortality in the 19th and early 20th centuries. *Journal of the Royal Society of Medicine, 99*, 593-563.

For an overview of American maternal mortality for a different, partially overlapping era (1935-2017), see Note 5 for Chapter 4 ("On the Evil Five").

(19)Rational self-interest dictates that women be in favor of high levels of government spending: It benefits them considerably and costs them little (at least in the short term). See Note 5 for Chapter 2 ("The Lists").

And they do! Women are more likely than are men to vote for candidates in favor of extensive social spending:

Chaturvedi, R. (2016, July 28). A closer look at the gender gap in presidential voting. *Pew Research Center*. Retrieved from https://www.pewresearch.org/

This voting pattern also relates to risk tolerance. Government programs reduce individual risk, and as has been explored previously, women are generally more risk-averse than men, and low-testosterone men are typically more risk-averse than men with higher levels of testosterone.

As for draconian family-court policies, both Republicans and Democrats have pushed for punitive measures against men; however, more female-oriented policies are promoted by the Democrats than the Republicans, which is to be expected by a party that generally attracts more women than does its opponent.

Both parties work to extract money from men for the benefit of women, but the Republican Party squeezes men in the working and middle classes hardest (through the family courts), whereas the Democratic Party tends to take an across-the-board approach, bleeding the working class, middle class, and upper class alike (through taxes).

(20) *Status* or *S-score* as examined later in this chapter.

(21) Although I did make use of the term in Chapter 4 ("On the Evil Five"), I have found *sexual market value* to be somewhat poorly defined. In this chapter—Chapter 9—I introduce the *HSP score*, which is far less ambiguous. HSP addresses a man's *(h)eight*, *(s)tatus*, and *(p)enis size*. Obviously, individual preferences vary, but these translate well across demographics and cultures.

As for strategy shifts—moving away from the *investment approach to relationships* to the *immediate return approach to relationships*—this ties to ever-rising ages of first marriage. When a women marries young, she is giving something of current value (her youth) in exchange for something of potential value (her husband's future earnings). When a women marries late, she is giving something of diminished value (her aging body) for something of immediate value (her husband's current earnings).

The more pronounced this age-delaying pattern becomes, the better a deal marriage becomes for women and the worse deal it becomes for men. Why men tolerate this arrangement is the real mystery.

(22) As for women being involved in work of little value, consider the human resources (HR), its composition, and its incompetence. See Note 5 for Chapter 6 ("On Work").

As for disclaiming responsibility, this is *hypoagency* in its purest form.

(23)

Fink, S. (2013). *Five days at Memorial: Life and death in a storm-ravaged hospital.* New York, NY: Crown Publishing.

(24) At the risk of further desecrating the remains of a thoroughly dead horse, I refer to yet another study that establishes that men are (on average) more competitive than women:

Niederle, M., & Vesterlund, L. (2007). Do women shy away from competition? Do men compete too much? *Quarterly Journal of Economics, 122*(3), 1067–1101.

The questions within the title are founded on an unnatural and ahistorical presumption—that men and women should adopt similar life strategies. Given differences in reproductive elasticity, it would be shocking if men *were not* more competitive than women.

As for women being more or less competitive against women than against men, the available research is limited, partially as a result of most athletic contests (as well as some intellectual ones, such as chess tournaments) being segregated by sex.

(25) Starring Jean-Claude Van Damme:

DiSalle, M. (Producer), & Arnold, N. (1988). *Bloodsport* [motion picture]. United States: The Cannon Group.

(26) The first and most obvious way to be stuck paying for a child who is not yours is to adopt him (or her). As for the matter paying child support for someone else's child—a child you did not adopt—this is where the matter of the *estoppel doctrine* comes into play.

In some states, a stepparent is obligated to pay his stepchild's living expenses if they live under the same roof. Normally, this obligation is terminated upon divorce; however, if the court determines that the stepchild has become dependent upon the stepparent (a totally subjective assessment), the stepparent can be ordered to continue paying expenses even after a divorce. The stepparent is *estopped* from discontinuing payments:

FreeAdvice Staff. (2019). Can a stepparent be required to pay child support? *FreeAdvice Legal.* Retrieved from https://family-law.freeadvice.com/family-law/

Miller, S.B. (2016, April 4). 2 Rare scenarios when stepparents are forced to pay child support. *Oak View Law Group.* Retrieved from https://www.ovlg.com/

(27) See Note 19 for Chapter 6 ("On Work"). Apparently, even women are not overly eager to mentor women.

(28) According to John Gottman, a well-known marriage researcher, displays of contempt are strong predictors of divorce. Although Gottman's research addresses marriage, there is no reason to believe that contempt is less toxic to any other type of relationship, including those in business:

Prooyen, E.V. (2017, August 25). This one thing is the biggest predictor of divorce. *The Gottman Institute.* Retrieved from https://www.gottman.com/

(29)
U.S. public becoming less religious. (2015, November 3). *Pew Research Center*. Retrieved from https://www.pewforum.org/

(30)The Touro Synagogue of Newport, Rhode Island, was opened in 1763—more than a decade before the United States came into existence. The original building stands. George Washington visited the facility and later wrote a letter to the congregation assuring them of their equality under the law and wishing them success:

Congregation Jeshuat Israel. (2019). Touro Synagogue history. Retrieved from https://www.tourosynagogue.org/

As for Eastern religions, joss houses (Chinese temples) have existed in the United States since at least the latter part of the 19th century. Some of those older temples, such as the Weaverville Joss House (California):

State of California. (2019). Weaverville Joss House. Retrieved from http://ohp.parks.ca.gov/

Muslims appear to have had a comparatively small presence in the United States until recently, but even they have been here for more than one hundred years.

(31)First, let us establish the validity of these criteria. Research confirms the obvious—that women prefer tall men with large penises:

Dell'Amore, C. (2013, April 9). Study tracks science of penis preference. *National Geographic*. Retrieved from https://news.nationalgeographic.com/

The numbers for the height table were derived from an estimated average height of about 5 feet and 9 inches and relying on a standard deviation of about three inches.

I have also slightly adjusted all numbers (by a few percent) to reflect the fact that *average is not good*. There is nothing inherently wrong with this pattern: Men have considerable reproductive elasticity, so it is not unreasonable for the average woman to expect to have sex with a man who is at least *a bit* better than the true average (keeping him may be another matter, but that has little to do with impregnation).

Possibly as a result of this, women have a tendency to rate most men as being *below average,* which is very likely an impossibility (depending upon if *average* is defined as the median or the mean).

The original article explaining all this was removed, but an archived version is still available:

Rudder, C. (2009, November 17). Your looks and your inbox. Retrieved from https://bit.ly/2kPP1xv

Next, is the matter of status.

Status can be either *economic* in origin (wealth or apparent wealth based) or non-economic in origin.

—*Economic status*—

A French study confirms that women responded more positively to advances by men who appeared to have money:

Mehta, V. (2012, July 19). Are women shallow? *Psychology Today.* Retrieved from https://www.psychologytoday.com/

This scale is based on earning, rather than accumulated wealth, simply because most Americans, even the high-earning ones do not have much in the way of savings, but money is money of course.

—*Non-economic status*—

When trying to quantify non-economic and non-anthropometric criteria, there is bound to be a certain level of guesswork involved. This uncertainty is only exacerbated by the limited research as to what defines non-economic status. Nevertheless, that women prefer dangerous men/bad boys is settled, and the reasons for their selection (at least from a historical/evolutionary perspective) are entirely sensible:

Live Science Staff. (2012, May 14). Why women choose bad boys. *Live Science. Retrieved from* https://www.livescience.com/

—Status in general—

It should be noted that *everyone* (men included) pay more attention to high-status men. High-status women do not receive commensurate attention:

DeWall, C.N., & Maner, J.K. (2008). High status men (but not women) capture the eye of the beholder. *Evolutionary Psychology, 6*(2), 328-341.

—Penis size—

According to a British study, average penis length is around 5.4 inches. For the purposes of the HSP model, I have slightly adjusted these numbers upward based on some limited research (and probably a bit of optimism) that the Stars and Stripes hang a bit longer than the Union Jack.

As for the upper limit, I have yet to find research on how big is too big, but anything sufficient to bruise a mare's womb is probably more than the average woman is likely to enjoy.

Average penis size:

Veale, D., Miles, S., Bramley, S., Muir, G., & Hodsoll, J. (2014). Am I normal? A systematic review and construction of nomograms for flaccid and erect penis length and circumference in up to15 521 men. *BJUI International, 115*(6), 978-986.

10) On Children

(1) As is the case with most ancient books, translations vary, I picked an older (and public domain) one:

The Buddha's 'first sermon.' (1917). Retrieved from http://www.columbia.edu/itc/religion/f2001/edit/docs/buddhas_first_sermon.htm

(2) Although little experimental research has been conducted, the rise of smartphones and electronics seems to correlate nicely with a

decline in sexual activity. Note the drop from 2007 to 2014, which roughly correlates with the introduction of the smartphone:

Twenge, J.M., Sherman, R.A., & Wells, B.E. (2017). Declines in sexual frequency among American adults, 1989–2014. *Archives of Sexual Behavior, 46*(8), 2389–2401.

This relationship between technology and decreased sexual activity is not inherently bad. One Indian politician advocated making televisions more readily available to poor families as a way of slowing population growth. This would seem to be a more humane method of controlling birthrates than forced sterilization:

Sidner, S. (2009, August 13). Less sex, more TV idea aired in India. *CNN*. Retrieved from http://edition.cnn.com/

(3) Of all methods of birth control, vasectomy is one of the most effective, and of all methods of vasectomy, cauterization is the best of the best.

Comparison of vasectomy to other methods of birth control:

Centers for Disease Control and Prevention. (n.d.). Effectiveness of family planning methods. Retrieved from https://www.cdc.gov/

Effectiveness of different methods of vasectomy:

Barone, M.A., Irsula, B., Chen-Mok, M., Sokal, D.C., & Investigator Study Group. (2004). Effectiveness of vasectomy using cautery. *BMC Urology, 4*(10).

(4) In addition to the rather obvious logic of this argument, there is the question of the overall value of bringing *anyone* into existence, at topic which has been considered at length:

Benatar, D. (2006). *Better never to have been: The harm of coming into existence.* New York, NY: Oxford University Press.

(5) Here is something one is not likely to be told: "Men with children . . . are more likely to be unhappy than men in relationships who don't have them." This is not to say that one

should not have children, only that happiness should not be expected from it:

Lott, T. (2014, 17 January). Has having children made me happier than I was before? *The Guardian*. Retrieved from https://www.theguardian.com/

(6) Pol Pot's death was *probably* a suicide:

Poole, T. (1999, January 21). Pol Pot 'suicide' to avoid US trial. *The Independent*. Retrieved from https://www.independent.co.uk/

As for Sade, his death was not much better:

Perrottet, T. (2015, February). Who was the Marquis de Sade? *Smithsonian.com*. Retrieved from https://www.smithsonianmag.com/

Of course, some actively malevolent bastards live and die well, but one should not count on it.

(7)

Khan, R. (2010, August 5). 1 in 200 men direct descendants of Genghis Khan. *Discover*. Retrieved from http://blogs.discovermagazine.com/

(8) Lest the pedants think I do not realize that *rape and pillage* did not originally have a sexual meaning, I refer them to a quote from J.R.R. Tolkien's *The Silmarillion*: "Few of the Teleri were willing to go forth to war, for they remembered the slaying at Swanhaven, and the raping of their ship . . . " (p. 301). Unless the enemies of the Teleri were both unusually perverse and unusually well-endowed, it is unlikely that this passage was written with a sexual meaning, with *rape* being something more akin to *plunder* in this case. For more about the divers meanings of *rape*, see Note 9 for Chapter 8 ("On Debt and Taxes").

Tolkien, J.R.R. (2002). *The silmarillion*. New York, NY: Random House. (Original work published 1977).

(9) Quite at odds with the popular stereotype of Genghis forcing those he conquered into absolute submission, he was fairly tolerant of beliefs that differed from his own:

McLynn, F. (2015). *Genghis Khan: His conquests, his empire, his legacy*. Philadelphia, PA: De Capo Press.

(10)As it stands now, single motherhood is *more* common than married motherhood in the African American community. The exact nature of the relationship that the children in these households have with their fathers is highly variable and poorly documented. However, that this trend—one of children being raised with limited interaction with fathers—is likely to continue is almost certainly beyond doubt:

Badger, E. (2014, December 18). The unbelievable rise of single motherhood in America over the last 50 years. *Washington Post*. Retrieved from https://www.washingtonpost.com/

As for those indifferent to welfare of Blacks, they may want to keep in mind that as go the souls of Black folk—in art, culture, slang, and music—so go the rest of us, if only somewhat later.

(11)I do not want to overstate this matter. The majority (75%) of children from single-parent households, do not suffer any major problems; however, the percentage who do suffer such problems (25%) is hardly trivial and is more than twice that found in children raised in married households:

Wilcox, W.B. (2012, July 20). The kids are not really alright. *Slate*. Retrieved from https://slate.com/

(12)Max Weber defined the state as a "human community that (successfully) claims the monopoly of the legitimate use of physical force within a given territory," but I would argue that his definition is too narrow. This is the *starting point* for the state. The ultimate purpose any state is to *claim the monopoly of the mind*. Regardless of how tolerant or classically liberal a government may be at its inception, it will eventually grow authoritarian and will attempt, possibly with some success, to establish the acceptable bounds of thought, knowledge, and moral values of the state's peoples.

(13)Some research suggests that parents feel more fulfilled (and possibly happier) than do non-parents, but some research suggest the opposite. This does not so much plainly contradict the relevant reference within Note 5 for this chapter as it suggests that the matter of happiness and parenthood is not settled:

Dick, J. (2014, September 11). Hands down, people without kids have better lives—except for this one major thing. *Quartz*. Retrieved from https://qz.com/

Other research:

Belkin, L. (2009, April 1). Does having children make you unhappy? *The New York Times*. Retrieved from https://nytimes.com/

Of course, almost every part of a man's life is likely to be miserable if he goes through a divorce (at least for a few years).

(14)For the 1:2 ration see Note 11 for Chapter 9 ("On Women"). For the 1:17 ratio see Note 12 for that same chapter.

(15)

Amundsen, B. (2014, May 9). A quarter of Norwegian men never father children. *ScienceNorway*. Retrieved from http://sciencenordic.com/

(16)All of these men may have been bested by lawyer, Latin lover, and revolutionary leader Fidel Castro, who supposedly slept with more than 35,000 women—about two a day for forty years. From each according to *her* ability (to bend over) to each according to *his* need (to bend her over). Had this aspect of Communism had been better advertised, there is little doubt we America would have succumbed to the Red Menace generations ago:

Windle, L. (2016, August 14). The lovers' league: The famous men who have slept with thousands of women . . . but who's bedded the most? *The Sun*. Retrieved from https://www.thesun.co.uk/

(17)There is some debate as to exactly how many children Mr. Hatchett has, but the number is almost certainly in excess of 21. Either way, his penis seems better able to bear the burden of many children than is his wallet, hence his efforts have his child support payments reduced:

Tennessee baby machine is a state inmate. (2012, May 21). *The Smoking Gun*. Retrieved from http://www.thesmokinggun.com/

(18)This 10% prediction is derived from research by the Rensselaer Polytechnic Institute. Unfortunately, this research provides no hint as to what happens to the bulk of the population if 10% hold a belief with absolute conviction and an equal number hold an opposing view with absolute conviction. Perhaps these two devoted groups will negate each other. Perhaps popular opinion bifurcates. Who knows?

DeMarco, G. (2011, July 25). Minority rules: Scientists discover tipping point for the spread of ideas. *Rensselaer Polytechnic Institute*. Retrieved from https://news.rpi.edu/

(19)See Note 10 for this chapter.

(20)The struggles of the children of immigrants are well known (which is not to say that a great many of them fail to achieve success):

Rieti, J. (2012, February 15). Children of immigrants caught between 2 cultures. *CBC*. Retrieved from https://www.cbc.ca/

(21)While children of immigrants are more likely to become terrorists than are their parents, it should be kept in mind that the overall number of those who do so is small:

Calamur, K. (2016, June 15). Are immigrants prone to crime and terrorism? *The Atlantic*. Retrieved from https://www.theatlantic.com/

(22)

Gann, C. (2012, July 24). After 30 years, unintended birth rate still almost 40 percent. *ABC News*. Retrieved from https://abcnews.go.com/

(23)There is little research on those who regret having children (possibly a result of an admission of this sort being taboo). These lists (while far from scientific) detail some common complaints:

Stockton, C. (2014, July 3). 15 parents explain what they regret about having children. *Thought Catalog*. Retrieved from https://thoughtcatalog.com/

Tepfenhart, O. (2016, August 5). Men speak out about why they regret having kids. *Rebel Circus*. Retrieved from https://www.rebelcircus.com/

There is quite a bit of overlap in these, but some differences can be found as well.

(24)Women may regret having children as much as men do. Perhaps they regret it even more. After all, no man has ever had his vagina destroyed by the birthing process.

At least one woman wrote about the horrors of having children. She is French, but that does not necessarily make her wrong:

Maier, C. (2008). *No kids: 40 good reasons not to have children*. (P. Watson Trans.). Toronto, Canada: McClelland & Stewart, Ltd.

11) On Isolation, Faith, and Dark Forests

(1) American productivity increased 96% during the Second World War, and corporate after-tax profits doubled:

Goodwin, D. (1992, Fall). The way we won: America's economic breakthrough during World War II. *The American Prospect*. https://prospect.org/

As for other industrial powers, rationing in England did not end until 1954. Presumably, the *losing* countries fared even worse:

Institute of Continuing Education. (2019). Wind of change: post-war Britain 1945–1965. *University of Cambridge*. Retrieved from https://www.ice.cam.ac.uk/

(2) Plenty of older Westerns had strong female characters. The *tough-as-nails woman* was not the product of a bunch of hairy-legged gender studies majors. Instead, it developed quite naturally. Consider these films and the year each one was released: *Forty Guns* (1957), *Johnny Guitar* (1954), *Rancho Notorious* (1952), and (my favorite of the bunch) *Destry Rides Again* (1939).

A great many other films included similar characters:

Chennault, N. (2013, November 18). Women in Westerns. *Great Western Movies*. Retrieved from http://thegreatwesternmovies.com

To their credit, these films portray the men and women as being *equals*, which makes for far more entertaining interactions than the current man-helpless-idiot/woman-living-god approach to writing male/female interaction. Interestingly, the actresses starring in these films—Joan Crawford and Marlene Dietrich—do a better job at projecting real ability than most modern actresses, and they manage this without all of the male characters around them being written as one-dimensional morons or man-children.

(3) The notion of the highly independent man of the western states (and the limitations of this idea) was written about at considerable length. One of the seminal works on the topic is historian Frederick Jackson Turner's collection of essays:

Turner, F.J. (1921). *The frontier in American history*. New York, NY: Henry Holt and Company. Retrieved from https://www.gutenberg.org/

As for the frontier states being exceptionally violent and populated by men incapable of working together, such may be as much a matter of myth as reality. There is a fair amount of evidence that the men of the American West were far more cooperative than commonly portrayed:

DiLorenzo, T.J. (2010). The culture of violence in the American West: Myth versus reality. *The Independent Review, 15*(2), 227–239.

(4) Focusing on the rise of superhero films (rather than Westerns and action films), long-time blogger Larry Kummer considers the isolated-man myth in relation to superheroes. His emphasis is different, but we come to similar conclusions:

Kummer, L. (2017, June 29). We like superheroes because we're weak. Let's use other myths to become strong. *Fabius Maximus*. Retrieved from https://fabiusmaximus.com/

(5) The Desert Fathers lived in relative isolation for years. Quite a few of their stories and saying have been compiled:

Monastery of Christ in the Desert. (2019). Timeless spiritual wisdom found in the sayings and stories of the early Christian monks of the desert. Retrieved from https://christdesert.org/prayer/desert-fathers-stories/

The Buddha meditated and lived in isolation before reaching enlightenment, although the amount of time there spent thus was fairly brief:

Lopez, D.S. (2019, August 22). Buddha: Founder of Buddhism. *Encyclopædia Britannica*. Retrieved from https://www.britannica.com/

Laozi also valued his peace and quiet. See Note 17 for Chapter 3 ("On Shaming and the Big Three").

Then there is the matter of wandering monks.

Ajaan Mun Bhuridatto spent years in the wilds of Southeast Asia and developed the Thai Forest Tradition of Buddhism, which emphasizes (among other things) aestheticism, meditation, and isolation:

Bhikkhu, T. (1999). The customs of the noble ones. *Access to Insight* Retrieved from https://www.accesstoinsight.org/

As for *wild men* of the American West, some of them referred to themselves as prospectors, but what they really appeared to want —more than gold—was to be left the hell alone. Men of similar dispositions lived closer to the Atlantic, but before the area was as crowded as it is today. It should be noted that such hermits were in the minority. Most men, even in the open West, did not desire such extreme isolation:

The Hermitary, & Meng-hu. (2011). Hermits in history: American. *Hermitary*. Retrieved from http://www.hermitary.com/

(6)

Liu, C. (2015). *The dark forest.* (J. Martinsen, Trans.). New York, NY: Tom Doherty Associates, LLC.

(7) Computers have been beating people at chess for quite some time. Their progress at learning the game of Go is more recent, but no less impressive. They are also doing quite well at poker and video games. Strictly speaking, poker is not a perfect information game; however, a strong poker player (human or machine) can do a good job of guessing the hands of other players based on probability and observations of opponents' behaviors:

Haridy, R. (2017, December 27). 2017: The year AI beat us at all our own games. *New Atlas*. Retrieved from https://newatlas.com

Computers fare poorly at games requiring extremely high degrees of intuition, and that is where we have our advantage.

(8) Of these ways to form social/community bonds, the role of arranged marriages may be underappreciated by modern man. The Mongols tribes had fairly elaborate rules for inter-group marriages. The relevant rank of each tribe determined if it provided wives or husbands to to the partnership. Genghis Khan was the product of one such inter-tribal marriages. See Note 9 for Chapter 10 ("On Children") for book reference.

(9) As to *who* is more responsible for the destruction of family—capitalists or communists—the answer is unclear. The communists proposed that the capitalists rather cynically protect family only to the extent that doing so serves economic ends. An excerpt from *The Communist Manifesto* outlines the Red's take on the matter:

> On what foundation is the present family, the bourgeois family, based? On capital, on private gain. In its completely developed form this family exists only among the bourgeoisie. But this state of things finds its complement in the practical absence of the family among the proletarians, and in public prostitution.
>
> . . .
>
> The bourgeois clap-trap about the family and education, about the hallowed co-relation of parent and child, becomes all the more disgusting, the more, by the action of Modern Industry, all family ties among the proletarians are torn asunder, and their children transformed into simple articles of commerce and instruments of labour.

Taken from:

Marx, K. & Engels, F. (1906). *The communist manifesto*. (S. Moore, Trans.). Chicago, IL: Charles H. Kerr & Company. Retrieved from https://books.google.com/

Marx and Engels wrote that "What the bourgeoisie therefore produces, above all, are its own grave-diggers," and they may have been even more right than they imagined. Far more than in the late

19th century, intact families appear to be a defining marker of the upper middle class alone, with the *petite bourgeoisie* having already seen its hearth and home disintegrated under the combined forces of consumerism, globalization, women's liberation, the family courts, and professional do-gooderism.

The communists urged that this destruction be inflicted upon families of *every* level, not just the working classes. Assuming current trends continue, they are almost certainly guaranteed to have their wish within a generation.

(10)Any number of people's and cultures have had their own versions of heaven, including the occasional heaven on earth, but these were places one found, usually after much searching. *Utopia*, as developed by Sir Thomas More, was different.

He described an imaginary place, a *Commonwealth of Nowhere*, but he developed the fiction as inspiration, rather than as simple fantasy. This—the idea that heaven on earth is a place to be *built* rather than discovered—is a radical notion. More's perfect island varied from modern realizations of a heaven built by man. Amongst other things, it was small—about 200 miles across at the widest point. The modern Commonwealth is massive and growing by the day. High technology has done much to obliterate space. Nevertheless, city-states have dynamics quite a bit different from those of nation states. Perhaps More's vision is not so much impossible as it is unscalable. What can be pleasant at one size can be horrible at another:

More, T. (1895). *Utopia*. (G. Burnet, Trans.). London, England: Cassell and Company, Limited. Retrieved from https://books.google.com/

(11)Taken from an (alleged) Edward Abbey quote and bastardized for my own ends.

(12)—*CAD versus CoSV*—

I may risk confusing my readers by using two superficially similar terms—Cult of the American Dream (CAD) and Church of the Sacred Vagina (CoSV)—but this metaphor choice is deliberate. Both suggest a connection to religion, and I would hold that CAD and CoSV are founded upon the same core belief: that happiness can only be provided by external agents. In this way, they remove the *locus of control* from the man and place it within the dominion of the employer, the woman, and the marketers.

To further build upon the metaphor, a cult is *a system of religious belief that is more or less secretive and that relies upon group-exclusive knowledge and customs and segregation (physical, psychological, or both) of its members from larger elements of society*. A church is simply *where one worships*. One worships vaginas at the CoSV and follows the practices of the CAD. Together, they may be thought of as being part of the overall *American Religion of Love and Optimism*.

—Love and marriage—

The idea that love is important to long-term sexual/marital relationships is relatively recent. To the extent that one did find love, it was far more likely to be in an affair than in a marriage. Important life decisions were more likely to be made by the head than the heart (or genitals, to put it more bluntly):

The Week Staff. (2012, June 1). How marriage has changed over centuries. *The Week*. Retrieved from https://theweek.com/

The Mongolians were just one of many groups to practice arranged (rather than romantic) marriages. See Note 8 for this chapter.

(13) There may not be many things upon which the American left and right can agree, but they do share a declining faith in American meritocracy. This is not to say that the CAD is dead, only that this element of its practice may be of diminishing importance. Even

religions change over time, and this change appears to have occurred fairly recently.

The difference between the two sides is that one group believes that our attempts at achieving meritocracy have failed, are immoral at heart, and should be replaced with something else—*equality*, a term with a meaning nearly as subjective as that of *good*. The other group believes that our attempts at achieving meritocracy have failed, are moral at heart, and should be replaced with an effective implementation of meritocracy:

Equality must prevail (the left):

Appiah, K.A. (2018 October 19). Sorting people by 'merit' will do nothing to fix inequality. *The Guardian*. Retrieved from https://www.theguardian.com

Meritocracy must prevail (the right):

Unz, R. (2012, November 28). The myth of American meritocracy. *The American Conservative*. Retrieved from https://www.theamericanconservative.com/

(14) The idea that frantically running from one place to the next and one task to the next is inherently good is a peculiar one. And it is not universal:

Bellezza, S., Paharia, N. & Keinan, A. (2016, December 15). Research: Why Americans are so impressed by busyness. *Harvard Business Review*. Retrieved from https://hbr.org/

This ties to workism but is not identical to it. See Note 4 for Chapter 1 ("The Rules").

(15)

Smart, N. (1998). *The world's religions*. (2nd ed.). New York, NY: Cambridge University Press.

(16) Sociologist Robert Putnam considered the role of work in relationship building. He found that some friendships are created

at work, but he was nearly as skeptical of the significance and durability of such relationships as I am:

Putnam, R.D., (2000). *Bowling alone: The collapse and revival of American community*. New York, NY: Simon & Schuster Paperbacks.

For additional references to work and friendship, see Note 18 for Chapter 6 ("On Work").

As for the notion of a *third place*—somewhere that is neither work nor home—the idea is relatively old, but may not be familiar to all:

Oldenburg, R. (1999). *The great good place: Cafes, coffee shops, bookstores, bars, hair salons, and other hangouts at the heart of a community*. New York, NY: Marlowe & Company.

(17) One reason for this pattern of assuming homosexuality may be that we overestimate the total number of homosexuals. Recent surveys suggest that the American public believes that around 25% of the population is homosexual. In reality, homosexuals probably make up no more than 5% of the population (and possibly less):

Franke-Ruta, G. (2012, May 31). Americans have no idea how few gay people there are. *The Atlantic*. Retrieved from https://www.theatlantic.com/

(18) American men may be somewhat *more* reserved than they were a few generations ago (at least around other men). We can only speculate as to the reasons. Personally, I suspect this is the product of both our isolation and the aforementioned overestimation of the prevalence of homosexuality. An additional factor may well be the decline of truly masculine work—that which is dark, dirty, and dangerous—and the growth of decidedly less masculine office work. Those who mine coal for twelve hours a day have already established their toughness. The pencil pusher's identity is built

upon graphite, the miner's upon coal. In this case, the more combustible form of carbon is superior to the other:

McKay, B. & McKay, K. (2008, August 24). The history and nature of man friendships. *The Art of Manliness*. Retrieved from https://www.artofmanliness.com/

(19) There is a clear stereotype that men are more hierarchical than women:

Mast, M.S. (2004, May). Men are hierarchical, women are egalitarian: An implicit gender stereotype. *Swiss Journal of Psychology, 63*(2), 107-111.

Unfortunately, it has very much become the fashion in academia to attack stereotypes as being inherently bad. Believing in stereotypes blindly certainly can be. What academics are more hesitant to acknowledge is that a great many stereotypes are based on truth. Of course, one should not take stereotypes as being *absolutely* true for all people, but as broad generalizations that are unlikely to be perfectly accurate in all cases:

Jussim, L. (2016, August 15). Truth in stereotypes: Social scientists dismiss them, but rather than being universally inaccurate, stereotypes are often grounded in reality. *Aeon*. Retrieved from https://aeon.co/

Although research on exactly who is more hierarchical is thin on the ground, good research does suggest that men are both more aggressive and faster to make peace after a conflict. This would certainly seem to lead to a different type of social order than one built by women:

Reuell, P. (2016, August 8). Resolving conflict: Men vs. women. *The Harvard Gazette*. Retrieved from https://news.harvard.edu/gazette/

Although none of the listed articles and research absolutely establish that men build more hierarchical social structures than men, they establish that men have *different* structures than do women, with greater emphasis on competition and aggression, and that men are *perceived* (stereotyped) as being more hierarchical than women. Research has also established that stereotypes oftentimes contain some very general truths. Thus, one can say with some confidence that men *probably* have different—more regimented, more effective competitive social structures—than do women.

(20)In regards to in-group bias, see Note 3 for Chapter 5 ("On Education"). In regards to agreeableness/passivity, see Notes 5 and 6 for that same chapter.

(21)Supposedly, H.L. Mencken said, "Love is the delusion that one woman differs from another." Perhaps he is right. If so, this delusion seems to be suffered far more by men than by women, who may be more realistic in their assessments of their own kind.

(22)Who actually devised the term *one-percenter* may never be known:

Dulaney, W.L. (2005, November). A brief history of "outlaw" motorcycle clubs. *International Journal of Motorcycle Studies*. Retrieved from https://motorcyclestudies.org/

(23)The structure and admissions procedures of motorcycle clubs (MC) are reasonably complex, with the lowest level being that of *hang around*—the name for both a period of time (the *hang-around period*) and a person (someone interested in joining the club). The hang-around period entails both proving one's worth to the group and demonstrating a good personality fit. After that, one becomes a *prospect*, which is something like a monastic novice:

Motorcycle Riding Club Education. (n.d.). Hang around. Retrieved from http://rcvsmc.net/id33.html

As for the rules of conduct within an MC, they entail all of the protocols listed in the chapter, with the sample bylaws establishing that any member is forbidden from sexually pursuing the *ol' lady* (girlfriend/wife/female sexual partner) of another member:

Motorcycle Riding Club Education. (n.d.). 1% bylaws example.
Retrieved from http://rcvsmc.net/id6.html

(24) Women have been allowed into the *sangha* (monastic orders) almost since Buddhism's beginning; however, the sexes were strictly segregated. The bhikkhu-sangha (community of ordained men) and bhikkhuni-sangha (community of ordained women) were also distinct in their operation and rules:

O'Brien, B. (2019, February 4). Maha Pajapati and the first nuns: The beginning of barriers? *Learn Religions*. Retrieved from https://www.learnreligions.com/

(25) Trappist monks follow *St. Benedict's Rule for Monasteries,* which despite the singular form—*rule*—consists of a great many of them. Different orders of monks follow different sets of rules. They are all generally quite stringent:

Benedict of Nursia. (1948). *St. Benedict's rule for monasteries.* (L. Doyle, Trans.). Collegeville, MN: The Liturgical Press. Retrieved from https://www.gutenberg.org/

Buddhist monks follow the *Vinaya.* There are several different versions of the text. The Theravada tradition (the oldest extant version of Buddhism) has the shortest list of instructions, of which there are about 230:

Vinaya pitaka. (2019). *Pali Canon Online.* Retrieved from http://www.palicanon.org/index.php/vinaya-pitaka

(26) The process for becoming a Trappist monk is variable. It can take a few years, or it can take far longer:

Order of Cistercians of the Strict Observance. (2019). Becoming a monk or nun. Retrieved from https://www.ocso.org/

Becoming a Buddhist monk is no easier. Again, the exact time required varies from person to person and temple to temple, but about three years appears to be the minimum:

Becoming a monastic. (2019). *Plum Village*. Retrieved from
 https://plumvillage.org/

(27)Most monastic orders do not have extraordinarily complex chains of command, but the Tibetan system is somewhat of an exception. It can be best understood with the use of a flowchart:

Tibetan religious hierarchy. (2018). *HierarchyStructure*. Retrieved
 from https://www.hierarchystructure.com/

The Trappists are part of the Roman Catholic Church, which has known layers of hierarchy, from bishops to archbishops to the cardinals all the way to the supreme pontiff.

(28)Tantric teachings are *esoteric* teachings. Some of them relate to sex, but many of them do not:

O'Brien, B. (2018, April 15). An introduction to Buddhist tantra:
 Transforming desire into enlightenment. *Learn Religions*.
 Retrieved from https://www.learnreligions.com/

(29)In regards to the Vinaya, see Note 25 for this chapter.

(30)See entirety of Note 25 for this chapter.

(31)Strict churches and religious orders can be more effective and provide more to their members than can the softer fell-good variety. As much as I would like to claim being the first person to notice this, I am not. An economist beat me to it. Presumably, this strictness/benefit relationship holds true for many types of groups:

Iannaccone, L.R. (1994). Why strict churches are strong.
 American Journal of Sociology, 99(5), 1180-1211.

(32)See Note 6 for Chapter 2 ("The Lists").

(33)If an increase in the number of women in a given field *causes* it to become less rigorous or if women are simply drawn to less-rigorous domains is open to debate. Either way, the correlation is strong (at least in colleges and universities). The number of women in a given area of study and the average SAT score of those entering that field correlate inversely.

SAT and intelligence correlate somewhat, but the lower average apparent levels of intelligence for female-dominated majors does not necessarily establish that women are less intelligent.

Olson, R. (104, June 25). Average IQ of students by college major and gender ratio. Retrieved from http://www.randalolson.com/2014/06/25/average-iq-of-students-by-college-major-and-gender-ratio/

In the military at least, the introduction of women appears to have led to the lowering of standards, if only the physical ones. Initially, this was a matter of having lower standards exclusively for women, which rubbed some people the wrong way. In the long term, it leads to the reevaluation of standards for both men and women, with the logic being that if women do not need to meet certain standards to function in a given environment, perhaps no one does:

Mulrine, A. (2015, May 29). All 8 women fail Ranger School: Some Rangers say standards should change. *The Christian Science Monitor*. Retrieved from https://www.csmonitor.com/

Yet women graduate college at higher rates than men and have higher grade point averages. So what is the overall effect of women on a field of study or professional endeavor?

More than anything else, women seem to find the middle. They excel when standards are calibrated for the statistical mean, just as they do poorly when standards are geared towards the exceptional. *Soft majors* (management, social work, et cetera) are about as average and middle-of-the-road as one can get. And there is nothing even *slightly* bold about going to college to study such things. Men are quite the opposite. *Army Ranger*, *physicist*, *mathematician*—these are professions in which only a few could ever realistically hope to find employment. Many men fail at such things, but most people who succeed in them are men.

In regards to women's academic performance, see Note 7 for Chapter 5 ("On Education"). In regards to *greater male variability*, see Note 18 for that same chapter.

(34) The growth of women in the workplace occurred along with growth of complicated regulatory schemes designed to reduce the risk of *discriminatory practices.* These schemes themselves necessitated the development of both government agencies (the Equal Employment Opportunity Commission, for example) and human resources as an industry and a corporate department. All of this regulation and management places considerable burdens on companies and leads to a fair amount of resentment:

Fast Company Staff. (2005, August 1). Why we hate HR. *Fast Company*. Retrieved from https://www.fastcompany.com/

As far as women's inferior upper-body strength, the evidence is essentially irrefutable:

Miller, A.E., MacDougall, J.D., Tarnopolsky M.A., & Sale D.G. (1993). Gender differences in strength and muscle fiber characteristics. *European Journal of Applied Physiology and Occupational Physiology, 66*(3), 254-262.

Additionally, women take off more sick time than do men and work fewer hours:

Swinford, S. (2014, February 25). Women are almost 42 per cent more likely to take sick days than men. *The Telegraph.* Retrieved from https://www.telegraph.co.uk/

Bureau of Labor Statistics. (2015, July 2). Time spent working by full- and part-time status, gender, and location in 2014. *TED: The Economics Daily*. Retrieved from https://www.bls.gov/

(35)Much as one would expect, there is a push to offer women a shorter work week than men (but for the same total pay). The most interesting point of the research backing up this argument is that it is based on the *supposedly* sexist assumption that women are less capable than men of engaging in honest work. Apparently, acknowledging this inferiority is fine *when doing so is convenient for women:*

Dinh, H., Strazdins, L., & Welsh, J. (2017). Hour-glass ceilings: Work-hour thresholds, gendered health inequities. *Social Science & Medicine, 76*, 42-51.

(36)Not only do people of different social classes have different life and practical educations, what they learn in the classroom is likely different. This was the case in even reasonably standardized grade-school curricula as of the early 1980s, although recent, more aggressive efforts to reduce inter-school inconsistency may have had some effect.

Anyon, J. (1981). Social class and school knowledge. *Curriculum Inquiry, 11*(1), 3-42.

(37)The practice of noting one's responses as they develop was not recently developed. Insight meditation, which has been practiced for millennia, teaches this—observation of the *arising and passing away* of physical sensations, thoughts, and emotional responses.

One need not meditate in the formal sense to develop a better sense of his mental processes and emotional reactions as they occur. Rather, this can be achieved through the simple mental exercise of acknowledging what one thinks and feels as thinking and feeling it.

A brief description of insight meditation and how to do it:

Goldstein, J. (2013, November 12). The four foundations of mindfulness. *Lion's Roar*. Retrieved from https://www.lionsroar.com/

12) On the Living, the Sick, and the Dead

(1) Futurist Ian Morrison wrote, "The Scots see death as imminent. Canadians see death as inevitable. And Californians see death as optional." Unfortunately, California Death Denial Disorder (CD^3) seems to have spread throughout the land. Perhaps we should take the Scottish approach. It is almost certainly more economical (as are most things Scots):

Emanuel, E.J. & Bekelman, J.E. (2016, January 19). Is it better to die in America or in England? *The New York Times*. Retrieved https://www.nytimes.com/

(2)

Kotz, D. (2010, October 7). Overmedication: Are Americans taking too many drugs? *U.S. News & World Report*. Retrieved from https://health.usnews.com/

(3)

The cost of dying: End-of-life care patients' last two months of life cost Medicare $50 billion last year: Is there a better way? (2010, August 5). *CBS News*. Retrieved from https://www.cbsnews.com/

(4)

James, J.T. (2013). A new, evidence-based estimate of patient harms associated with hospital care. *Journal of Patient Safety,* 9(3), 122-128.

(5)

Kochanek, K.D., Murphy, S.L., Xu, J., & Arias, E. (2019). Deaths: Final data for 2017. *National Vital Statistics Reports, 68*(9), 35-36.

(6) Several versions and hardware bundles of the IBM PC were offered, and prices varied. My inflation-adjusted price is for one of the less lavish models:

Stengel, S. (2019). IBM Personal Computer (PC). *Steve's Old Computer Museum*. Retrieved from http://oldcomputers.net/

(7) As the quality of automobiles improves, the average time they are driven before being replaced increases:

Walsworth, J. (2016, November 22). Average age of vehicles on road hits 11.6 years. *Automotive News*. Retrieved from https://www.autonews.com/

(8) Physician Atul Gawande has some relevant insight into the limits of life and medicine:

Gawande, A. (2014). *Being mortal: Medicine and what matters in the end*. New York, NY: Metropolitan Books.

(9) Although *some* innovation has taken place over the last 50 years, it has almost certainly been of less economic and cultural significance than the innovations of 1920 to 1970:

Rotman, D. (2016, April 6). Tech slowdown threatens the American dream. *MIT Technology Review*. Retrieved from https://www.technologyreview.com/

(10) For comparison, more than 8,000,000 citizens of the Soviet Union died in WWII, whereas slightly more than 400,000 Americans did. Although the population of the two political entities was not identical (making comparison of the numbers not perfectly comparable), they were close enough so that the Soviets could still be said to have suffered a massively disproportionate loss of life:

Research starters: Worldwide deaths in World War II (n.d.). *The National WWII Museum*. Retrieved from https://www.nationalww2museum.org/

(11) The odds of dying in a "motor vehicle incident" (a broad term, admittedly) are about 1/133. The odds of dying in a terrorist-attack conducted by a foreign-born terrorist are 1/45,808. Considered from this perspective, the most destructive act any conservative

Muslim state as ever done to Americans is sell them the oil required to keep their vehicles running:

Mosher, D., & Gould, S. (2017, January 31). How likely are foreign terrorists to kill Americans? The odds may surprise you. *Business Insider*. Retrieved from https://www.businessinsider.com/

(12) No projectile made of steel should be shot at a steel backstop. The projectile *will* bounce. Lead deforms. Steel bounces. Those who wish to practice shooting with a BB gun should use an appropriate BB pellet trap. Heed this advice or risk losing an eye!

(13) Interestingly, Sunzi also emphasized (at least as much as I do) the importance of facing death as motivation:

> Throw your soldiers into positions whence there is no escape, and they will prefer death to flight. If they will face death, there is nothing they may not achieve."

The Art of War, as useful as it may be, cannot be blindly applied to all parts of life. Some of its wisdom is quite compatible with the Rules. Other parts are better suited to different times, places, and circumstances.

For source of Sunzi quote, see Note 20 for Chapter 5 ("On Education").

13) On Addiction

(1) Only one source exists for the 5%/80% statement, but it is widely reported and treated as authoritative:

The American Society of Interventional Pain Physicians (ASIPP) fact sheet. (n.d.) *American Society of Interventional Pain Physicians*. Retrieved from https://tinyurl.com/y3hfphcc

As for opioid deaths, the Centers for Disease Control provides the accepted estimate:

Centers for Disease Control and Prevention. (2019, June 27). Drug overdose deaths. Retrieved from https://www.cdc.gov/

(2) Fortunately, Americans appear to be getting a bit more realistic by the generation. Perhaps this will make us a saner people:

Fottrell, Q. (2018, April 3). **For the first time, young Americans have less optimism than those aged 55 and older.** *MarketWatch.* Retrieved from https://www.marketwatch.com/

Overall belief in the power of meritocracy—at the core of much optimism and the CAD—is also declining. See Note 13 for Chapter 11 ("On Isolation, Faith, and Dark Forests").

(3) The Hazelden Betty Ford Foundation has long perpetuated the disease-as-addiction model, an overview of which is provided by said organization:

Ranes, B. (2016, March). **The brain disease model of addiction.** *Butler Center for Research.* Retrieved from https://www.hazeldenbettyford.org/

(4) One cannot fairly describe *preliterate cultures* as a monolith. Their individual customs, attitudes towards violence, and diet vary greatly. Some of the more famously violent cultures have achieved homicide rates to put the most brutal of drug lords to shame. The myth of the *universally* peaceful savage is just that—a myth:

Keeley, L.H. (1996). *War before civilization: The myth of the peaceful savage.* New York, NY: Oxford University Press.

Others, such as the Moriori were pacifistic (or nearly so). These seem to be somewhat exceptional relative to their blood-soaked technological peers:

Frost, N. (2018, March 6). **The sad story of the Moriori, who learned to live at the edge of the world.** *Atlas Obscura.* Retrieved from https://www.atlasobscura.com/

Despite their many differences, few of the members of these groups were overweight (prior to the introduction of the European diet, that is). Finally, it should be noted that there is some debate as to if American society is more or less violent than it was a century ago.

We are almost certainly less violent than we were 10,00 years ago, but general trends to do necessitate entirely smoothly lines. See Note 3 for Chapter 11 ("On Isolation, Faith, and Dark Forests") for some discussion of historical rates of violence in the American West.

(5) Chinese researchers found that anger, particularly strong anger (rage), spread far faster than joy on social media. Social issues—food safety, corruption, et cetera—and diplomatic issues—such as conflict with Japan—were found to be the genesis of most anger in China. As for what riles people in the United States, the issues likely differ. Either way, anger spreads quickly, probably about as much in *meatspace* as in the digital realm:

Fan, R., Zhao, J., Chen, Y., Xu, K. (2014). Anger Is more influential than joy: Sentiment correlation in Weibo. *PLOS ONE, 9*(10), 1-8.

(6)

White elephant. (2019). *Merriam-Webster.* Retrieved from https://www.merriam-webster.com/

(7)

Elephant basics. (2019). *The National Elephant Center*. Retrieved from http://www.nationalelephantcenter.org/learn

(8)

Boyle, A. (2015, May 27). Physicist Leon Lederman's Nobel Prize medal sells for $765,000. *NBC News.* Retrieved from https://www.nbcnews.com/

(9)

Head, J. (2015, December 16). Defaming a dog: The ways to get arrested for lese-majeste in Thailand. *BBC News.* Retrieved from https://www.bbc.com/

(10) Some alcoholics and drug addicts *spontaneously recover* (much as someone with cancer may go into spontaneous remission). This appears to be about the only way that one can survive true alcohol or drug addiction, with most treatments not doing much good:

Johnson, B.A. (2010, August 8). We're addicted to rehab. It doesn't even work. *Washington Post*. Retrieved from http://www.washingtonpost.com/

(11) Most research suggest that at least 50% of *drug addiction* is the result of genetics. (Note that there are other kinds of addiction —to sex, gambling, and just about anything else imaginable) Changing environment and behaviors are important, but a genetic vulnerability remains a genetic vulnerability:

Price, M. (2008, June). Genes matter in addiction. *Monitor on Psychology, 39*(6). Retrieved from https://www.apa.org/monitor/

Referencing this may seem to contradict my earlier assertion that much addiction is *not a disease* (main text circa Note 3).

It does not.

First, there are many kinds of addiction. *Drug addiction* is just one subset of a larger category of behaviors and diagnoses. Second, *addiction* is a broadly used term, one that I believe is seriously *overused*. Many of the people who are categorized as *addicts* suffer from the problem PIED. As for true drug and alcohol addicts, they suffer from a serious and unfortunate ailment. Their odds of living tolerable lives are not good.

14) On Being a Bastard

(1) This is the idea behind the *selfish gene*, the theory of which *does not* argue that there is a gene that makes one selfish, but that the genes of an organism strive to survive, even if doing so is deleterious to the carrier organism. *The organism exists to serve the genes, not the genes to serve the organism.*

Writer and futurist Stewart Brand argued that "information wants to be free . . . and expensive." He was referring to human-generated information and the tension between the declining cost of information transmission and the economic incentives to keep valuable information as expensive as possible. Assuming that one regards genes as information, the rule in the natural world is slightly different: *Information wants to survive, no matter how great the expense to the organism that carries it*. This *information-survival imperative* (ISI) may well to be *anti-entropy*, or at least the closest thing in existence to it. It is *this*—the ISI—that can lead to sacrifice for the benefit of those with whom one shares genes.

In the modern era, the ISI has transmogrified into *malignant altruism*—a disease that appears to affect Western men almost exclusively, largely to the detriment of their society—through a complex interaction of instinct and social conditioning.

The selfish gene:

Ridley, M. (2016). In retrospect: The selfish gene. *Nature, 529*, 462-463. Retrieved from https://www.nature.com/

Information wants to to be free:

Clarke, R. (2012). Information wants to be free . . . Retrieved from http://www.rogerclarke.com/II/IWtbF.html

(2) The peak year for homicide in the United States was 1980, with a rate of slightly more than 10/100,000. Although 2016 rates (about 6/100,000) were still higher than those of 1950 (about 5/100,000), the America of today is far safer today than it was in the age of Pac-Man.

The very real fear of crime during the 1980s (and the belief that it would increase without end) was reflected in the fiction of the day, hence *Escape From New York*, a 1981 film in which a future (1997) New York City is portrayed as a massive and astoundingly violent prison.

Were the film to have been more accurate in its predictions (and set a bit later in the future), it would have been titled *Escape From the New York Sugary Drinks Portion Cap Rule*.

As for firearms and restrictions on gun ownership, the National Instant Criminal Background Check System (NICS) was put in place in 1998, making weapons somewhat more difficult to obtain than they were in decades past.

Homicide rates since 1950:

Statista Research Department (2019, August 1). Deaths by
   homicide per 100,000 resident population in the U.S. from
   1950 to 2016. *Statista*. Retrieved from
   https://www.statista.com/

National Instant Criminal Background Check System:

National Instant Criminal Background Check System (NICS)
   (n.d.). *Federal Bureau of Investigation*. Retrieved from
   https://www.fbi.gov/

(3) Nicotine is quite a bit more toxic than one might think. Even *handling* large amounts of tobacco can lead to nicotine poisoning:

Blosser, F. (1993, July 8). NIOSH issues warning to tobacco
   harvesters. *Centers for Disease Control and Prevention. The
   National Institute for Occupational Safety and Health*.
   Retrieved from https://www.cdc.gov/niosh/

(4) In effect, being a *nice guy* puts one in a fragile position. Being a bastard puts one in an *antifragile* position (or at least a *resilient* one). *Antifragility* is defined as the inverse of fragility:

'Fragility' can be defined as an accelerating sensitivity to a harmful stressor: this response plots as a concave curve and mathematically culminates in more harm than benefit from random events. 'Antifragility' is the opposite, producing a convex response that leads to more benefit than harm.

Taken from:

413

Taleb, N.N. (2013). 'Antifragility' as a mathematical idea. *Nature,*
494, 430.

Nice-guy status is extremely sensitive to random occurrences or behavior. Thus, it is fragile. *Bastardry* exhibits both resilience and antifragility. It is resilient in that it is somewhat tolerant of error (in this case, *not being a bastard*). It is also likely to benefit from random events. Self-interest, carelessness, or simple fatigue can all lead to behavior that amplifies one's bastard reputation. Nice-guy status, however, must be guarded and maintained almost entirely without lapse.

(5) Note 9 for Chapter 12 ("On the Living, the Sick, and the Dead") covers 50 years of innovation (1920-1970), which would seem to be a good match for a 1970-2019 comparison. I include the list below (covering a slightly different, but overlapping, time span) to reinforce my point. Were one to chart these achievements relative to a scale of global bastardry, it would likely reveal a *peak bastard/peak innovation* overlap:

First motion picture:	1888
First transatlantic radio transmission:	1901
First powered flight:	1903
Bohr atomic model:	1913
Tetanus toxoid vaccines:	1924
Programmable digital computer (ENIAC):	1943-1946
First atomic bomb:	1945
First supersonic flight:	1947
Salk polio vaccine:	1953
First satellite launch:	1957
First human spaceflight:	1961
Motion picture invention:	

Casey, K. (2013, August 29). The mystery of Louis Le Prince, the father of cinematography. *The National Science and Media Museum*. Retrieved from https://blog.scienceandmediamuseum.org.uk/

Radio:

History.com Editors. (2019, January 31). Guglielmo Marconi. *History.com*. Retrieved from https://www.history.com/

First airplane flies:

History.com Editors. (2019, July 17). This day in history (December 17): First airplane flies. *History.com* Retrieved from https://www.history.com/

Bohr atomic model:

De Leon, N. (n.d.). The Bohr atom. Retrieved from http://www.iun.edu/~cpanhd/C101webnotes/modern-atomic-theory/Bohr-model.html

Tetanus vaccine:

World Health Organization. (2017). Tetanus vaccines: WHO position paper—February 2017. *Weekly Epidemiological Record, 92*(6), 53–76. Retrieved from https://www.who.int/wer/

First digital computer:

What Was the First Digital Computer? (2019). *wiseGEEK*. Retrieved from https://www.wisegeek.com

First atomic bomb:

History.com Editors. (2019, July 28). This day in history (July 16): The first atomic bomb test is successfully exploded. *History.com* Retrieved from https://www.history.com/

First supersonic flight:

First supersonic flight. (2019). *Guinness World Records*. Retrieved from https://www.guinnessworldrecords.com/

Salk polio vaccine:

History.com Editors. (2019, July 28). This day in history (March 26): Salk announces polio vaccine. *History.com*. Retrieved from https://www.history.com/

First satellite launch:

Garber, S. (2007, October 10). Sputnik and the dawn of the space age. *NASA History*. Retrieved from https://history.nasa.gov/

First manned spaceflight:

Bell, E. (n.d.). Vostok 1. *NASA Space Science Data Coordinated Archive*. Retrieved from https://nssdc.gsfc.nasa.gov/

(6)

Kantor, J., & Streitfeld, D. (2015, August 15). Inside Amazon: Wrestling big ideas in a bruising workplace. *The New York Times*. Retrieved from https://www.nytimes.com/

(7)

Baime, A.J. (2014, June 2). Henry Ford's reign of terror: Greed and murder in Depression-era Detroit. *Salon*. Retrieved from https://www.salon.com/

(8)

Bates, D. (2015, May 5). Exclusive: How McDonald's 'founder' cheated the brothers who really started empire out of hundreds of millions, wrote them out of company history—and left one to die of heart failure and the other barely a millionaire. *Daily Mail*. Retrieved from https://www.dailymail.co.uk/

(9)

Winfrey, G. (2015, October 9). Why Steve Jobs was so mean to employees. *Inc*. Retrieved from https://www.inc.com/

Love, D. (2011, October 26). 16 examples of Steve Jobs being a huge jerk. *Business Insider Australia*. Retrieved from https://www.businessinsider.com.au/

15) On Liberation

(1) Estimates of median American home size vary somewhat from one publication to the next. *The Motley Fool* provides a middle-of-the-road number:

Housel, M. (2013, September 13). How the average American home has changed in the last 40 years. *The Motely Fool*. Retrieved from https://www.fool.com/

(2) Although one may debate exactly what constitutes *quality construction*, the vulnerability of stick-frame structures to fire is understood. Masonry construction is less vulnerable, which is why New York City banned the erection of wooden buildings many years ago:

Fox, J. (2019, February 13). Why America's new apartment buildings all look the same. *Bloomberg Business*. Retrieved from https://www.bloomberg.com/

Despite all of these known risks—fire hazards, et cetera—Americans continue to build and buy giant tinderboxes and call them homes. The Germans, in contrast, use better materials but build smaller structures:

Josey, C. (n.d.). Find out the differences between American vs German homes: It's where the heart is. *WorldThruOurEyes*. Retrieved from https://worldthruoureyes.com/

(3) This number—7.7 billion—is the 2019 estimate:

Worldometers. (2019). World population (2019 and historical). Retrieved from https://www.worldometers.info/

Of course, even 0.000001% of the population—about 77 people —being of any concern to you is a high number, but such is not entirely out of the realm of possibility.

(4) This is hardly an original observation, but it is worth repeating:

Mackey, M. (2014, February 18). Want to succeed? Learn to fail. *The Fiscal Times*. Retrieved from http://www.thefiscaltimes.com/

(5) *Zen* was probably rejected closer to 121 times, although differing accounts provide slightly different numbers:

Wamsley, L. (2017, April 24). 'Zen And The Art of Motorcycle Maintenance' Author Robert M. Pirsig Dies At 88. *NPR*. Retrieved from https://www.npr.org/

Carrie is a far cry from the record holder for rejections, but given the book's tremendous profitability, the number of rejections —30—is somewhat surprising. Of course, that which made it uniquely profitably might well have made it difficult for publishers to categorize:

Temple, E. (2017, December 22). The most-rejected books of all time (of the ones that were eventually published). *Literary Hub*. Retrieved from https://lithub.com/

References

—A—

Abraham, C. (2018, April 28). Designated scholarships overwhelmingly favour women. *The Globe and Mail*. Retrieved from https://www.theglobeandmail.com/

Agnew, R. (2015, June 18) Feminist porn: Putting female desire in the picture? *The Irish Times*. Retrieved from https://www.irishtimes.com

Albright, T., & Rakoff, J. (2015, January 30). Eyewitnesses aren't as reliable as you might think. *Washington Post*. Retrieved from https://www.washingtonpost.com/

Alter, C. (2016, April 22). U.S. suicide rate rising precipitously, especially among women. *Time*. Retrieved from https://time.com/

The American Society of Interventional Pain Physicians (ASIPP) fact sheet. (n.d.) *American Society of Interventional Pain Physicians*. Retrieved from https://tinyurl.com/y3hfphcc

Amnesty International publishes policy and research on protection of sex workers' rights. (2016, May 26). Retrieved from https://www.amnesty.org/

Amundsen, B. (2014, May 9). A quarter of Norwegian men never father children. *ScienceNorway*. Retrieved from http://sciencenordic.com/

Anderson, A. (2015, June 9). After the government takes his life savings, this 22-year-old fights for justice. *The Daily Signal*. Retrieved from https://www.dailysignal.com/

Andersson, E. (2019, March 15). The Supreme Court didn't put the nail in civil asset forfeiture's coffin. *ACLU*. Retrieved from https://www.aclu.org/blog/

Andrews, E. (2018, August 30). 7 early robots and automatons. *History.com*. Retrieved from https://www.history.com/

Andriotis, A., Brown, K., & Shifflett, S. (2019, August 1). Families go deep in debt to stay in the middle class. *The Wall Street Journal*. Retrieved from https://www.wsj.com/

Angel, H. (2010, July 8). Are you closer to your best friend than your husband? Hannah was—and here she evokes a magical bond every woman will recognise. *Daily Mail*. Retrieved from https://www.dailymail.co.uk/

Anyon, J. (1981). Social class and school knowledge. *Curriculum Inquiry, 11*(1), 3-42.

Apicella, C.L., Dreber, A., Campbell, B., Gray, P., Hoffman, M., & Little, A.C. (2008). Testosterone and financial risk preferences. *Evolution and Human Behavior, 29*(6), 384-390.

Appiah, K.A. (2018 October 19). Sorting people by 'merit' will do nothing to fix inequality. *The Guardian*. Retrieved from https://www.theguardian.com

Arden, R. & Plomin, R. (2006). Sex differences in variance of intelligence across childhood. *Personality and Individual Differences, 41*(1), 39-48.

Arum. R., & Roksa, J. (2011). *Academically adrift: Limited learning on college campuses*. Chicago, IL: The University of Chicago Press.

Arum, R., & Roksa, J. (2011, January 18,). Are undergraduates actually learning anything? *The Chronicle of Higher Education*. Retrieved from https://www.chronicle.com/

Asimov, N. (2008, February 29). Quaker teacher fired for changing loyalty oath. *SFGate*. Retrieved from https://www.sfgate.com/

Associated Press. (2010, April 28). One-third of married women say their pet is a better listener than their spouse, poll finds. *Los Angeles Times*. Retrieved from https://www.latimes.com/

Association of American Universities. (2015, September 3). AAU climate survey on sexual assault and sexual misconduct (2015). Retrieved from https://www.aau.edu/

Aziz, O., Gemmell, N., & Laws, A. (2013, June). The distribution of income and fiscal incidence by age and gender: Some evidence from New Zealand. *Victoria University of Wellington*. Retrieved from https://papers.ssrn.com/

—B—

Badger, E. (2014, December 18). The unbelievable rise of single motherhood in America over the last 50 years. *Washington Post*. Retrieved from https://www.washingtonpost.com/

Baime, A.J. (2014, June 2). Henry Ford's reign of terror: Greed and murder in Depression-era Detroit. *Salon*. Retrieved from https://www.salon.com/

Bates, D. (2015, May 5). Exclusive: How McDonald's 'founder' cheated the brothers who really started empire out of hundreds of millions, wrote them out of company history—and left one to die of heart failure and the other barely a millionaire. *Daily Mail*. Retrieved from https://www.dailymail.co.uk/

Barnett, E. (2014, October 1). Stella McCartney's right: Women can use their 'weakness' as a form of strength. *The Telegraph*. https://www.telegraph.co.uk/

Barone, M.A., Irsula, B., Chen-Mok, M., Sokal, D.C., & Investigator Study Group. (2004). Effectiveness of vasectomy using cautery. *BMC Urology, 4*(10).

Becoming a monastic. (2019). *Plum Village*. Retrieved from https://plumvillage.org/

Bejjanki, V.R., Zhang, R., Li, R., Pouget, A., Green, C.S., Lu, Z., & Bavelier, D. (2014). Action video game play facilitates the development of better perceptual templates. *PNAS, 111*(47), 16961-1696. Retrieved from https://www.pnas.org/

Belkin, L. (2009, April 1). Does having children make you unhappy? *The New York Times*. Retrieved from https://nytimes.com/

Bell, E. (n.d.). Vostok 1. *NASA Space Science Data Coordinated Archive*. Retrieved from https://nssdc.gsfc.nasa.gov/

Bellezza, S., Paharia, N. & Keinan, A. (2016, December 15). Research: Why Americans are so impressed by busyness. *Harvard Business Review*. Retrieved from https://hbr.org/

Benatar, D. (2006). *Better never to have been: The harm of coming into existence*. New York, NY: Oxford University Press.

Benedict of Nursia. (1948). *St. Benedict's rule for monasteries*. (L. Doyle, Trans.). Collegeville, MN: The Liturgical Press. Retrieved from https://www.gutenberg.org/

Bethune, B. (2019, January 15). Are Baby Boomers the suicide generation? *Maclean's*. Retrieved from https://www.macleans.ca/

Bhikkhu, T. (1999). The customs of the noble ones. *Access to Insight* Retrieved from https://www.accesstoinsight.org/

Blosser, F. (1993, July 8). NIOSH issues warning to tobacco harvesters. *Centers for Disease Control and Prevention. The National Institute for Occupational Safety and Health*. Retrieved from https://www.cdc.gov/niosh/

Bois, P. (2017, December 18). No surprise here: Feminist witchcraft on the rise. *The Daily Wire*. Retrieved from https://www.dailywire.com/

Boyle, A. (2015, May 27). Physicist Leon Lederman's Nobel Prize medal sells for $765,000. *NBC News*. Retrieved from https://www.nbcnews.com/

Britt, R.R. (2006, June 23). Americans lose touch, report fewer close friends. *Live Science*. Retrieved from https://www.livescience.com/

Brown, P. (2014, September 8). Parents' house seized after son's drug bust. *CNN*. Retrieved from https://www.cnn.com/

Brown, V.B. (2018, October 12). Thanks for not raping us, all you 'good men.' But it's not enough. *Washington Post*. Retrieved from https://www.washingtonpost.com/

The Buddha's 'first sermon.' (1917). Retrieved from http://www.columbia.edu/itc/religion/f2001/edit/docs/buddhas_first_sermon.htm

Bureau of Labor Statistics. (n.d.) Household data annual averages: Employed persons by detailed occupation, sex, race, and Hispanic or Latino ethnicity. Retrieved from https://www.bls.gov/cps/

Bureau of Labor Statistics. (2015, July 2). Time spent working by full- and part-time status, gender, and location in 2014. *TED: The Economics Daily*. Retrieved from https://www.bls.gov/

Bureau of Labor Statistics. (2017, May 22). 69.7 percent of 2016 high school graduates enrolled in college in October 2016. *TED: The Economics Daily*. Retrieved from https://www.bls.gov/

—C—

Calamur, K. (2016, June 15). Are immigrants prone to crime and terrorism? *The Atlantic*. Retrieved from https://www.theatlantic.com/

Carnevale, A. P., & Smith, N. (2018). Balancing work and learning: Implications for low-income students. *Georgetown University Center on Education and the Workforce*. Retrieved from https://cew.georgetown.edu/

Casey, K. (2013, August 29). The mystery of Louis Le Prince, the father of cinematography. *The National Science and Media Museum*. Retrieved from https://blog.scienceandmediamuseum.org.uk/

Cash, J. (n.d.). "Success is having to worry about every damn thing in the world, except money." *AZ Quotes*. Retrieved from https://www.azquotes.com/

Catey, H. (2016, April 18). 45% of Americans pay no federal income tax. *MarketWatch*. Retrieved from https://www.marketwatch.com/

Centers for Disease Control and Prevention. (n.d.). Effectiveness of family planning methods. Retrieved from https://www.cdc.gov/

Centers for Disease Control and Prevention. (2019, June 27). Drug overdose deaths. Retrieved from https://www.cdc.gov/

Chamberlain, G. (2006). British maternal mortality in the 19th and early 20th centuries. *Journal of the Royal Society of Medicine, 99*, 593-563.

Chandler, D.P. (1999). *Brother number one: A political biography of Pol Pot*. Boulder, CO: Westview Press.

Chapman, B.P., Duberstein, P.R., Sörensen, S., & Lyness, J.M. (2007). *Personality and Individual Differences, 43*(06), 1594–1603.

Charan, R. (2014, July–August). It's time to split HR. *Harvard Business Review*. Retrieved from https://hbr.org/

Chaturvedi, R. (2016, July 28). A closer look at the gender gap in presidential voting. *Pew Research Center*. Retrieved from https://www.pewresearch.org/

Chen, J. (2019, Jun 30). Investment. *Investopedia*. Retrieved from https://www.investopedia.com/

Chen, J., Lu, S., & Vekhter, D. (n.d.). Strategies of play. Retrieved from https://cs.stanford.edu/people/eroberts/courses/soco/projects/1998-99/game-theory/Minimax.html

Chennault, N. (2013, November 18). Women in Westerns. *Great Western Movies*. Retrieved from http://thegreatwesternmovies.com

Choi, C. (2012, March 7). Primate police: Why some chimps play the cop. *Live Science*. Retrieved from https://www.livescience.com/

Clarke, R. (2012). Information wants to be free . . . Retrieved from http://www.rogerclarke.com/II/IWtbF.html

Click, M.A. (2009). *It's 'a good thing': The commodification of femininity, affluence, and whiteness in the Martha Stewart phenomenon.* (Doctoral dissertation). Retrieved from https://scholarworks.umass.edu/

Cochrane, K. (2013, May 24). Women in art: why are all the 'great' artists men? *The Guardian*. Retrieved from https://www.theguardian.com/

Cole, M.A. (2009, August). 55 ways to lose your license. *Bench & Bar of Minnesota*. Retrieved from http://lprb.mncourts.gov/

Conger, D., & Long, M.C. (2010). Why are men falling behind? Gender gaps in college performance and persistence. *The Annals of the American Academy of Political and Social Science, 627*(1), 184-214.

Congregation Jeshuat Israel. (2019). Touro Synagogue history. Retrieved from https://www.tourosynagogue.org/

Consideration. (2015, September 12). *Legal Dictionary*. Retrieved from https://legaldictionary.net/

Coontz, S. (2010, June 16). Divorce, no-fault style. *The New York Times*. Retrieved from https://www.nytimes.com

Cooper, P. (2017, February 22). How unlimited student loans drive up tuition. *Forbes*. https://www.forbes.com/

Coren, M.J. (2011, September 20). Foldit gamers solve riddle of HIV enzyme within 3 weeks. *Scientific American*. Retrieved from https://www.scientificamerican.com/

The cost of dying: End-of-life care patients' last two months of life cost Medicare $50 billion last year: Is there a better way? (2010, August 5). *CBS News*. Retrieved from https://www.cbsnews.com/

Costa, P.T., Terracciano, A., & McCrae, R.R. (2001). Gender differences in personality traits across cultures: Robust and surprising findings. *Journal of Personality and Social Psychology, 81*(2), 322-331.

Counseling, feelings, and the roles of husband and wife. (2018, October 29). *Lazy Mother Musings*. Retrieved from https://lazymothermusings.wordpress.com/

Crouch, D. (2015, March 14). Swedish prostitution law targets buyers, but some say it hurts sellers. *The New York Times*. Retrieved from https://www.nytimes.com/

—D—

Davis, J., & Mazumder, B. (2017, July). The decline in intergenerational mobility after 1980 (WP 2017-05). *Federal Reserve Bank of Chicago*. Retrieved from https://www.chicagofed.org/

Deaner, R.O., Balish, S.M.., & Lombardo, M.P. (2016). Sex differences in sports interest and motivation: An evolutionary perspective. *Evolutionary Behavioral Sciences, 10*(2), 73-97.

Defense Language Institute Foreign Language Center. (2018). General catalog 2019-2020. Retrieved from http://www.dliflc.edu/

De Leon, N. (n.d.). The Bohr atom. Retrieved from http://www.iun.edu/~cpanhd/C101webnotes/modern-atomic-theory/Bohr-model.html

Dell'Amore, C. (2013, April 9). Study tracks science of penis preference. *National Geographic*. Retrieved from https://news.nationalgeographic.com/

DeMarco, G. (2011, July 25). Minority rules: Scientists discover tipping point for the spread of ideas. *Rensselaer Polytechnic Institute*. Retrieved from https://news.rpi.edu/

Department of Justice and Equality. (2016, December 20). Check if you are an Irish citizen by birth or descent. Retrieved from http://www.inis.gov.ie/en/INIS/Pages/citizenship-by-birth-descent

Deresiewicz, W. (2014). *Excellent sheep: The miseducation of the American elite*. New York, NY: Free Press.

DeVore, C. (2018, December 19). Fatal employment: Men 10 times more likely than women to be killed at work. *Forbes*. Retrieved https://www.forbes.com/

DeWall, C.N., & Maner, J.K. (2008). High status men (but not women) capture the eye of the beholder. *Evolutionary Psychology, 6*(2), 328-341.

Dick, J. (2014, September 11). Hands down, people without kids have better lives—except for this one major thing. *Quartz*. Retrieved from https://qz.com/

Diep, F. (2017, June 14). 8,000 years ago, 17 women reproduced for every one man. *Pacific Standard*. Retrieved from https://psmag.com/environment/

DiLorenzo, T.J. (2010). The culture of violence in the American West: Myth versus reality. *The Independent Review, 15*(2), 227–239.

DiMartino-Booth, D. (2017, April 12). Bonds backed by auto loans look toxic. *Bloomberg Opinion*. Retrieved from https://www.bloomberg.com/opinion

Dinh, H., Strazdins, L., & Welsh, J. (2017). Hour-glass ceilings: Work-hour thresholds, gendered health inequities. *Social Science & Medicine, 76*, 42-51.

DiSalle, M. (Producer), & Arnold, N. (1988). *Bloodsport* [motion picture]. United States: The Cannon Group.

Dixon, D. (2014). *Endless question: Youth becomings and the anti-crisis of kids in global Japan.* (Doctoral dissertation). Retrieved from http://scalar.usc.edu/students/endlessquestion/index

Dobbs, R., Madgavkar, A., Manyika, J., Woetzel, J., Bughin, J., Labaye, E., . . . Kashyap, P. (2016, July). Poorer than their parents? Flat or falling incomes in advanced economies. *McKinsey Global Institute.* Retrieved from https://www.mckinsey.com/

Drexler, P. (2014, March 4). Can women succeed without a mentor? *Forbes.* Retrieved from https://www.forbes.com/

Duke University Student Affairs. (2019). Student sexual misconduct policy and procedures: Duke's commitment to Title IX. Retrieved from https://studentaffairs.duke.edu/

Dulaney, W.L. (2005, November). A brief history of "outlaw" motorcycle clubs. *International Journal of Motorcycle Studies.* Retrieved from https://motorcyclestudies.org/

Dunbar, R.I. (1993). Coevolution of neocortical size, group size and language in humans. *Behavioral and Brain Sciences, 16,* 681-735.

—E—

Edkins, G. (2018, June 1). Collapse of the nuclear family should be applauded due to the 'new reality' of single and same-sex parents, says top family court judge. *Daily Mail.* Retrieved from https://www.dailymail.co.uk/

Ekaterina W. (2012, March, 19). Marketing to women: How to get it right. *Fast Company.* Retrieved from https://www.fastcompany.com/

Elephant basics. (2019). *The National Elephant Center.* Retrieved from http://www.nationalelephantcenter.org/learn

Emanuel, E.J. & Bekelman, J.E. (2016, January 19). Is it better to die in America or in England? *The New York Times*. Retrieved https://www.nytimes.com/

Erickson, A. (2018, October 2). An Italian professor set out to prove 'physics was built by men.' He ended up suspended. *Washington Post*. Retrieved from https://www.washingtonpost.com/

Ethics Unwrapped. (2019). Veil of ignorance. *McCombs School of Business*. Retrieved from https://ethicsunwrapped.utexas.edu/glossary

Evarts, B. & Stein, G. (2019, March). US fire department profile – 2017. *National Fire Protection Association*. Retrieved from https://www.nfpa.org/

—F—

Fan, R., Zhao, J., Chen, Y., Xu, K. (2014). Anger Is more influential than joy: Sentiment correlation in Weibo. *PLOS ONE, 9*(10), 1-8.

Fast Company Staff. (2005, August 1). Why we hate HR. *Fast Company*. Retrieved from https://www.fastcompany.com/

Feeney, N. (2014, June 29). Pentagon: 7 in 10 youths would fail to qualify for military service. *Time*. Retrieved from https://time.com/

Fink, S. (2013). *Five days at Memorial: Life and death in a storm-ravaged hospital*. New York, NY: Crown Publishing.

First supersonic flight. (2019). *Guinness World Records*. Retrieved from https://www.guinnessworldrecords.com/

Folger, J. (2019, February 6). What is the relationship between inflation and interest rates? *Investopedia*. Retrieved from https://www.investopedia.com/

Fottrell, Q. (2018, April 3). For the first time, young Americans have less optimism than those aged 55 and older. *MarketWatch*. Retrieved from https://www.marketwatch.com/

Fox, J. (2019, February 13). Why America's new apartment buildings all look the same. *Bloomberg Business*. Retrieved from https://www.bloomberg.com/

Frailich, R. (2018, November 29). Your home is not an investment. *Forbes*. Retrieved from https://www.forbes.com/

Franke-Ruta, G. (2012, May 31). Americans have no idea how few gay people there are. *The Atlantic*. Retrieved from https://www.theatlantic.com/

FreeAdvice Staff. (2019). Can a stepparent be required to pay child support? *FreeAdvice Legal*. Retrieved from https://family-law.freeadvice.com/family-law/

Fresh Out—Life After The Penitentiary (2014, June 2). *Differences between federal and state prison systems—What are they?* Retrieved from https://www.youtube.com/

Frost, N. (2018, March 6). The sad story of the Moriori, who learned to live at the edge of the world. *Atlas Obscura*. Retrieved from https://www.atlasobscura.com/

—G—

Gann, C. (2012, July 24). After 30 years, unintended birth rate still almost 40 percent. *ABC News*. Retrieved from https://abcnews.go.com/

Garber, S. (2007, October 10). Sputnik and the dawn of the space age. *NASA History*. Retrieved from https://history.nasa.gov/

Garfield, E. (2019). The Clarivate Analytics impact factor. *Clarivate Analytics*. Retrieved from https://clarivate.com/

Gawande, A. (2014). *Being mortal: Medicine and what matters in the end*. New York, NY: Metropolitan Books.

Gee, A. (2017, September 28). Facing poverty, academics turn to sex work and sleeping in cars. *The Guardian*. https://www.theguardian.com/

Gersen, J.G. (207, September 20). Laura Kipnis's endless trial by Title IX. *The New Yorker*. Retrieved from https://www.newyorker.com/

Giang, V. (2012, February 13). There's a big difference between your work friends and your real friends. *Business Insider*. Retrieved from https://www.businessinsider.com/

Giles, L. (1910). *Sun Tzu on the art of war*. London, England: Luzac & Co.

Goble, B.V. (2014). A long bet: By 2040, the percentage of U.S. citizens of traditional college age who are attending postsecondary educational institutions in the United States will drop at least 50% from the level reported for the 2011/2012 academic year. *Long Bets*. Retrieved from http://longbets.org/676/

Goldberg, S. (1989, July 5). Numbers don't lie: Men do better than women. *The New York Times*. Retrieved from https://www.nytimes.com/

Goldstein, J. (2013, November 12). The four foundations of mindfulness. *Lion's Roar*. Retrieved from https://www.lionsroar.com/

Goodwin, D. (1992, Fall). The way we won: America's economic breakthrough during World War II. *The American Prospect*. https://prospect.org/

Goyer, M. (2019). Five decades of American female pilots statistics. How did we do? *Institute for Women of Aviation Worldwide*. Retrieved from https://womenofaviationweek.org/

Gracen, J. (2000, September 20) Andrea Dworkin in agony. *Salon*. Retrieved from https://www.salon.com/

431

Graeber, D. (2018). *Bullshit jobs: A theory.* New York, NY: Simon & Schuster.

Guo, J. (2014, December 11) Women are dominating men at college. Blame sexism. *Washington Post.* Retrieved from https://www.washingtonpost.com/

Gvozdenodic, V. (2013). *Beauty and wages: The effect of physical attractiveness on income using longitudinal data.* (Master's thesis). Retrieved from https://digitalcommons.pace.edu/

Gyatso, G. K. (2008). *Introduction to Buddhism.* Glen Spay, NY: Tharpa Publications. (Original work published 1992).

—H—

Haridy, R. (2017, December 27). 2017: The year AI beat us at all our own games. *New Atlas.* Retrieved from https://newatlas.com

The Hart Law Firm. (2019). Major causes of physician license revocations in Texas. Retrieved from https://www.thehartlawfirm.com/blog/

Hartocollis, A. (2017, July 9). Long after protests, students shun the University of Missouri. *The New York Times.* Retrieved from https://www.nytimes.com/

Head, J. (2015, December 16). Defaming a dog: The ways to get arrested for lese-majeste in Thailand. *BBC News.* Retrieved from https://www.bbc.com/

The Hermitary, & Meng-hu. (2011). Hermits in history: American. *Hermitary.* Retrieved from http://www.hermitary.com/

Hess, A. (2017, November 15). Harvard Business School professor: Half of American colleges will be bankrupt in 10 to 15 years. *CNBC.* Retrieved from https://www.cnbc.com/

History.com Editors. (2019, January 31). Guglielmo Marconi. *History.com.* Retrieved from https://www.history.com/

History.com Editors. (2019, July 17). This day in history (December 17): First airplane flies. *History.com* Retrieved from https://www.history.com/

History.com Editors. (2019, July 28). This day in history (March 26): Salk announces polio vaccine. *History.com.* Retrieved from https://www.history.com/

History.com Editors. (2019, July 28). This day in history (July 16): The first atomic bomb test is successfully exploded. *History.com* Retrieved from https://www.history.com/

Housel, M. (2013, September 13). How the average American home has changed in the last 40 years. *The Motely Fool.* Retrieved from https://www.fool.com/

Human Rights Watch. (2007, December 15). US: Federal statistics show widespread prison rape. Retrieved from https://www.hrw.org/

—I—

Iannaccone, L.R. (1994). Why strict churches are strong. *American Journal of Sociology, 99*(5), 1180-1211.

Informa UK Limited (2019). Journal of Gender Studies. Retrieved from https://tandfonline.com/toc/cjgs20/current

Institute of Continuing Education. (2019). Wind of change: post-war Britain 1945–1965. *University of Cambridge.* Retrieved from https://www.ice.cam.ac.uk/

Intelligent machines: Call for a ban on robots designed as sex toys. (2015, September 15). *BBC News.* Retrieved from https://www.bbc.com/

—J—

James, J.T. (2013). A new, evidence-based estimate of patient harms associated with hospital care. *Journal of Patient Safety, 9*(3), 122-128.

433

Johnson, B.A. (2010, August 8). We're addicted to rehab. It doesn't even work. *Washington Post*. Retrieved from http://www.washingtonpost.com/

Josey, C. (n.d.). Find out the differences between American vs German homes: It's where the heart is. *WorldThruOurEyes*. Retrieved from https://worldthruoureyes.com/

Jussim, L. (2016, August 15). Truth in stereotypes: Social scientists dismiss them, but rather than being universally inaccurate, stereotypes are often grounded in reality. *Aeon*. Retrieved from https://aeon.co/

—K—

Kacperczyk, A., Sanchez-Burks, J., & Baker, W.E. (2011, November 17). Social isolation in the workplace: A cross-national and longitudinal analysis. Retrieved from https://papers.ssrn.com/

Kantor, J., & Streitfeld, D. (2015, August 15). Inside Amazon: Wrestling big ideas in a bruising workplace. *The New York Times*. Retrieved from https://www.nytimes.com/

Karlan, D., & Zinman, J. (2005, October). Elasticities of demand for consumer credit. (Paper 926). *Yale University Economic Growth Center*. Retrieved from https://www.semanticscholar.org/

Keeley, L.H. (1996). *War before civilization: The myth of the peaceful savage*. New York, NY: Oxford University Press.

Kelly, K. (2017, July 5). Are witches the ultimate feminists? *The Guardian*. Retrieved from https://www.theguardian.com/

Kevane, M.J., & Sundstrom, W.A. (2016). *Public libraries and political participation, 1870-1940*. Santa Clara, CA: Santa Clara University. Retrieved from https://scholarcommons.scu.edu/

Key, S. (2017, November 13). In today's market, do patents even matter? *Forbes*. Retrieved from https://www.forbes.com/

Khan, R. (2010, August 5). 1 in 200 men direct descendants of Genghis Khan. *Discover*. Retrieved from http://blogs.discovermagazine.com/

Khazan, O. (2018, February 18). The more gender equality, the fewer women in STEM. *The Atlantic*. Retrieved from https://www.theatlantic.com/

Kinsella, E. (2017, November 29). A new study shows that most artists make very little money, with women faring the worst. *Artnet News*. Retrieved from https://news.artnet.com/

Kitchener, C. (2017, August 22). When it's hard for women to find male mentors. *The Atlantic*. Retrieved from https://www.theatlantic.com/

Kochanek, K.D., Murphy, S.L., Xu, J., & Arias, E. (2019). Deaths: Final data for 2017. *National Vital Statistics Reports, 68*(9), 35-36.

Konnikova, M. (2014, October 7). The limits of friendship. *The New Yorker*. Retrieved from https://www.newyorker.com/

Korte, G. (2019, February 25). Q&A: A judge has ruled the male-only military draft unconstitutional. What happens now? *USA Today*. Retrieved from https://www.usatoday.com/

Kotz, D. (2010, October 7). Overmedication: Are Americans taking too many drugs? *U.S. News & World Report*. Retrieved from https://health.usnews.com/

Kraemer & Kraemer. (2019). Panamanian citizenship. Retrieved from https://kraemerlaw.com/en/immigration/panamanian-citizenship/

Kroll. L. & Dolan, K.A. (2019, March 5). Billionaires: The richest people in the world. *Forbes*. https://www.forbes.com/

Kulp, K. (2017, October 14). Boomers worry they can't sell those big suburban homes when the time comes. *CNBC*. Retrieved from https://www.cnbc.com/

Kummer, L. (2017, June 29). We like superheroes because we're weak. Let's use other myths to become strong. *Fabius Maximus*. Retrieved from https://fabiusmaximus.com/

—L—

LaBianca, J. (2019, May 2019).These people donated millions after they died—But no one knew they were rich. *Reader's Digest*. Retrieved from https://www.yahoo.com/

LaCapria, K. (2016, April, 22). Do 643,000 bankruptcies occur in the U.S. every year due to medical bills? *Snopes*. Retrieved from https://www.snopes.com/

Larivière, V., & Gingras, Y. (2009). The decline in the concentration of citations, 1900–2007. *Journal of the American Society for Information Science and Technology, 60*(4), 858-862.

LeanIn. (2019). Men, commit to mentor women. Retrieved from https://leanin.org/mentor-her

Lee, J.A. (1973). *Colours of love: An exploration of the ways of loving*. Toronto, Canada: New Press.

Lewis, C.S. (1963, 21 December) We have no right to happiness. *The Saturday Evening Post, 236,* 10-12

Lewis, C.S. (2013). *The allegory of love.* New York: Cambridge University Press. (Original work published 1936).

Lin, S. (2019, April 23). The story of Laozi's servant. *The Epoch Times.* https://www.theepochtimes.com/

Liu, C. (2015). *The dark forest.* (J. Martinsen, Trans.). New York, NY: Tom Doherty Associates, LLC.

Live Science Staff. (2012, May 14). Why women choose bad boys. *Live Science. Retrieved from* https://www.livescience.com/

Livingston, G. (2014, December 22). Fewer than half of U.S. kids today live in a 'traditional' family. *Pew Research Center.* Retrieved from https://www.pewresearch.org/

Loewus, L. (2017, August 15). The nation's teaching force is still mostly white and female. *Education Week*. Retrieved from https://www.edweek.org/

Lopez, D.S. (2019, August 22). Buddha: Founder of Buddhism. *Encyclopædia Britannica*. Retrieved from https://www.britannica.com/

Lott, T. (2014, 17 January). Has having children made me happier than I was before? *The Guardian*. Retrieved from https://www.theguardian.com/

Love, B.J. (2014). Do university patents pay off? Evidence from a survey of university inventors in computer science and electrical engineering. *Yale Journal of Law and Technology, 16*(2), 285-343.

Love, D. (2011, October 26). 16 examples of Steve Jobs being a huge jerk. *Business Insider Australia*. Retrieved from https://www.businessinsider.com.au/

Lukianoff, G. & Haidt, J. (2015, September). The coddling of the American mind. *The Atlantic*. Retrieved from https://www.theatlantic.com/

—M—

Mackey, M. (2014, February 18). Want to succeed? Learn to fail. *The Fiscal Times*. Retrieved from http://www.thefiscaltimes.com/

MacLellan, L. (2017, July 14). One of the most common questions in American small talk is considered rude in much of the world. *Quartz*. Retrieved from https://qz.com/

Maeder, J. (2017, August 14). When 'flower child' feminist and failed playwright Valerie Solanas shot Andy Warhol. *New York Daily News*. Retrieved from https://www.nydailynews.com/

Maier, C. (2008). *No kids: 40 good reasons not to have children*. (P. Watson Trans.). Toronto, Canada: McClelland & Stewart, Ltd.

Malito, A. (2017, May 7). Why the lifetime earnings of American men are on a slow, inexorable decline. *MarketWatch*. Retrieved from https://www.marketwatch.com/

Marx, K. & Engels, F. (1906). *The communist manifesto*. (S. Moore, Trans.). Chicago, IL: Charles H. Kerr & Company. Retrieved from https://books.google.com/

Mast, M.S. (2004, May). Men are hierarchical, women are egalitarian: An implicit gender stereotype. *Swiss Journal of Psychology, 63*(2), 107-111.

McCurry, J. (2017, January 5). Japanese company replaces office workers with artificial intelligence. *The Guardian*. Retrieved from https://www.theguardian.com/

McDonald, M.M., Navarrete, C.D., & Vugt, M.V. (2012). Evolution and the psychology of intergroup conflict: The male warrior hypothesis. *Philosophical Transactions of the Royal Society B, 367*, 670-679.

McKay, B. & McKay, K. (2008, August 24). The history and nature of man friendships. *The Art of Manliness*. Retrieved from https://www.artofmanliness.com/

McLeay, M., Radia, A., & Thomas, R. (2014, March 14). Money creation in the modern economy. *Bank of England*. Retrieved from https://www.bankofengland.co.uk/

McLynn, F. (2015). *Genghis Khan: His conquests, his empire, his legacy*. Philadelphia, PA: De Capo Press.

Mehta, V. (2012, July 19). Are women shallow? *Psychology Today*. Retrieved from https://www.psychologytoday.com/

Merz, T. (2014, June 26). Women are 'more controlling and aggressive than men' in relationships. *The Telegraph*. Retrieved https://www.telegraph.co.uk/

Miller, A.E., MacDougall, J.D., Tarnopolsky M.A., & Sale D.G. (1993). Gender differences in strength and muscle fiber characteristics. *European Journal of Applied Physiology and Occupational Physiology, 66*(3), 254-262.

Miller, S.B. (2016, April 4). 2 Rare scenarios when stepparents are forced to pay child support. *Oak View Law Group.* Retrieved from https://www.ovlg.com/

Miller, S.G. (2016, December 13). 1 in 6 Americans takes a psychiatric drug. *Scientific American.* Retrieved from https://www.scientificamerican.com/

Mintz, S., & McNeil, S. (2019). Courtship in early America. *Digital History.* Retrieved from http://www.digitalhistory.uh.edu/

Monastery of Christ in the Desert. (2019). Timeless spiritual wisdom found in the sayings and stories of the early Christian monks of the desert. Retrieved from https://christdesert.org/prayer/desert-fathers-stories/

More, T. (1895). *Utopia.* (G. Burnet, Trans.). London, England: Cassell and Company, Limited. Retrieved from https://books.google.com/

Morgan, J. (2013, 24 October). Women 'better at multitasking' than men, study finds. *BBC News.* https://www.bbc.com/

Morrell, A. (2016, October 28). A Wharton professor explains why you shouldn't consider buying a home an investment. *Business Insider.* Retrieved from https://www.businessinsider.com/

Mosher, D., & Gould, S. (2017, January 31). How likely are foreign terrorists to kill Americans? The odds may surprise you. *Business Insider.* Retrieved from https://www.businessinsider.com/

Motorcycle Riding Club Education. (n.d.). 1% bylaws example. Retrieved from http://rcvsmc.net/id6.html

Motorcycle Riding Club Education. (n.d.). Hang around. Retrieved from http://rcvsmc.net/id33.html

Mulrine, A. (2015, May 29). All 8 women fail Ranger School: Some Rangers say standards should change. *The Christian Science Monitor*. Retrieved from https://www.csmonitor.com/

—N—

National Instant Criminal Background Check System (NICS) (n.d.). *Federal Bureau of Investigation*. Retrieved from https://www.fbi.gov/

National Institute of Environmental Health Sciences (n.d.) Details for high impact journal: Superfund research program: The New England Journal of Medicine (impact factor: 70.670). Retrieved from https://tools.niehs.nih.gov/srp/publications/

NewCars. (2019). Auto financing: It's all about the benjamins. Retrieved from https://www.newcars.com/how-to-buy-a-new-car/auto-financing.html

Newcastle University. (2016, February 8). Nature's mirror: The code for chirality. *Science Daily*. Retrieved from https://www.sciencedaily.com/

Newport, E.L. (1990). Maturational constraints on language learning. *Cognitive Science*, 14, 11-28.

Niederle, M., & Vesterlund, L. (2007). Do women shy away from competition? Do men compete too much? *Quarterly Journal of Economics, 122*(3), 1067–1101.

Ny, R. (2013, February 27). 4x as many scholarships for women — a disadvantage for men? *NerdWallet*. Retrieved from https://www.nerdwallet.com/

—O—

O'Brien, B. (2018, April 15). An introduction to Buddhist tantra: Transforming desire into enlightenment. *Learn Religions*. Retrieved from https://www.learnreligions.com/

O'Brien, B. (2019, February 4). Maha Pajapati and the first nuns: The beginning of barriers? *Learn Religions*. Retrieved from https://www.learnreligions.com/

Ohnuma, R. (2014, June 30). Buddhism and the family. *Oxford Bibliographies in Buddhism*. Retrieved from https://dx.doi.org/10.1093/obo/9780195393521-0201

Oldenburg, R. (1999). *The great good place: Cafes, coffee shops, bookstores, bars, hair salons, and other hangouts at the heart of a community.* New York, NY: Marlowe & Company.

Olick, D. (2019, June 20). Falling mortgage rates are heating home prices this summer. *CNBC*. Retrieved from https://www.cnbc.com/

Olson, R. (104, June 25). Average IQ of students by college major and gender ratio. Retrieved from http://www.randalolson.com/2014/06/25/average-iq-of-students-by-college-major-and-gender-ratio/

Order of Cistercians of the Strict Observance. (2019). Becoming a monk or nun. Retrieved from https://www.ocso.org/

Ouazad, A., & Page, L. (2013, July 3). Students' perceptions of teacher biases: Experimental economics in schools (INSEAD Working Paper No. 2013/66/EPS). Retrieved from https://ssrn.com/

—P—

Palermo, E. (2014, February 25). Who invented the printing press? *Live Science*. Retrieved from https://www.livescience.com/

Pappas, S. (2011, August 14). As schools cut recess, kids' learning will suffer, experts say. *Live Science*. Retrieved from https://www.livescience.com/

Patel, D. (2017, July 17). The pros and cons of outsourcing. *Forbes*. Retrieved from https://www.forbes.com/

Peddicord, K. (2015 May 12).Enjoy a low-cost retirement in Southeast Asia. *U.S. News & World Report*. Retrieved from https://money.usnews.com/

Perrottet, T. (2015, February). Who was the Marquis de Sade? *Smithsonian.com*. Retrieved from https://www.smithsonianmag.com/

Persell, C.H. (1990). Socialization. *introsocsite: Introduction to Sociology*. Retrieved from https://www.asanet.org/

Plateris, A.A. (1973 December). 100 years of divorce statistics: 1867-1967 (HRA 74-1902). *National Center for Health Statistics*. Retrieved from https://www.cdc.gov/

Plitt, L. (2013, November 27). Marcos Rodriguez Pantoja: Did this man live with wolves? *BBC News*. Retrieved from https://www.bbc.com/

Poole, G. (2015, August 6). Homelessness is a gendered issue, and it mostly impacts men. *The Telegraph*. Retrieved from https://www.telegraph.co.uk/

Poole, T. (1999, January 21). Pol Pot 'suicide' to avoid US trial. *The Independent*. Retrieved from https://www.independent.co.uk/

Porter, T. (2017, April 28). What is fentanyl, the drug linked to thousands of deaths in North America? *Newsweek*. Retrieved from https://www.newsweek.com/

Price, M. (2008, June). Genes matter in addiction. *Monitor on Psychology, 39*(6). Retrieved from https://www.apa.org/monitor/

Prooyen, E.V. (2017, August 25). This one thing is the biggest predictor of divorce. *The Gottman Institute*. Retrieved from https://www.gottman.com/

Putnam, R.D., (2000). *Bowling alone: The collapse and revival of American community*. New York, NY: Simon & Schuster Paperbacks.

PwC. (2017, March). *UK economic outlook*. Retrieved from https://www.pwc.co.uk/

—Q—

Qin, A. (2015, October 25). 'Kingdom of daughters' in China draws Tourists to its matrilineal society. *New York Times*. https://www.nytimes.com/

—R—

Rampell, C. (2015, February 17). Why do Americans go to college? First and foremost, they want better jobs. *Washington Post*. https://www.washingtonpost.com/

Ranes, B. (2016, March). The brain disease model of addiction. *Butler Center for Research*. Retrieved from https://www.hazeldenbettyford.org/

Rapacon, S. (2019, January 29). 15 worst college majors for a lucrative career. *Kiplinger*. Retrieved from https://www.kiplinger.com/

Rapacon, S. (2019, February 5). 25 best college majors for a lucrative career. *Kiplinger*. Retrieved from https://www.kiplinger.com/

Rape. (2019). *Dictionary.com*. Retrieved from https://www.dictionary.com/

Reid, R. (2018, April 6). Over half of women prefer their best friend to their husband. *Metro*. Retrieved from https://metro.co.uk/

Research starters: Worldwide deaths in World War II (n.d.). *The National WWII Museum*. Retrieved from https://www.nationalww2museum.org/

Reuell, P. (2016, August 8). Resolving conflict: Men vs. women. *The Harvard Gazette*. Retrieved from https://news.harvard.edu/gazette/

Ridley, M. (2016). In retrospect: The selfish gene. *Nature, 529,* 462-463. Retrieved from https://www.nature.com/

Rieti, J. (2012, February 15). Children of immigrants caught between 2 cultures. *CBC*. Retrieved from https://www.cbc.ca/

Rocheleau, M. (2017, March 6). Chart: The percentage of women and men in each profession. *The Boston Globe*. Retrieved from https://www.bostonglobe.com/

Rotman, D. (2016, April 6). Tech slowdown threatens the American dream. *MIT Technology Review*. Retrieved from https://www.technologyreview.com/

Rowlands, M. (2012). *Can animals be moral?* New York, NY: Oxford University Press.

Rudder, C. (2009, November 17). Your looks and your inbox. Retrieved from https://bit.ly/2kPP1xv

Rudman, L.A., & Goodwin, S.A. (2004). Gender differences in automatic in-group bias: Why do women like women more than men like men? *Journal of Personality and Social Psychology, 87*(4), 494-509.

—S—

Sacks, G. (2002, November 19). Why males don't go to college. *ifeminists.com*. Retrieved from http://www.ifeminists.com/

Sakulku, J., & Alexander, J. (2011). The impostor phenomenon. *International Journal of Behavioral Science, 6*(1), 73-92.

Sauro, J. (2019). Fundamentals of statistics 2: The normal Distribution: Introducing the normal distribution. *Usable Stats*. Retrieved from https://www.usablestats.com/

Schumacher, H. (2019, March 18). Why more men than women die by suicide. *BBC News*. Retrieved from http://www.bbc.com/

Sidner, S. (2009, August 13). Less sex, more TV idea aired in India. *CNN*. Retrieved from http://edition.cnn.com/

Silver, M. (2015, February 16). Sexual desire often fades in relationships. *The Sydney Morning Herald*. Retrieved from https://www.smh.com.au/

Simpson, R. (2011, December 15). Iraq War casualties—By gender as of end of combat missions. *The American War Library*. Retrieved from http://www.americanwarlibrary.com/

Singh, G.K. (2010). Maternal mortality in the United States, 1935-2007: Substantial racial/ethnic, socioeconomic, and geographic disparities persist. *U.S. Department of Health and Human Services*. Retrieved from http://www.mchb.hrsa.gov/

Slack, J. (2014, February 19). It's the end of the nuclear family . . . and that's no bad thing, insists Supreme Court judge who says he fears watching couples take their wedding vows. *Daily Mail*. Retrieved from https://www.dailymail.co.uk/

Smart, N. (1998). *The world's religions*. (2nd ed.). New York, NY: Cambridge University Press.

Smith, H. (2013). *Men on strike: Why men are boycotting marriage, fatherhood, and the American dream—and why it matters*. New York, NY: Encounter Books.

Snow, C.E., & Hoefnagel-Höhle, M. (1978). The critical period for language acquisition: Evidence from second language learning. *Child Development, 49*(4), 1114-1128.

Sommers, C.H. (2000). *The war against boys: How misguided feminism is hurting our young men.* New York, NY: Touchstone.

Starr, S. (2012). Estimating gender disparities in federal criminal cases. *University of Michigan Law School.* Retrieved from https://repository.law.umich.edu/

State of California. (2019). Weaverville Joss House. Retrieved from http://ohp.parks.ca.gov/

Statista Research Department (2019, August 1). Deaths by homicide per 100,000 resident population in the U.S. from 1950 to 2016. *Statista.* Retrieved from https://www.statista.com/

Stengel, S. (2019). IBM Personal Computer (PC). *Steve's Old Computer Museum.* Retrieved from http://oldcomputers.net/

Sterbenz, C. (2015, May 16). Here's a surprising look at the average serial killer. *Business Insider.* Retrieved from https://www.businessinsider.com/

Stockton, C. (2014, July 3). 15 parents explain what they regret about having children. *Thought Catalog.* Retrieved from https://thoughtcatalog.com/

Stolba, S.L. (2019, April 12). Baby Boomers prove high debt doesn't equal bad credit. *Experian.* Retrieved from https://www.experian.com/blogs/ask-experian/

Stone, L. (2018, September 6). Study: If trends continue, all men may be infertile by end of century. *The Federalist.* Retrieved from https://thefederalist.com/

Susskind, R., & Susskind, D. (2015). *The future of the professions: How technology will transform the work of human experts.* New York, NY: Oxford University Press.